With a flexible financial solution, life can be fun with a daredevil scamp.

Insurance, banking or investment: no matter which it is, every Fortis company believes in flexible solutions. Not just for the short term, but also for the distant future.

Because no two people want the same thing, because children always do the unexpected and because no one can look ten years into the future.

The Fortis group includes AMEV, Fortis Bank and MeesPierson. They can provide additional information.

If you would like to know more about the Fortis group, please call us on 31 (0)30 257 65 48.

FORTIS

Solid partners, flexible solutions

WE ARRANGED THE FINANCE TO TAKE COMMUNICATION TO NEW DEPTHS.

You're tendering to supply a new global submarine communication system for the UK Ministry of Defence. You need a lead financial advisor – one equipped to deliver a complex, innovative and high profile project. Enter the Public-Private Partnership specialists at PricewaterhouseCoopers. We're leaders in the structuring of defence projects using private capital. We introduced equity partners to the consortium. We arranged the debt finance. And we steered the project safely into port in record time.

www.pwcglobal.com/pfp

PRICEWATERHOUSE COOPERS 🅟

THE WORLD IN 2002

EDITOR: Dudley Fishburn

MANAGING EDITOR: Harriet Ziegler
DEPUTY EDITOR: Stephen Green
EDITORIAL ASSISTANT: Fenella Crane
RESEARCHER: Ian Curry
DESIGN AND ART DIRECTION: Bailey and Kenny
DESIGN ASSISTANCE: Anita Wright,
Edgar Gonzalez
CHARTS AND MAPS: Michael Robinson,
Edgar Gonzalez, Russ Street
ILLUSTRATIONS: Derek Cousins,
Geraldine Spence
PICTURE EDITOR: Juliet Brightmore
ADVERTISING DIRECTOR: John Dunn
CIRCULATION DIRECTOR: Des McSweeney
PRODUCTION: Katy Greenway, Carrie
Goldsworthy, Andrew Rollings
FOREIGN RIGHTS: Hutton-Williams Agency
ASSOCIATE PUBLISHER: David Gill
PUBLISHER: David Hanger
ENTERPRISES DIRECTOR: Martin Giles

ISBN 0 86218 188 7

Where opinion is expressed it is that of the
authors and does not necessarily coincide
with the editorial views of the publisher or
The Economist.

All information in this magazine is verified
to the best of the authors' and the
publisher's ability. The Economist
Newspaper Limited does not accept
responsibility for any loss arising from
reliance on it.

PHOTOGRAPHIC SOURCES: AFP; Associated
Press; Bridgeman Art Library; Christie's
Images; Corbis/David Samuel Robbins;
FPG International/Getty Images; Empics
Nottingham; Foster and Partners /Richard
Davies/ Nigel Young; Frank Spooner
Picures/Gamma; Image Bank/Getty
Images; Images of India Picture
Agency/Rajesh Vora; Impact Photos;
IPG/Katz Pictures/Tom Stoddart;
Katz Pictures/Max Alexander/Serge
Attal/Donatello Brogioni/George
Steinmetz; Network
Photographers/Gideon Mendel;
PA Photos; PA Photos/EPA; Panos
Pictures/Jeremy Horner;
Still Pictures/David Hoffman; Colin Thomas.

Printed by TPL Printers (UK) Ltd
(Kidderminster, England)
Reprographics by Mullis Morgan Group Ltd
Printed on UPM-Kymmene Star 80gsm

The Economist

25 St James's Street, London, SW1A 1HG
Telephone: 020 7830 7000
E-mail: theworldin@economist.com
Internet: http://www.theworldin.com

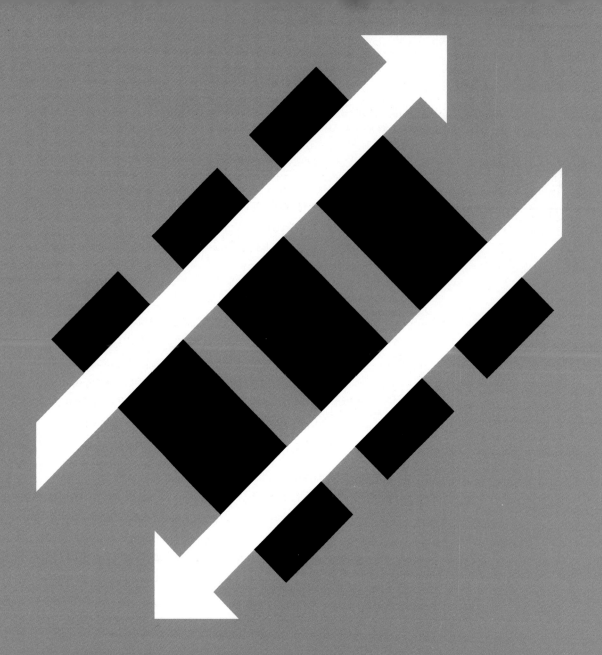

Go for index trackers.

POLITICS

ECONOMICS

HEADACHES

MANAGEMENT

IDEAS

imagine

waste isn't wasted ... waste is wanted ... waste volume becomes trading volume .

++ USED GLASS +£ 32,81 ++
55 +++ WASTE PAPER +

1898	1964	1980	1990	2001	Moving ideas
RWE is founded	RWE operates largest waste incineration plant in Germany	First recycling plant for raw materials	New procedure for measuring CFC emissions from refrigeration appliances	First fully-automatic plant for sorting waste paper	www.rwe.com +49 18 01/40 50 60

RWE
One Group. Multi Utilities.

Electricity. Gas. Water. Recycling. Services.

2002 will be a year of convalescence. The dust will blow away from the military attacks on Afghanistan, leaving the world on edge. America will prevail. Terrorists will doubtless strike again, with much drama but to less effect. Organised, co-ordinated terrorism, however, will stop. America's war will go underground: noisy bombardments being replaced by the careful, plodding work of intelligence. America's eventual success will no sooner be established in 2002 than it will start to unravel. That is the way of democracy. Expect a return to "normalcy": allies will fall out over the political settlement that must follow the war. President George Bush's popularity at home, high at the start of the year, will dwindle with the approach of the congressional elections in November: the Democrats will strengthen their control.

The world economy will be in convalescence too, though the wounds of 2001 will repair themselves. There will be no prolonged recession. Recovery, when it comes in the second half of the year, will be rapid in both the United States and Europe. Interest rates will climb as the year progresses.

Britain, though expecting a terrorist attack of some kind, has little reason to fear 2002. It will have a strong government, unchallenged throughout the year. Its economy, while suffering with the world, is in robust shape; and the country, now perhaps the most cosmopolitan and the most porous in the world, has good intelligence services. Less travel will keep Britons locked in the crowded island's traffic jams; expect everyone, however, to take a relaxed week off in June to celebrate Queen Elizabeth's 50th anniversary on the throne. The one political disagreement, mounting to a noisy crescendo at the end of 2002, will be over whether the British government should call a referendum to decide on ditching the local currency for the euro.

The new European currency arrives in the pockets of 300m EU citizens on January 1st. It will be the talk on every tongue for the first months of the year. Apart from being an enormous logistical exercise, the psychological effects—first shock, then pride—will be profound. Europe will have changed irrevocably and Britain will be envious. The humdrum business of politics—the elections in Germany and France—will seem as nothing compared with this momentous reality.

If there is a semblance of peace in the world, it will not come to Israel, where violence will be embedded in daily life. But for the Middle East and the Muslim world in general, America's war on terrorism will galvanise that huge majority of the population—and its leadership—that seeks a modern way of life. It will be a time of reform and progress; a time to cast off clerics and dictators everywhere.

The World in 2002 will appear in 14 languages and 90 countries. Some of our forecasts will be wrong; most, I hope, will be valuable. Last year we predicted that Afghanistan would be 2001's most wretched country. We do not guess who will win soccer's World Cup final on June 30th, but we do predict that in a hostile, divided world some one billion people will watch the game; one in which, interestingly, there is no element of American culture. Globalisation brings its refreshing moments of unity.

Dudley Fishburn
Editor, *The World in 2002*

For most people the horizon is as far as they can see. But for us it represents the threshold to an unseen world of new opportunities. As one of the world's foremost managers of capital and risk, we are constantly searching for solutions that lie beyond the obvious. With financial and intellectual reservoirs of great depth and breadth to draw from, we combine insight, knowledge and original thinking to create new opportunities. We do it for ourselves. We can do it for you.

Solutions beyond the obvious.

Swiss Re

Europe's day of change

The new currency that arrives in the pockets of 300m people will alter forever Europe's view both of itself and of the world, predicts **Gideon Rachman**.

The first banknotes and coins will start circulating in the 12 countries that have adopted the new currency on new year's day. There will be a period of up to two months—varying from country to country—in which old and new currencies will circulate side by side. But by March it will be euros only. This is a breathtakingly ambitious—indeed unprecedented—undertaking. It is a massive economic experiment. And, although the British (who are staying out of the project, for now) still sometimes try to pretend otherwise, the euro is also in the words of Joschka Fischer, the German foreign minister, a "profoundly political project". It will be both a symbol and a driver of European integration. When the war in Afghanistan is long forgotten, this event will have silently shifted the balance of the world.

Europe's "ever closer union" has been unfolding for 50 years, but the averagely inattentive European could be forgiven for not really noticing. Many of the most important developments—common tariffs and single-market legislation for example—have been technical in nature. Even those aspects of integration that do touch the ordinary citizen—disappearing customs posts, a common passport—do not crop up in day-to-day life.

The future of the European Union will ride on the success or failure of the new currency. A successful euro will create a genuine pan-European identity—both inside and outside the EU. "Europe" will have a tangible everyday existence, and people living in the Union will have more of a sense of common endeavour. Those countries that are outside the project, notably Britain, will start to feel restless, forced to the margin of continental influence. An unsuccessful euro, by contrast, would cause enormous tensions within the Union.

But what will constitute success or failure? For the past two years much attention has been focused on the external value of the currency, above all against the dollar. In 2002 that issue will fade and the euro may break back through the symbolic level of parity with the dollar. In the first few weeks in which the new money is circulating, attention will instead switch to the ease or otherwise of the transition to notes and coins.

The logistics are indeed daunting. Some 14.5 billion banknotes and 50 billion coins will have to be distributed to 300m people across an area stretching from Portugal to Finland. Inevitably, there will be some horror stories. For a while it will take longer for people to make usually simple purchases, as they hand in their national currencies and get their change in unfamiliar coins and notes. One prediction: there will be scarcely any other topic of conversation in the shops and streets of Europe for the first months of 2002. The press—particularly the British

Gideon Rachman: Brussels correspondent, *The Economist*

press—are certain to seize upon any stories that reflect the sense of shock and anger that many Europeans will feel as they wrestle with the unfamiliar coins.

But barring a real logistical disaster—which seems unlikely—the political and economic fate of the euro will not be determined by the smoothness with which notes and coins are introduced; nor by its value against the dollar. Instead, by the second half of 2002, the real point of debate will be whether the currency's arrival has created the need and momentum for further European integration. For some time leading figures within the Union, such as Romano Prodi, the commission president, have been calling for an "economic government" for Europe. The implication is that the euro area will need stronger political institutions to forge the common economic policies necessitated by a single currency. In 2002 this debate will merge with the new debate on Europe's constitutional future that will have been launched by the European Union at a summit in Belgium in December 2001.

A club with tough rules

The discussion about economic governance will be given a tangible focus by emerging tensions over the euro area's Stability and Growth Pact, and its impact on the national budgets of the 12 countries sharing the currency. The pact was adopted essentially at Germany's behest to ensure that all members of the club follow responsible fiscal policies. In normal times they are meant to aim for national budgets that are "in balance or surplus". Deficits are allowed in recessions, but if they exceed 3% of GDP the other members of the European Union can levy punitive fines. The idea is that by waving such a big stick the Union will enforce fiscal responsibility, and prevent any one country's profligacy creating inflationary problems for the other members of the euro zone.

But the potential political and economic difficulties are also apparent. By joining a monetary union, nations have already voluntarily surrendered two instruments traditionally used for national economic management—the power to vary interest rates and to devalue the national currency. The Stability and Growth Pact severely restrains the third major tool—fiscal policy.

The European Commission is empowered to monitor the fiscal policies of its members. Worryingly the euro zone's big three—Italy, Germany and France—could all be in line for reprimands in 2002. That is because in worsening economic conditions they are all likely to find it hard to meet the budgetary commitments they have made to their euro-zone partners. The pact embodies the central question which will determine the fate of the single currency. Will the benefits of the euro—convenience, more trade and investment, the fostering of European identity—outweigh the constraints it imposes on national freedom of action? The answer to that question will be played out over the course of a decade. □

His mind is abroad, his matter at home

A year of living dangerously

It will take all of President Bush's strength to stop America lapsing back into domestic quarrels, warns John Micklethwait.

The war on terrorism will dominate American political life for the first months of 2002 but then, inevitably, the tug of domestic matters will force the attention of Washington as the mid-term elections in November come into view. The first big electoral test of George Bush's presidency would, in any normal time, be decided on the basis of domestic issues—the economy, education, health care.

In one sense, this calendar and the prejudice towards the domestic still stands, despite the events of September 11th. Mid-term elections tend to be even more local than presidential ones. When the voters of South Carolina come to decide who will succeed the finally retiring 99-year-old Strom Thurmond, the race will be decided on the basis of recent quarrels over video-poker and the Confederate flag, and the state of local schools. The elections also give the Democrats a real chance to change America's political map. In the Senate, which the Democrats have controlled since June 2001 by one seat, the Republicans have to defend 20 seats, the Democrats only 13. The Democrats will also be hoping to overturn the Republicans' slender majority in the House. And among the 36 gubernatorial contests, 23 have Republican incumbents.

But, even against the inexorable pull of competitive politics, it is clear that something has changed. Come next

John Micklethwait: United States editor, *The Economist*

November, Mr Bush, by his own admission, is still likely to be in the trenches fighting a prolonged "war against terrorism"; and that war will reach far beyond America's borders. The conduct of foreign policy may not be the main issue, but it will matter more than in any election since the Vietnam war. Many Americans will look on this prospect with gloom. The period before September 11th when their country's airwaves were preoccupied by the travails of congressman Gary Condit (the Modesto Lothario) now seems idyllic; even the Florida election fiasco looks relatively benign. The period between the end of the cold war and the arrival of Osama bin Laden and anthrax—roughly, the two Clinton presidencies—now seems something of a golden age.

America rediscovers diplomacy

Nobody who cares about America could welcome the cloud that has engulfed it. But its reabsorption in the wider world is overdue. Looking back, America's involvement on the world stage before the terrorist attacks now seems oddly lopsided. Economically, it was fully engaged. It played an active role in lowering trade barriers and spreading capitalism. Globalisation became synonymous with American companies. But, politically, it was more reticent. While the older George Bush had set about creating a New World Order, Mr Clinton's foreign policy was a more reactive business. Having started by virtually ignoring the subject, Mr Clinton seemed better at managing crises than preventing them. And he was not helped by a Republican Congress that enjoyed spurning the United Nations.

For many of America's allies, the second Bush presidency started off in an even worse direction—"unilaterally" dismissing a string of international treaties and promising to push ahead with a missile-defence shield, regardless of the anti-ballistic missile treaty. In most cases, the new president was merely making plain the differences that Mr Clinton had preferred to fudge. But his style was abrupt and diplomacy seemed low on his list of priorities. On September 10th, the cover of *Time,* wondered, "Where have you gone, Colin Powell?" The next day, the world changed—and, ever since, the secretary of state has been on a spree of alliance-building. America has reached out to the other big powers, Russia and China. It has taken a new interest in trying to solve old problems, such as Palestine and Kashmir.

America's central challenge in 2002 will be to maintain this momentum. This may become increasingly difficult. At home, many Americans may prefer to retreat behind the country's own walls: to boost security on airlines, to take a tougher line on immigration and to keep clear of foreign escapades. Isolationism has always had its supporters: George Washington believed that America's policy should be "to steer clear of permanent alliances with any portion of the foreign world." Many foreigners too would prefer an inward-looking

America. Indeed, they have already made the argument that the World Trade Centre attacks were the inevitable result of American imperialism. Such dissenting voices will only grow louder if the war against terrorism goes badly.

Yet America must stay involved for three reasons. First, the war against terrorism makes no sense without an active international component. No wall—not even Mr Bush's missile shield—can insulate America from attacks. And, as the 1990s showed, a reactive foreign policy carries risks of its own. One reason why Mr bin Laden emerged as a threat is because America did too little to chase him down; one reason why the Taliban seized power in Afghanistan is because the West did too little to help the country after the Russians left.

The second reason is to do with geopolitical opportunism. In its perverse, bloody way, September 11th has given Mr Bush a chance to tackle some of the world's thornier problems. Some of the opportunities—the development of a Palestinian state alongside Israel, the possibility of smarter sanctions against Iraq—tie directly into grievances (perceived or real) in the Arab world. But there is also room to look at wider questions—such as relations with Russia and the future of the United Nations. Such meddling contains dangers of its own; but it is a risk worth taking. The final reason is to do with what some call the American way. For the past half-century, the United States has been a benevolent superpower, overseeing a worldwide increase in prosperity and freedom. The attacks of 2001 were a bloody assault on that tradition. If 2002 sees America retreat back into its shell, the terrorists will have won their greatest victory. □

A modern Muslim world

The days of oligarchical Islam are ending, predicts **Brian Beedham**. A Reformation is on the way.

No: fingers crossed, we are not heading for the dread Clash of Civilisations, the Revenge of Allah, the Last Crusade. For all the horrors and hysteria since September 11th, Muslims and westerners can still one day hope to be good neighbours to each other, perhaps even shoulder-to-shoulder allies if 21st-century China turns out to be the era's real problem and a danger for both of them.

Although, in a general way, men like Osama bin Laden can ride on the turbulent waves of anti-western resentment that wash through the Muslim world, a growing number of clearer-eyed Muslims have begun to realise that most of this turbulence has its causes in a fading past; and these clearer-

Brian Beedham: associate editor, *The Economist*

eyed Muslims also see that, though there will always be some religion-based differences between Islam and the West, there are a lot of things in "the western way of life" they would like to share: which will not be helped by a Clash of Civilisations. The tide, in short, is going to turn.

One of Mr bin Laden's aims last September, he said, was to solve the Israel-Palestine problem. By that he meant the removal of Israel from the map; he did not kill several thousand people just to urge a change of a few dozen square miles in a future Israel-Palestine border. But most Palestinians, says Yasser Arafat, accept the continued existence of Israel; and the same is true of most other Arab governments, the most notable exception being Iraq's Saddam Hussein.

Mr bin Laden was in similar company in the other part of his explanation for the attack on America. He hated the presence of American soldiers on the holy soil of Saudi Arabia. But those soldiers went there to rescue Kuwait, and protect Saudi Arabia, from Saddam Hussein; and they would not still be there unless most Saudis still wanted their protection. On both counts, pious bin Laden and dictator Saddam make an odd, and rather isolated, couple.

There is also, to be sure, that genuine, wider tug of angry, anti-western Muslim envy. A millennium ago Islam was a sparkling civilisation next door to a crude medieval Europe. These crude Europeans then bloodily sacked its holy places in Jerusalem; borrowed Islam's science, its mathematics and its arts to bring about their Renaissance; rose to dominate most of the rest of the globe; and eventually scooped up the majority of Muslims into their European empires. Fair cause for resentment.

But those European empires disappeared half a century ago. The United States, now the chief target of Muslim envy, has huge power, but it is not power exercised by colonial governors and bayonets; it is economic power, based on the workings of a free-market economy in which people buy and sell what they want. It is not America that decides the price of Arab oil; it is Muslims who decide whether or not they want to eat at their local McDonald's. It is hard for fair-minded people to resist the conclusion that, if most Muslim countries are still poor and powerless, it is chiefly the fault not of outsiders but of their own incompetent, self-serving or corrupt rulers.

Islam's Renaissance

Here is the heart of the matter. A lot of Muslims, following this train of thought, have decided that they want their own Renaissance: a rebirth, a revival, of Islam's splendours. Some of these people are peasant ideologues of the Taliban sort, or violent fanatics like Mr bin Laden. But most are not.

The clear-minded Muslim revivalists—a fairer word than "fundamentalist"—are men and women who know far more about the western world than their parents and grandparents did, thanks to television, telephones, the Internet and the rest of today's distance-destroying technology. They deplore some of what they see (so much sex, so much emphasis on material luxury) but then so do quite a lot of westerners. And there are other things that these revivalists can honestly admire. They like the idea that governments should be answerable to the people they govern. They long for the Muslim world's economies to grow more efficient, provided the efficiency is tempered by compassion. They are happy to embrace modernity so long as they can remain good Muslims; they want girls to wear scarves, but the girls can cheerfully work at the computer as they wear the scarves.

The trouble is that, to achieve these things, a Muslim revival has to change the Muslim world's existing structures of power. The rigidities that keep Muslim politics so undemocratic, and Muslim economics so incompetent, do not have their origin in the Koran. In the Koran, God commended the idea of individual responsibility ("No man can bear another man's burdens"), and God's economic ideas were plainly of the free-market sort.

But, in the centuries after Muhammad transcribed God's word, Muslims allowed the interpretation of his word to fall into the hands of the *ulema*, the tiny, all-male, more or less self-selected little groups of scholars who claim a monopoly of knowing what God meant—not only in spiritual matters, but earthly ones as well. Theological authoritarianism and authoritarian politics predictably went hand in hand. If there is to be a modern Islam, every Muslim's God-given right to individual responsibility will have to break free of this antique oligarchy. Islam needs its Reformation, too.

Such things do not happen overnight. They take even longer to achieve after a war started by a violent fanatic and his peasant-ideologue allies. But the tide is turning, and these two Peoples of the Book, Islam and the West, are not doomed to be enemies for ever. □

Traditional yet contemporary

The economic consequences of terror

The usual economic tinkering with taxes, spending or interest rates will be of little use in 2002, argues **Clive Crook**. Confidence will be the key.

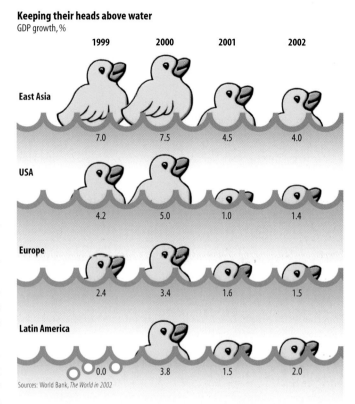

Keeping their heads above water
GDP growth, %

	1999	2000	2001	2002
East Asia	7.0	7.5	4.5	4.0
USA	4.2	5.0	1.0	1.4
Europe	2.4	3.4	1.6	1.5
Latin America	0.0	3.8	1.5	2.0

Sources: World Bank, *The World in 2002*

A recession in the United States is now a certainty. For the first three months, and perhaps for the first six months, of 2002, the American economy will be shrinking. What matters is how deep, how long and how contagious this slowdown proves to be—and what to do about it. Much depends on whether there are more big attacks on America and its allies. The material effects of terrorist action are beside the point: even the terrible destruction in Manhattan was minuscule when measured against the totality of America's economic assets. The issue is confidence—America's greatest economic vulnerability. Even as output growth slowed over the past year, with stockmarkets slumping and hopes for the fabled "new economy" in retreat, shoppers in the United States kept spending. That was enough, just, to keep the economy afloat. The attacks on New York and Washington hit a slowing, struggling economy where it was most at risk.

If the outrage of September 11th is a one-off, America and its trading partners can hope, with luck, to see growth recover quickly, even if (or especially if) the initial drop in output is severe. If things turn out this way, the resilience of the economy will take people by surprise, as after previous downturns. Some of the expansionary measures now planned by Congress and the Federal Reserve will go too far, just like the relaxation of policy after the stockmarket crash of 1987. But if there are more big attacks, everything changes: the loss of confidence will be deeper and more prolonged.

In 2002, therefore, the most important tool of economic policy will not be taxes, public spending or even interest rates, but the steps America and its allies take at home and abroad to fight terrorism. If those measures fail, fiscal and monetary policy will be unable to do much about the resulting collapse in confidence; if they succeed, dramatic changes in fiscal and monetary policy will not be needed. This 2002 redefinition of "economic policy"—which renders the orthodox expertise of economists almost redundant—is only one of the ways in which, after September 11th, the world has changed.

But wars are good for the economy, aren't they? They can be, in a way. Wars spur economic growth, as conventionally measured, if they involve enormous military spending and mobilisation of personnel. Wars like that cure unemployment, at least. Yet, by the yardstick of the work that people would prefer to be doing, or the goods that they would rather be consuming, the increase in economic activity seen during wartime is almost entirely waste, and on a colossal scale. Whatever happens, this "war" will not be as "good" for the economy as conventional large-scale military conflict.

A better guide is the limited war against Saddam Hussein after the invasion of Kuwait in 1990. The Gulf war, mainly through its effect on confidence, helped to push the United States into recession: in the last quarter of 1990 the economy shrank by 3% at an annual rate, reflecting sharp drops in both consumer spending and business investment. This time, the shock to American confidence is greater. America has learned that its enemies can cause enormous damage within the country's borders. Terrorists are harder to confront than Saddam Hussein: he, at least, had territory to invade and assets to destroy. And the global economic context is worse too. Japan is stagnating, at best, and growth in Europe is sluggish, whereas in 1990 the world outside America was doing well.

In response, America's Fed and other monetary authorities around the world are lowering interest rates—which is right. On fiscal policy, though, mistakes are being made. The main thing is to let the so-called automatic stabilisers work. (As economies slow, tax revenues dwindle and social spending goes up, automatically reducing budget surpluses or adding to budget deficits, as the case may be.) The right thing is to

Clive Crook: deputy editor, *The Economist*

let this happen, even if it means breaking the specious rules of budget prudence that have become modish in Britain, where the chancellor has made a lot of his "golden rule" of budget policy, and in Europe's single-currency area, where taxes and spending are governed by the ill-advised "stability pact".

Neutralising the automatic stabilisers would be one mistake. Yet to go much beyond just letting them work, as America will, with big new spending programmes and tax cuts, has little to recommend it either. In the short term, the effect will be small in any case: spending takes time to come on stream, and lower taxes will fail to spur spending while confidence is low. In the longer term, it will either be beside the point (if confidence is permanently impaired) or surplus to requirements (if confidence recovers). America has a pile of revenues to spend, and although it will do no great harm to spend it, especially if the measures are temporary, it will do little good either. In dealing with the economic consequences of the war against terrorism, the front line will not be in finance ministries, but in public confidence. □

Civil society

You'll hear it mentioned ever more often, but what is it? asks **John Grimond**.

Far away and long ago, there was something called polite society. You might not have wanted to be a member of it, but you knew what it was. There was, and indeed is, also the civil service, and everyone has always known what that is. Today there is something that appears to be a hybrid of these two creatures, called civil society. It is universally talked about in tones that suggest it is a Great Good, but for some people it presents a problem: what on earth is it? Unless you know, how can you tell if you would want to join it?

One possible clue is that civil society is often mentioned in the same breath as democracy. A recent book by David Blunkett, Britain's home secretary, for instance, is subtitled "Renewing Democracy and Civil Society". Democracy is a familiar concept, but what might the other be? The five chapters offer no explanation.

Michael Edwards, of the Ford Foundation in New York, brings rather more rigour to the question. "Analytic or structural definitions", he says, "stress the importance of forms: social organisations and networks, the 'third sector', or, more broadly, the arena in which citizens come together to advance the interests they hold in common." This apparently includes all organisations between the family and the state, with the exception of business (so presumably the Mafia is excluded, though maybe not Osama bin Laden's al-Qaeda). But if you thought that you were getting a handle on the idea, Mr

Edwards confuses matters by saying that there is also a "cognitive" definition, which stresses the importance of norms: trust, tolerance, co-operation and all those things that make a society "civil", which he defines in turn as "a way of being and living that is different from the rationality of either state or market" (back comes the Mafia?).

The academics who see civil society as a fertile new subject to exploit—the authors of "Global Civil Society 2001" excitedly call it the "most important social-science (re)discovery of the 1990s"—have found a splendid intellectual genealogy for the concept. It all began with the Greeks, apparently, and was then taken up by Adam Ferguson (an 18th-century Scot), Hegel, Marx, de Tocqueville, Gramsci and a variety of Central Europeans and Latin Americans. But what is it? "One thing that helps to explain the present universal popularity of civil society is its very fuzziness: it can be all things to all people," according to "Global Civil Society 2001".

In short, there is no definition. It is tempting, therefore, to dismiss the entire idea as a woolly expression for woolly-minded people. That, however, would be too charitable. In the absence of a definition, judge civil society by the company it keeps. Note that civil society crops up in association with many of the most flabby expressions of voguish punditry: governance, which is just another word for government (Mr Edwards is the Ford Foundation's "director of governance and civil society"); community leaders (lobbyists); social capital (something nice); and the international community (an assortment of busybodies and do-gooders who come together as a wonderful family only in the imagination).

And who promotes, indeed feeds and flourishes, on these vacuous expressions? One group in particular: NGOs, otherwise known as non-governmental organisations, an international community if ever there was one. Or, if you stop to think about it, the "third sector" that stands between the family and the state: yes, civil society is just another term for NGOs, the sometimes admirable, sometimes maddening, always self-appointed, often unaccountable, ubiquitous practioners of all political arts except that of contesting and winning elections. You have been warned. □

John Grimond: foreign editor, *The Economist*

FUJITSU COMPUTERS
SIEMENS

SCENIC

Susie keeps secrets

Susie knows that information is a corporate resource and, like the people you employ, of immense value.

That's why, at Fujitsu Siemens, we put special emphasis on security, and build it in to our computers from the start. It's part of our commitment to enable your people to serve your customers.

Fujitsu Siemens SCENIC PCs use the latest, high-performance Intel® processors, up to Intel® Pentium® 4 processors. Find out more about the range from sleek, ultra-portable notebooks to super-scalable servers at **www.fujitsu-siemens.co.uk**

Fujitsu Siemens Computers use genuine Microsoft® Windows®
http://www.microsoft.com/piracy/howtotell

Work Orange

Because the way we work is changing.

Because work is something you do
not somewhere you go.

Because the world will be wirefree.™

You're not tied to a desk or the limit
of anyone else's ambition.

Because nine to five is irrelevant.

You're on email, voice mail, the internet,
the extranet and you can share ideas
using portable, pocketable, high speed
everything.

Today you can achieve more in an hour
than your father did in a week.

And tomorrow you'll use systems that
will talk to each other without even getting
you involved.

Because it's OK to derive as much satisfaction
from your labour as your leisure.

Because you're standing at the threshold
of a boundless, liberating future.

And because you want to be in business with
a company that believes wirefree™ technology
isn't just changing the way we're organised,
it's changing the way we think.

Don't you?

To find out how to Work Orange call 0800 731 3330
or visit www.orange.co.uk/business

The future's bright. The future's Orange.

DIARY FOR 2002

January

Euro notes and coins arrive in the shops and pockets of 12 European countries.

Spain takes on the presidency of the EU.

Portuguese foreign minister, Jaime José Matos de Gama, becomes chairman of Europe's Organisation of Security and Co-operation.

The Basel Committee of rich-country bank supervisors publishes its new proposals on capital adequacy.

Abdel Basset Ali Mohammed al-Megrahi appeals his conviction for the Lockerbie bombing.

New Orleans hosts the 36th Superbowl for a record ninth time.

The World Economic Forum meets in Davos, Switzerland.

Queen Margarethe II celebrates 30 years on the Danish throne.

The EU's dolphin-friendly ban on drift-net fishing enters into force.

February

Parliamentary and presidential elections in Costa Rica.

Winter Olympics in Salt Lake City.

Carnival in Rio de Janeiro.

Chinese new year 4700: the year of the horse.

The heir to the Dutch throne, Willem-Alexander, Prince of Orange, marries in a civil ceremony.

February 28th—the last date for the removal of national currencies in the euro zone.

March

Parliamentary elections in Ukraine, Chad, Jamaica and the Bahamas. Presidential election in Zimbabwe. The end of the line for Robert Mugabe?

Hong Kong's Legislative Council is re-elected by 800 wise men and women. The Basic Law allows for real democratic elections in 2007.

Muslim new year 1423.

Uttar Pradesh, India's largest state, goes to the polls. Expect the ruling BJP to lose and the national government to wobble.

Swiss referendum on whether to join the United Nations. If successful, it will become the 190th member.

March 24th—the 74th Academy awards, the Oscars, in Los Angeles.

April

Parliamentary election in Hungary.

Japan's schools lower the starting age for learning English from 13 to six.

The IMF and World Bank meet: will recovery be in sight?

Indian schools end compulsory animal dissection.

American and Vietnamese officials hold their first conference on Agent Orange, a toxic defoliant used during the Vietnam war.

The World Curling Championship, North Dakota.

Starting this month, all cars sold in the EU will have to be recycled by their manufacturers at the end of their lives.

The London and Paris marathons.

May

Presidential elections in France and Colombia. Parliamentary election in the Netherlands.

EU and Latin American leaders meet in Madrid.

The soccer World Cup kicks off in South Korea and Japan. Look out for France and Argentina.

June

Parliamentary elections in the Czech Republic, Algeria and Papua New Guinea. Presidential and parliamentary elections in Bolivia.

June 26th—Canada hosts a meeting of the G8 in Kananaskis, Alberta.

EU summit in Seville, Spain.

Queen Elizabeth II celebrates 50 years on the British throne.

Sweden, Denmark and Finland eliminate limits on travellers importing alcohol and tobacco.

July

Denmark takes on the presidency of the EU.

The Commonwealth Games in Manchester, England.

The Tour de France, the shortest ever, starts in Luxembourg; 3,400km later, the winner arrives in Paris.

August

The 56th Edinburgh International Festival.

Nike takes on the merchandising operation of Manchester United, Britain's top football team, in a deal worth £303m.

12,000 people throw 100,000kg of over-ripe tomatoes at each other to mark harvest thanksgiving in Bunyol, Spain.

September

Presidium election in Bosnia-Hercegovina. Parliamentary elections in Sweden, Slovakia and Germany.

World Summit on Sustainable Development in Johannesburg.

Russia conducts its first post-Soviet census.

September 11th—first anniversary of the terrorist attack on the World Trade Centre in New York. The world will still be recovering.

The Chinese Communist Party's 16th Congress. Hu Jintao will be appointed party secretary. Jiang Zemin will remain in control.

October

Presidential and parliamentary elections in Brazil and Ecuador. Parliamentary election in Pakistan.

The leaders of the Asia Pacific Economic Co-operation (APEC) group meet in Puerto Vallarta, Mexico.

The decennial World Space Congress meets in Houston.

40th anniversary of release of The Beatles' first single, "Love Me Do".

November

November 5th—Americans go to the polls to elect a new House of Representatives, a third of the Senate and 36 state governors.

Presidential election in Slovenia. Parliamentary election in Morocco.

NATO meets in Prague, and expands eastwards.

December

Presidential election in South Korea.

Pakistan's Ghazi Barotha hydroelectric station becomes fully operational.

World Scouting Jamboree in Thailand.

A total solar eclipse plunges Africa and Australia into darkness.

EU summit in Denmark. Greece then assumes the presidency.

infrastructure: it starts with you.

When you left the office last night, you worked for a medium-sized, independent company with ten smoothly running accounts across Europe.

When you walked in this morning, you were greeted by an e-mail announcing that you've just landed a new piece of business—which happens to be bigger than all your current customers.

What's at the top of today's priority list? Figure out how to expand your supply chain and create distribution channels to service all of your client's retail locations around the world. And could you do it by tomorrow, thank you?

Hopefully, you've got an infrastructure that's built on technology that works around *your* needs, not the other way around. It should be standards-based, so you're limiting your risk. Adaptable, so you can quickly adjust to change. Reliable, so you're up and running without a problem.

At HP, we engineer infrastructure that starts with you—your business, your issues, your opportunities. So you can easily respond as your business expands, contracts or takes off in new directions.

Servers that are designed to address the critical nature of an always-on Internet infrastructure. Software that puts your entire network within easy reach of your keyboard. Storage that enables you to transparently scale your capacity. Service professionals to help you quickly design and deploy flexible solutions and infrastructures. As well as the support resources to help keep them running around the clock.

HP infrastructure solutions are based in the real world of business. Because the last time we checked, that's where we all work. Visit us at hp.co.uk/infrastructure.

invent

not here.

HOLMES POIROT & MARLOWE

Private Detectives

If you were searching for the perfect detective agency, 'Holmes, Poirot & Marlowe' would probably fit the bill. But what if you are looking for a dream team of the world's top investment managers? Well, we can help. As a major institutional investor, we offer you access to the world's top investment managers. We have cherry-picked the best, no matter where they work, to manage assets on our behalf. In effect, creating an investment dream team exclusive to Coutts clients. At times of market volatility, Coutts investment strategy to reduce risk through diversification has proven very effective. Why not track us down by calling on 020 7753 1963 or visit www.coutts.com/dreamteam

*British Muslims
at play*

A delightfully stodgy people

Anthony King

The British people will go about their lives as normal in 2002 regardless of the war on terrorism and the repercussions it may have at home. Tony Blair will not need to instruct them to. They would never think of doing anything else. Doggedness, patience and a certain stoicism remain British virtues. Like everyone else in the civilised world, Britons during 2002 will be apprehensive. The British government's unqualified support for America's war against terrorism makes Britain an obvious target. Britons will fear attacks on Canary Wharf and Big Ben like those on the Pentagon and the World Trade Centre. They will be aware of the ever-present threats of biological or chemical attack.

But they will keep their fears to themselves. Already in 2001, while American airports and aeroplanes were half empty, Britons caught the shuttles to London and Edinburgh, kept their business appointments in Milan and Düsseldorf and flew on holiday to Las Palmas and Tenerife. Budget airlines reported increased traffic. There was no boom in the sale of gas masks.

Part of the explanation lies in "Been there, done that". Folk memories of the 1940s Blitz are only now beginning to fade. More recently, repeated acts of IRA terrorism launched against civilian targets in Britain—including Canary Wharf—have inured the British to random deaths, disrupted communications and police cordons. Polls show that most Britons make no distinction between the IRA and al-Qaeda. Green terrorism is no better than crescent-shaped.

Britain's national self-image will also play a part. To feel fear is one thing, to show it another. Not good form. Un-British. Churchill remarked during the war that the British were the only people who liked to be told how bad things were—to be told the worst. Nothing has changed. Britain's stiff upper lip in 2002 will still refuse to quiver.

Nor will there be a significant change in a Briton's attitude towards his Muslim neighbour. Americans see Islam as foreign. Britons see it as domestic. Pakistanis play good cricket and as often as not for the local village team. The British empire used to be a great Islamic power, even if most Britons did not see it quite that way. Tens of millions of Muslims in Iraq, Palestine, Egypt, Somaliland, Zanzibar, Nigeria, the Sudan, Malaya and India were British subjects—in fact, if not always in form.

Many of their descendants still are. Two million Muslims live in and around London, the Midlands and the north of England—3.3% of the population. The east London rag trade, once dominated by Jews, is now dominated by Bangladeshi Muslims. The local food, once Kosher, is today Halal. East London Muslims remain, for the time being, poor. So do many Muslims in northern former cotton towns such as Bradford and Oldham. But most prosper; some are millionaires. There are as many Muslims, per head of population, as native whites in Britain's universities.

Racial tension occasionally flares, especially in the

2002

A good year for Northern Ireland: the fourth without a bomb. With the IRA's brand of terrorism isolated, expect Protestant extremists to behave badly but the economy to do well.

Anthony King: professor of government at Essex University; election commentator for the BBC and regular contributor to the *Daily Telegraph*

25

north of England. In 2002 such tension could mount if the war against terrorism is portrayed—by either side—as a war against Islam. But most native Britons, in their usual casual way, regard their Muslim neighbours as un-problematic (even when they are able to tell Muslims apart from Hindus, Buddhists and Sikhs).

Polls, including those taken after September 11th, indicate that most Britons think Muslims have fitted well into British society. Few imagine that British Muslims are terrorists or terrorist sympathisers. Islam is still seen as a peaceful religion. The war against terrorism will continue in 2002, but in Britain it will not be a holy civil war. □

The magic economy

Anatole Kaletsky

One of the few economic predictions that was not overturned by the extraordinary events of 2001 was that Britain would be a star performer among the advanced industrial countries. In fact, an excellent economic performance from Britain has been a long-odds wager that a betting man could have placed successfully each year since 1993. The question now is whether Britain's winning streak will be maintained for ten years running. The chances are that it will.

Despite the many ominous signs of world recession, the widespread manufacturing lay-offs and the heavy blows suffered by the financial, media and transport industries in the autumn, the British economy will again prove surprisingly resilient. In fact, Britain in 2002 will probably be the fastest-growing country in the G8 for the second year running. The bad news is that, as in 2001, this world-beating economy will only be the best of a particularly bad bunch.

Even if the OECD's forecasters prove too gloomy in their projection that growth in the advanced capitalist countries will slump to just 1.2% in both 2001 and 2002, the year ahead is clearly destined to be the worst since the 1991 recession, when the OECD's annual growth rate fell to the same level. Against this dismal background, Britain's performance would be quite creditable if it merely achieved the 1.6% growth rate forecast by the OECD. The official 2.25% to 2.75% growth range which the Treasury uses for budget planning—and will shade

Anatole Kaletsky: columnist on *The Times* and director of Kaletsky Economic Consulting

down only slightly in its 2002 forecasts—may, for a while, appear to be out of sight. Yet by the second half of the year, Gordon Brown's apparently rosy forecasts will look quite realistic and perhaps even a bit tame.

Looking beyond 2002, Britain's economic potential may be constrained by some very fundamental problems. These will hurt economic performance, both in absolute terms and relative to the rest of Europe for years ahead. Low productivity, an inadequate transport infrastructure and decades of under-investment in public services will start causing problems again as soon as the British economy returns to its trend rate of growth. This will mean serious upwards pressure on taxes in the absence of major reforms in public-service financing, especially of the health service. In 2002, however, the focus will be on Britain's economic virtues, rather than its vices, because it will be doing considerably better than any other countries in the G8.

Why will Britain outperform? The reasons for Britain's temporary advantage over America are obvious. Britain was much less exposed than America to the boom-bust cycle in technology stocks that entered the bust phase in 2001, and it did not suffer the devastating blow of September 11th. But why will Britain outdo its European neighbours, for the seventh time in ten years? The reasons can be divided into three groups: good policy, good luck and good economic structure.

Starting with policy, the Bank of England is under a legal obligation to pursue an activist approach to managing demand. Britain's symmetrical monetary policy target—inflation must neither exceed nor undershoot the 1.5% to 3.5% target range—means that the Bank treats economic weakness and inflationary overheating as equally threatening. The European Central Bank (ECB), by contrast, is mandated to worry only about inflation. As a result, British businesses and consumers know they can rely on monetary stimulus if the economy weakens.

In addition to a proactive monetary policy, Britain has the advantage of the strongest public finances in Europe and is not constrained by the European Monetary Union's Stability and Growth Pact. Unlike Germany and France, which are under pressure from the European Commission and the ECB to pursue the economic idiocy of tightening fiscal policy in a downturn, the British government will stick to its ambitious targets for expanding public spending and allow automatic fiscal stabilisers to

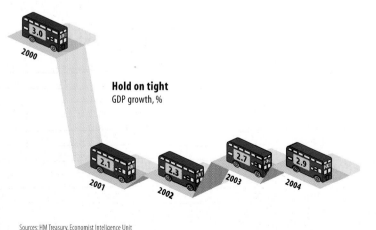

Hold on tight
GDP growth, %

3.0 — 2000
2.1 — 2001
2.3 — 2002
2.7 — 2003
2.9 — 2004

Sources: HM Treasury, Economist Intelligence Unit

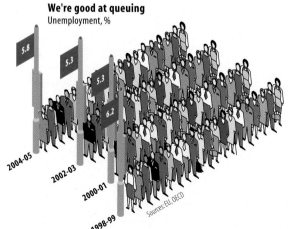

We're good at queuing
Unemployment, %

5.8 — 2004-05
5.3 — 2002-03
5.3 — 2000-01
6.2 — 1998-99

Sources: EU, OECD

IS THAT YOU?

MONT BLANC

Teamwork builds business

Integrated financial solutions
whatever your game

At WestLB we focus on delivering winning solutions worldwide. Our financial expertise, proven by our track record for creative solutions, could make the deciding difference to your game. Team up with WestLB and profit from our knowledge of the global business playing field.

www.westlb.com

A golden crown

It will be a right royal knees-up. From Friday May 31st, for four full days, Britain will be on holiday. Don't expect any business calls to be returned and don't be surprised if the official break extends to an unofficial week. The United Kingdom will be partying, toasting Her Majesty the Queen's 50th year upon the throne: the golden jubilee.

The country's love of royalty has much diminished over the years (though, in truth, there is no weight in the republican movement) but its love of a celebration has lessened not at all. For all the cynicism that understandably sticks to public figures, the queen is hugely respected. Seventy-five per cent of Britons cannot remember a time when she was not on the throne. The newspaper industry will, of course, turn out reams of sentimental pap. This should not disguise the quieter, firmer regard in which she is held by the nation.

Royalty and the tourist industry always march happily together. Hers will be a one-

The party girl

woman battle to lure back the foreign traveller scared away by war and pestilence. There will be a royal tour of the kingdom starting in May and a service of thanksgiving in St Paul's cathedral on June 4th. Appropriately, a huge horse show will be put on at

Windsor castle.

These will be the official events (doubtless, as is traditional, all in the pouring rain). But the more telling homage will be over pints of beer in pubs across the land when the average Brit will say "God bless her." □

---

work in full.

Turning to good luck, the British economy will be kept afloat in 2002 by several sources of strong demand that will happen to come into play at just the right time. Employment, for example, is bound to suffer from the downturn in manufacturing and finance, but the job losses will be largely offset by a big hiring boom in the social services, especially in health and education. A lot of the new jobs, though funded by the taxpayer, will be created in the private sector.

Consumer spending will slow by a percentage point or more from the torrid real growth rate of 6% which continued—to the consternation of the many Cassandras in the British financial establishment—right through the dotcom massacre, the foot-and-mouth epidemic and the terrible autumn of 2001. But the slowdown in private consumption in 2002 will be partly offset by higher government consumption and investment in infrastructure and construction, which will be boosted by low interest rates. Indeed, property and construction will remain two of the strongest businesses of the British economy.

A third piece of good fortune is the steady consolidation of the European financial and business service industries in London. This is the consequence of a fortuitous combination of the globalisation of all financial markets, and the dominance of English as the universal business language, with the creation of the euro and the gradual completion of the 1992 single-market project. The result of this confluence of factors is that London has become the unquestioned financial centre of the European market and the world's most important time zone.

Ironically, therefore, Britain will be among the biggest financial beneficiaries of the single-currency project, despite the government's current reluctance to adopt the euro as legal tender. Although the prime minister, Tony

Blair, will blow hot and cold on the euro issue, a decision will almost certainly be postponed until after the next general election, in 2005 or 2006.

Finally, consider the deeper structural foundations of Britain's improved economic performance. The most important are the labour market and competition reforms launched by Margaret Thatcher in the 1980s and continued (rather surprisingly) under a Labour government. These reforms have gradually changed Britain from a backward-looking country that was overly dependent on industries in long-term decline, into a very diverse economy. They have created a fairly deregulated and competitive business environment, at least by European standards. They have also transformed a unionised, class-ridden, reactionary army of industrial warriors into a flexible, individualistic workforce that is willing to learn new skills, accepts changes in status and is still fairly cheap by European standards, even with the pound at its present exalted exchange rate. As a result, highly publicised job losses in a few troubled industries, ranging from steel making and electronics to tourism and investment banking, will be offset by less noticeable gains in many other parts of the economy. And the employment gains will again exceed the losses, as the British economy re-accelerates in the spring or summer of 2002. The new-found diversity and

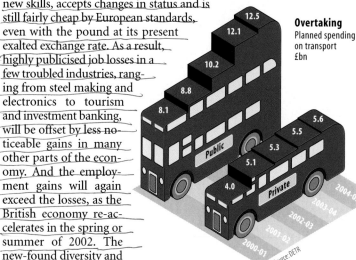

Overtaking
Planned spending on transport
£bn

Public
Private

12.5
12.1
10.2
8.8
8.1
4.0
5.1
5.3
5.5
5.5
5.6

2000-01
2001-02
2002-03
2003-04
2004-05

Source: DETR

flexibility of Britain's industrial structure will also help to keep the current-account deficit down to a manageable 2.5% of GDP, despite the continued strength of sterling.

Britain's ability and willingness to embrace change will not, on its own, guarantee rapidly rising standards of living. To match German, French or American levels of productivity in the long term will require more than deregulation, labour-market flexibility and sensibly pragmatic demand management. To become a truly first-rank economy, Britain will also need higher and better investment, improved management training, superior skills in the labour force, and many other of the mysterious factors that seem to contribute to outstanding levels of efficiency and productivity growth elsewhere. But those are challenges for the next decade. In the turbulent 12 months ahead, Britain's unusual flexibility will make it a world-beating economy. □

Why Britons will turn away from Westminster

Anthony King

A new fissure will develop in British politics in 2002. Isolated cracks are already appearing. They will merge by the end of the year to form a single—and potentially dangerous—fault line. British democracy will not be threatened. Respect for the country's democratic politicians, and for authority in general, almost certainly will be.

Traditionally, the main line of division in British politics has been the one familiar throughout Europe: left v right, labour v capital. But, in Britain as elsewhere, that line of division has largely disappeared. Consumer affluence and social mobility has silenced the guns of the class war. Throughout Europe, the traditional left-wing parties have changed in response. In Britain, New Labour, despite retaining the word "Labour" in its name (a

charming anachronism), makes no special appeal to the working classes. Labour in 2002 will remain an unashamedly pro-capitalist party.

Britain's Conservatives have no idea what to make of all this. They have become a party of pure opposition. Worse, British voters have no idea what to make of the Conservatives. Once the party of sound economic management, they stumbled badly in the 1990s. Once the party of noblesse oblige, they have now shed both their nobility (literally as well as morally) and their traditional top-down sense of obligation. It is clear what they are against: foreigners, welfare scroungers and the Labour Party, which keeps hammering them at elections. But it is not remotely clear to anyone—including themselves—what they are for.

And 2002 will only prolong the Conservatives' agony. To be sure, they will make gains in the May local elections but the turnout will be laughable and the Liberal Democrat Party's gains will appear just as impressive. More to the point, the Tories at the end of the year will look no more plausible as an alternative government than they did at the beginning. The fact that their new leader, Iain Duncan Smith, is a dull fellow is unimportant; successful politicians are often dull. What matters is that he has no clear conception—or indeed any conception—of how to engineer a Tory recovery. He will have fewer followers at the end of the year than at the beginning. Already some of the most able and voter-friendly Conservatives have declined, or not been asked, to serve in his shadow cabinet. Thus, Mr Duncan Smith's shadow cabinet in 2002 will consist almost entirely of has-beens and never-weres managed by never-will-bes. A few Conservatives of the broad church will defect to other parties. More will become internal exiles.

The Tories' failure to regroup and recover would be serious in any event: an adversarial political system like the British one needs real adversaries—at least two electable parties—if it is to function properly. What makes it more serious is that Tony Blair's Labour government, despite being re-elected with a huge parliamentary majority in 2001, is neither loved nor respected. Sure, it has managed the economy with reasonable competence; but its morals are dodgy (few in Britain credit either its promises or its press releases) and it has signally failed to do what most voters both expected and wanted it to do: namely, improve the quality of basic public services. The health service needs invasive surgery. Schools suffer chronic teacher shortages. Britain's roads, railways and urban mass transit systems have become a national joke—a bad one.

The result is a political vacuum. On the one hand, New Labour and the Blair government is discredited. On the other, only hard-core Conservatives (and not even all of them) dream of some future Tory restoration. The people have nowhere to turn to vent their frustration. More precisely, they have nowhere to turn within the conventional political order. Of course, they can cast protest votes for the Liberal

WITH THESE CRACKS I DON'T THINK IT HAS MUCH APPEAL

ANTIQUES ROAD SHOW

Democrats, but where will that get them? Even the Liberal Democrats' leader, Charles Kennedy, is too realistic to hold out the prospect of a Lib Dem government.

There are already signs of just how frustrated millions of Britons will become. In September 2000, high petrol prices led to protesters blockading oil depots. Severe fuel shortages ensued. Motorists might have been expected to resent the inconvenience they were subjected to, but instead they—and almost everyone else in the country— sided with the protesters. At the election in June 2001, a retired doctor with no previous political experience ran against one of Tony Blair's junior ministers. The doctor's nominal protest was against the closure of local hospital facilities, but most voters knew he was really protesting against "them". The doctor won. On the same day, some 40% of Britain's eligible electors failed to turn out. The turnout was the lowest in peacetime since 1874. Not all the non-voters were malcontents, disaffected from all the main political parties. But a large proportion were.

In 2002, to an even greater extent, the main line of political division in Britain will lie, not between traditional right and left, but between political class and the people, between all of "us" and all of "them". Popular disaffection will grow, especially as the government fails— as it must fail in the short term—to deliver on its promises of improved services. The impending economic downturn will only compound the disaffection.

How precisely the new fissure in British politics will manifest itself no one knows. But expect derisory turnouts in local elections and local referendums, street protests against everything from world capitalism to (again) rising fuel prices, more racial incidents and an increased level of industrial unrest. Some strikes will be directed against employers. More will be directed at the Blair government, as it seeks to reform the public sector.

Only one force can prevent such eruptions of popular discontent in 2002: a sustained United States-led war against terrorism, with the British feeling either threatened or directly involved. Under those circumstances, Britons would certainly re-engage with their political leadership. It would be temporary, however, and not enough to disguise the deeper, more divisive emotions of a people ever more disinclined to give either credit or moral support to their political system. □

Next stop London

The unhappy heart of rural England

Clive Aslet

One of the big subjects in Britain in 2002 will be the future of the countryside. Prince Charles said as much in 2001, and the government confirmed it by appointing Lord Haskins, Labour peer, millionaire and chairman of Northern Foods, as the supremo who will direct the restructuring of agriculture. Lord Haskins has little in common with the organic prince, a champion of the family-owned farm. Under the Haskins regime, small farmers, whose bones have already been shaken by the disasters of BSE, swine fever, and foot-and-mouth disease, will be rattled further. Farm acreages, already larger than those on the continent, will continue to get bigger. More owner-farmers will opt out of farming, preferring to sell

Clive Aslet: editor,
Country Life; author of
"A Horse in the Country"
(Fourth Estate)

One hundred years of childhood

Among all these predictions for 2002, cast your mind back 100 years. What are the lasting monuments of 1902? It was a year of wealth, prosperous imperialism in Britain, envious expansion in Germany, raucous American economic growth and festering terrorist movements in Eastern Europe and Russia.

Amid all this bustle, no one would have predicted that a little-known and retiring London spinster was to create that year's most memorable image: "Peter Rabbit". This is not mere nostalgia. In 2002, millions of copies of Beatrix Potter's tale will be sold in the West and Japan. Few indeed will be the homes that don't have either this tale (not 1,000 words long) or some product derived from it under their roof.

Two other children's books were published in 1902, both of which still flourish. Conan Doyle's most famous Sherlock Holmes story, "The Hound of the Baskervilles", sits on many an adolescent's bookshelf. And 1902 was also the year that Rudyard Kipling, having just returned to England, published the "Just-so Stories".

Who can now recall how the Kaiser strutted or which crises swirled around Theodore Roosevelt's White House? But who cannot recall an absurd but charming tale of a naughty rabbit and his siblings, Flopsy, Mopsy and Cotton-tail? It is a lesson in modesty that the strutters and players of 2002 would do well to remember. □

up or have their land farmed by a contractor.

In terms of the national economy, none of this matters very much. Agriculture contributes only around 1% to the economy. Following job losses of some 20,000 a year, it is no longer a big employer, even in rural areas. Successive food scares have undermined trust between farmers and the consumer. While almost every Parisian knows someone who works the land, many young English urbanites appear to hate the rural lobby.

They have a smidgen of a point. Leaving aside the devastation of tourism as well as agriculture caused by foot-and-mouth, the countryside has not done so badly. More new businesses are started in the countryside each year than in towns. The reason? The countryside is where entrepreneurs, like many other people, want to live. It is easy for rural lobbies such as the Countryside Alliance to talk up the problems of rural dwellers, not least because those problems caused by distance from the hospitals and other services in towns can never go away. But the rate of decline in rural life has, in some areas, slowed to a standstill. Only two or three rural schools will close in 2002, compared with 30 a year during the 1980s and 1990s. A £40m ($58m) fund has been established to help schools with less than 200 pupils.

Only 70% of parishes still have a shop, but those village shops that do survive qualify for a 50% relief on property taxes. More money is being spent on agri-envi-

ronmental schemes to safeguard wildlife habitats and open footpaths. Traditionally the countryside does better from Labour governments, open to the charge of not understanding it, than from Tory ones. For all their rural parliamentary seats, successive Conservative administrations did it few favours.

There has even been some progress in reviving rural markets. Five years ago there were no farmers' markets in the United Kingdom; now there are over 200. However, though the government officially backs the revival of market towns, the reality is that the supermarket giants will put high-street shops under still greater pressure during 2002. Supporters of the alternative food economy have to contend with the British shoppers' reluctance to spend more at the check-out. While the average family spent 30% of its income on food in the 1950s, that figure has now fallen to around 10%. This is extraordinarily low. Not only do the French spend considerably more on food, so does the average American family. Other issues are similarly hard to resolve. Public transport is dire, with only one in four rural parishes having so much as a daily bus service. Relative poverty, more sporadic in the country than in towns and therefore more difficult to tackle, will increase in 2002. House prices will too.

Surveys show that most Britons would, in an ideal world, live in the countryside. Family fragmentation, with children leaving home earlier, couples divorcing and

London's great expectations

A bubble for babble

London will stir, quietly but mightily, in 2002. The capital's movement, although not invisible, will require an observant eye to spot. It will happen deep underground, behind hoardings and scaffolds, and—most important—on the desks of London's planners and property developers. Look for it especially around the edge of central London. King's Cross, Paddington and Battersea will all be revived.

The bureaucrats of the Greater London Authority, who are planning much of this change, will settle into the new glass-panelled City Hall, located south of the Thames, just op-

posite the City. Ken Livingstone, London's mayor, will be back in the kind of headquarters that both main political parties have tried for so long to prevent him from having.

London needs one thing above all: a solution to the creaking public-transport system. It will not seem so to the wretched passenger, but finally a solution is being found. At the centre of the government's plans is Cross Rail, a fast, limited-stop rail line that will connect east and west London. It is designed to take pressure off the London Underground. Much delayed, the £3.8 billion ($5.5 billion) project will finally begin to take form

in 2002 as financing and planning start in earnest.

Expect to see busy preparations for the capital's new traffic policy. When it is introduced in 2003, this will seek to charge drivers each day they enter the city centre by car. The technology should allow vehicles to be charged automatically. Cameras and computer-recording equipment will spring up in the streets. There will be a period of chaos on the roads as they are made bus-friendly. The experiment, the biggest of its kind, will be watched by other world cities.

Over in Battersea, a long-empty power station will be developed into an exclusive housing and leisure complex. Plans will also be finalised for a bridge between Battersea and Pimlico, for pedestrians and bikes. Expect the Millennium Bridge, which gracefully spans the river between St Paul's and Tate Modern, to be open at last, cured of its propensity to wobble. Alongside it will be the Jubilee Bridge, a new pedestrian link connecting Cannon Street with the South Bank, that will open in June. So, even if the roads are all dug up, and the tubes are not working, there will still be some interesting new London walks. □

old people living longer, have already generated a need for several million new homes. The surge in immigration has put the housing stock under still greater pressure. Perhaps two-thirds of new homes in Britain will be built on brown-field, or previously developed, land. That still leaves an awful lot that must go on green-field sites. Building new housing estates in the countryside will inevitably create tensions, and perhaps another bone of contention between the government and rural dwellers.

2002 well may see government sympathy for the countryside running thin. Politicians noted that the foot-and-mouth disease did not dent the prime minister's popularity. This may lead them to conclude they can do as they like. They would, however, be rash to play with the visceral emotions of traditional country dwellers. All of them feel hard done by. Watch out. □

New wealth and old

Martin Vander Weyer

As times change, so do the relativities of wealth and influence. In the darker world of 2002, Britain will not fulfil the glowing economic forecasts that were commonplace a year or two ago; nor will it live up to the chancellor, Gordon Brown's oft-repeated claim to have defeated the cycle of boom and bust. There will still be more wealth, old and new, than ever before, with more than 150,000 sterling millionaires—but much of it will not be where it was once expected to be.

The bursting of the technology bubble, the slump of the stockmarket and the terrorist attacks on America put paid not only to many potential fortunes, but to an anything's-possible entrepreneurial mood that came with them. Tony Blair's election victory in 2001 might have suggested easy times ahead for an elite of wealthy media and business figures who held influence in New Labour. But three months later, armed conflict and global recession gave the government a new seriousness and diminished their sway.

The most stable wealth in Britain in 2002 will be old wealth. The property boom which had seen London house prices rising in mid-2001 at an annual rate of around 15% will see a sharp deceleration—hit particularly by a decline in buying power among City executives. But a healthy economy and prevailing low interest rates will make a 1991-style property crash unlikely, and London's continuing importance as a financial centre may underpin the luxury rental market, long dominated by American expatriates. All of which means that the fortunes of London's historic landlords—the Duke of Westminster, who owns Mayfair and Belgravia, Earl Cadogan in Chelsea and the Howard de Walden family in Marylebone, estimated to be worth £6.5 billion between them—are safe as houses. Indeed, almost anyone who owns an unmortgaged home in central London will probably count

as a millionaire.

Opportunities to make one's fortune in finance will be scarce. If the stockmarket does not recover some of its bounce, traders and corporate financiers will be among the biggest losers in 2002. At least 30,000 investment bankers worldwide were expected to lose their jobs by the end of 2001. There are more redundancies to come and the March 2002 bonus season will be the leanest for years.

Conversely, as with property, old fortunes will fare better: the Fleming and Schroder families, for example, both sold large parts of their businesses in 2000 when the going was good, and hold £1 billion to show for it. And in the middle-ranking professional classes, there will be ample fees for the partners of City law firms such as Clifford Chance—perhaps, as has become common in the United States, defending banks and brokers against disgruntled investors. Top accountants at firms such as PricewaterhouseCoopers will also stay prosperous, notably those who specialise in insolvency. Even the top echelons of the civil service should remain comfortable: a recent survey showed that 5% of British millionaires work in the public sector.

But who will be ahead of the pack in 2002? Certainly not the new breed of Internet and telecoms entrepreneurs. Those with the most sensible business models—such as Charles Dunstone of the Carphone Warehouse chain—have the best chance of survival. Low-cost airlines such as Stelios Haji-Ioannou's easyJet—provided it can operate normally—should fare well. In periods of low consumer confidence, the high-street winners are value-for-money supermarkets, cheap-clothing stores and DIY chains: that should mean a safe year for the Sainsbury fortune, and for newer names such as John Hargreaves of the Matalan discount chain. There will also be opportunities for takeover players: Guy Hands, a former Nomura financier, and Philip Green, a retail entrepreneur, are men to watch.

A downturn will also prove the mettle of Britain's Asian entrepreneurs. With tight-knit family management and strong cost-control, their business model is well designed for adversity. In food, textiles and low-tech manufacturing, and in electronic and pharmaceutical retailing, their prominence will increase. Brothers Vijay and Bikhu Patel in health care and the Almahomed family in plastic-bag manufacturing offer good examples.

Wealth will continue to accrue to stars of sport and entertainment: television chefs, footballers and pop stars. Perhaps 2002 will produce another J.K. Rowling, whose Harry Potter books are said to have made her $100m. But celebrity fortunes are one-in-a-million. In 2002 prosperity will come more easily to those with feet-on-the-ground businesses. And it will reside most with those who have put faith in Britain's most traditional store of wealth: bricks and mortar. □

The world is their oyster
Number of dollar billionaires

USA 269
Germany 28
Switzerland 15
France 16
Britain 12
Japan 29

Sources: Forbes, The World in 2002

2002

A gentleman's club is no longer his own. The Athenaeum in London, 178 years after its founding, admits women.

Martin Vander Weyer: associate editor of the Week and contributor to the Daily Telegraph

**The 2001 BMW
5 Series**

www.bmw.co.uk
Tel. 0800 325 600

**The Ultimate
Driving Machine**

These BMWs are similar in many ways. They share the same chassis. They all have near perfect weight distribution.

Models featured: The 2001 5 Series range with the new 6-cylinder, V8 and 400bhp engines. Prices from £23,540. Prices correct at time of going to press. For information

They're all rear-wheel drive. Which means they're all built for performance. It's just that some are hotter than others.

regarding financial services available to business users, please contact your local BMW dealer.

Alain de Botton, essayist and philosopher, foresees new shapes for old paranoias

Status anxiety

"It will be a year when many people's self-esteem will suffer along with their economic fortunes"

We're so accustomed to the sober statistical language of modern economics that there's a danger of losing a sense of the human stories stirring beneath it. A growth of x% in a nation's GDP refers in essence to an increase in the number of overcast Saturday afternoons in which people have returned from the shops with a scented candle or a new fridge freezer. And beneath an economic slowdown lies not just a decrease in the amount of money in wallets, but also a complex, troublesome range of feelings in what the poets have called the heart.

2002 will be a year of slowdown, perhaps a year of profound recession. In previous centuries, in the economies of what is now called the industrialised world, this would have meant death on an important scale. For most readers of *The World in 2002*, recession will not mean starvation, but it may mean an outbreak of what sociologists have awkwardly termed "status anxiety".

All societies are arranged hierarchically and all of us are endowed with a specific status. In feudal times, status was determined by birth. You were a noble or a peasant because your father had been. There was little social mobility, downwards or upwards. Economies were sluggish. Wealth was tied up in land, fortunes were (wars or the whims of a monarch aside) slow to make and relatively slow to lose.

Life was grim for most, but there was one great psychological consolation for the state of affairs: one was not responsible for one's status. It was bad being a peasant, but peasanthood hadn't come about because one had failed an exam, left a boss unimpressed or misread the stockmarket. Peasanthood was a condition ascribed at birth by society or, as one would hear on Sundays, by a benevolent God, who was in any case sure to right things in the next world.

The 18th century changed all that, with two events in particular: the American and French revolutions. Behind both lay an ideology of social movement. People were, it was said by Rousseau and others, born equal. Some utopian thinkers understood this to mean that they should live equally too. But, a few experiments aside, it was generally held that they should start off equally and then find a place in the hierarchy according to their own virtues (at making money).

A consequence of this ideology was a new understanding of success and failure. Expressed in its crudest way by 19th-century social Darwinists, the rich were fitter than the poor and the successful (in business) were "better" than the failures.

Ascribing status by achievement rather than birth has released enormous energies and talents. But, during recessionary periods, when one is facing unemployment or hard times, the method is also an enormous generator of status anxiety. The poor of old were not responsible for their poverty. The poor and the bankrupt of new have a harsher psychological landscape to contend with. They are to blame or at least feel to blame for their condition. It is no coincidence that in the United States, the country that has most firmly embraced a meritocratic ideology, the two most successful publishing genres are books on how to get rich and books on how to recover one's self-esteem. Expect strong sales of the latter in 2002. It is when one has tried to get rich and failed that the need to feel better about oneself becomes paramount. As Emile Durkheim pointed out in his famous essay, "On Suicide", the material consequences of failure are less in modern society, but the psychological consequences are far greater (hence the high rate of suicide in developed countries).

It will be a year when many people's self-esteem will suffer along with their economic fortunes. If you are what you earn, then many of us will feel not just poorer but less worthy—and the unworthiness will arguably be more of a problem than the poverty. Our troubles will be part of a global downturn, but this won't help to shift the humiliation of being fired. We will fear that in the eyes of a world that loves winners, we have become losers.

Who's for denial?

What will people do with their status anxiety? We can expect to see a resurgence of two manoeuvres of mind in 2002. First, people will divert their status anxiety outwards, they will seek an explanation for their troubles that does not only refer to their own shortcomings. Instead of bearing all the blame for failure, it will be "global capitalism", "government" or "the markets". Paranoid theories will thrive alongside more acute criticisms of the economic order. One writer will successfully harness the slack left by the collapse of the old left-wing ideology and produce a brilliant critique of the economic system.

Expect a second manoeuvre of mind to combat status anxiety. People will try to separate their sense of worth from their financial achievements. They will rebut the idea that the most important thing about who they are is the place they occupy in the financial hierarchy. Historically in the West, there have been two great intellectual attempts at this kind of separation, Stoicism and Christianity, and neo-versions of both will thrive.

For the Stoic philosopher Seneca (writing in the 40s AD), the wise should never judge themselves according to wealth. For wealth is a gift of the goddess of Fortune and she is a fickle and irrational creature. We should not take her too seriously when we are rich or when she has made us poor.

Similarly, for St Augustine, true Christians do not esteem themselves more when they are at the top of the social pole than at the bottom. The true hierarchy of merit among people has nothing to do with the official worldly hierarchy. Both views will seem particularly comfortable in 2002. □

Europe takes the plunge

Lionel Barber

Europe, which seems at times to change so slowly, will have a revolutionary year. Over 300m citizens of the European Union will have new euro notes and coins arriving in their pockets in January. By the end of February they will have lost the national currencies of a lifetime. The psychological and economic landscape of the continent will be changed forever. A second revolution, almost as big, will occur later in the year. The full 15 members of the club will decide on a batch of new entrants from Central, Eastern and Southern Europe, most likely to join by 2004.

This enlargement will redraw the political map of Europe. But it will also mark the launch of a constitutional debate about legitimacy and democratic accountability. In the past, Europe's leaders have paid lip-service only; now they cannot escape a serious debate.

The reason is that eastern enlargement will break the precedent of controlled expansion. In the past, starting with the entry of Britain, Denmark and Ireland in 1973, the EU has preferred to enlarge modestly. In 1986, Spain and Portugal followed the earlier entry of Greece. In 1995, the EU welcomed Austria, Finland and Sweden. Barring unexpected complications, the list of prospective members this time round will include at least five, possibly eight or, at a stretch, ten members. The favoured few are likely to include the Czech Republic, Cyprus, Hungary, Slovenia and at least one Baltic state, probably Estonia. The list may also include Latvia, Lithuania, Malta, Poland and Slovakia. Only Bulgaria, Romania and Turkey will be left behind.

A "big bang" enlargement brings to the fore the issue of how to organise an EU of 20-plus countries. Thanks to pressure from Germany, the EU is expected to launch a convention in spring 2002 made up of constitutional experts, national parliamentarians and members of

the European Parliament to discuss power-sharing in a wider Union.

The convention will fall short of the 1787 version in Philadelphia—where are Europe's Madisons?—and it will most certainly not lead to a fully fledged constitution. But unlike previous debates, that have taken place between experts behind closed doors, it will involve public exchanges under the watchful eye of a heavyweight chairman, possibly even a former European prime minister. The convention will open in the spring and will last at least 12 months. Top of the agenda will be how best to share power between the central decision-making bodies in Brussels, the national parliaments and the regions. German experts have suggested a catalogue of responsibilities, but this seems too elaborate. Expect a more general declaration of principle.

The convention will examine the case for a new body to scrutinise EU legislation to check if it is too intrusive. It may suggest taking the selection of the president of the European Commission, the EU executive, out of the hands of Europe's leaders. One idea is to let candidates head the slate of European Parliament groups in the 2004 elections. This would mark a belated effort to restore the authority of the commission which, under its president, Romano Prodi, has lost the role of political beacon in Europe which it enjoyed 15 years ago under Jacques Delors.

Still, we should not assume that enlargement is a done deal. 2002 will involve difficult negotiations between the current 15 members and the applicant countries over the two issues that matter most: regional aid and the common agricultural policy.

The poorer EU countries—notably Greece, Portugal and Spain—have made clear that they will not countenance an enlargement which, in the words of former

2002
NATO meets in Prague and will approve expansion to the east. Welcome the Baltic states and a couple of lucky others to the alliance.

Lionel Barber: editor of the European edition of the *Financial Times*

Who gives, who takes
Annual net contributions to, and receipts from, the EU budget, €m

Contributors
Germany 11,700
Britain 5,400
The Netherlands 1,800
Sweden 1,200
France 1,000

Beneficiaries
Belgium 1,100
Ireland 1,800
Portugal 2,700
Greece 3,700
Spain 6,700

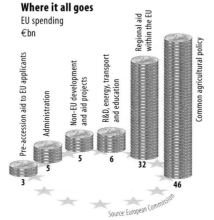

Where it all goes
EU spending €bn

Pre-accession aid to EU applicants 3
Administration 5
Non-EU development and aid projects 5
R&D, energy, transport and education 6
Regional aid within the EU 32
Common agricultural policy 46

Source: European Commission

Spanish premier Felipe Gonzalez, takes place on the back of their own farmers. Richer countries such as France and Germany have made the same point. Germany, nominally one of the most enthusiastic supporters of enlargement, is also worried about the impact on its poorer eastern regions. So expect a loud crisis as the climax nears in the enlargement negotiations. The prospective entry of Cyprus, the perennial powderkeg, is certain to provoke tensions between Greece and Turkey, especially if only the Greek half of the island is deemed fit for membership. Another source of tension is Poland, the biggest country by population and the most important in geo-political terms. Through a combination of arrogance and incompetence in previous administrations, Poland has fallen behind other applicants in meeting the *acquis communautaire*, the accumulated rules of the club, and could fail to make the "first wave" of entrants.

The threat of a crisis weighs heavier because of the electoral calendar in Europe. In the spring, France begins the first round of presidential elections with Jacques Chirac, the farmers' best friend, standing for re-election against the likely Socialist candidate, prime minister Lionel Jospin. In the autumn, Gerhard Schröder, Social Democratic chancellor, is running for re-election in Germany. Both countries will find it hard to block the entry of Poland. So one possibility is that the EU member states could order a "pause", delaying future membership for the select few for a few months until Poland is ready. This would trigger a furore among other applicant countries, most of which have been anxiously waiting for membership since the collapse of communism more than a decade ago.

Britain is also watching the European electoral calendar warily. The British government will be counting on Spain to further the cause of liberalisation, particularly once the centre-right government moves into the rotating EU presidency on January 1st 2002. Its hopes are pinned on the EU summit in Barcelona in March 2002. This will review progress on the March 2000 Lisbon summit, which set an ambitious timetable for boosting European competitiveness in biotechnology, energy and information technology. Britain would dearly like to use Barcelona as a showcase for the argument that Europe is moving Britain's neo-liberal way. This would form an important part of a future campaign to persuade the British people to join the euro. □

2002
More Anglo-Saxon capitalism for Germany. The 50% capital-gains tax on sales of corporate equity is scrapped, creating an incentive for reduced cross-shareholdings. The junk-bond market could benefit as companies issue high-yield debt to finance acquisitions.

Who's generous?
Annual asylum acceptances per million population

Italy 26
France 115
UK 176
Sweden 1,028
Germany 122
Denmark 97

Sources: Eurostat, *The World in 2002*

Barbara Beck: surveys editor, *The Economist*

Is Germany stuck?

Barbara Beck

If there is one prediction about Germany that can be made with certainty, it is that its politics in the coming year will not be boring. On September 22nd the Germans go to the polls to deliver their judgment on the Social Democratic/Green coalition government they voted in four years earlier, when they made a break from 16 years of Christian Democratic rule. In 1998, the mandate they gave their new chancellor, Gerhard Schröder, was far from overwhelming: a majority for his government in the Bundestag (the lower house of parliament) of just 16. How will he fare in 2002?

His first year in office was a litany of disasters that convinced many people he would remain a one-term chancellor. His reputation as a *Macher* (man of action), earned in his previous job as premier of Lower Saxony, took a steep dip. But his problems seemed to concentrate his mind, and he had soon re-established himself as a tough and effective political wheeler-dealer. He used those qualities to start tackling the *Reformstau* (backlog of reforms) with which his veteran predecessor, Helmut Kohl, had been unable to get to grips. First, Mr Schröder launched a five-year programme of tax reforms, starting in 2001, designed to make the German economy more flexible and more competitive. Next, and less boldly, he had a go at Germany's increasingly unaffordable state-pension system, encouraging more private provision. He also made a start on the politically sensitive problem of immigration into Germany.

But as 2001 wore on, he gradually changed his image from "man of action" to "steady hand". The choice was not entirely his. After a bright start to the year, the economic climate was increasingly gloomy. Unemployment was starting to rise again. Given the need to woo the trade unions, Mr Schröder may have judged this the wrong moment to tackle Germany's inflexible labour markets. Indeed, recent legislation has arguably made them even more inflexible.

But Mr Schröder is bound to upset the trade unions anyway by failing to reduce unemployment as promised. By the next election, he repeatedly said, it would come down to below 3.5m (from about 4m when he took office). But despite a plethora of work-creation schemes, it is still running at around 3.9m, or about 9% of the workforce, and has recently been rising again. One reason is precisely that labour markets remain unreformed, so employers are wary about hiring people they may not easily be able to shed again. Another is that the integration of Germany's eastern *Länder* has proved much slower and more difficult than originally expected. More than a decade after unification, and despite the expenditure of hundreds of billions of D-marks, the economy of eastern Germany is lagging well behind. Unemployment there is roughly twice the west German level.

But the main trouble is the economic slowdown that started in the spring of 2001. By the summer, forecasters were rapidly revising their growth predictions for that year from close to 3% to successively lower figures. In early autumn the International Monetary Fund came up

A qualified welcome

Barbara Beck

Germany is not an immigration country. German politicians have been intoning this mantra for decades, in the face of mounting evidence to the contrary. Since 1955, some 30m immigrants have come to Germany. Many have gone back to where they came from, but the country is still home to the biggest number of foreigners in Europe: a total of over 7m, more than 9% of the population. This total includes about 2m people from within the EU (who have an automatic right of entry), but it excludes 3m ethnic German immigrants from the former Soviet Union, who were welcomed with open arms even though many of them could not speak German when they arrived.

2002 may be the year when Germany officially acknowledges that it has become an immigration country after all—not because it has taken pity on foreigners who want to come in, but because it has realised that it needs a large number of extra workers that its home market cannot supply. An independent commission reported in July 2001 that the country was having trouble filling jobs and would be suffering acute labour shortages across all sectors by 2010. Moreover, if current demographic trends continue, by 2050 Germany's present population of 82m will have dropped to below 60m. Nearly half the adult population will then be above retirement age, and there will be far too few workers to pay for all those pensions.

One answer, the commission suggested, would be to allow in large numbers of well-qualified immigrants from outside the European Union. The German chancellor, Gerhard Schröder, took a first step in that direction in 2000, when he launched a "green-card" scheme to admit up to 20,000 IT specialists a year from countries such as India. It met with much opposition. Now the commission is suggesting much larger numbers—50,000 a year to begin with, and rising—and says that many of them should be able to settle in Germany permanently.

Otto Schily, Germany's interior minister, is now trying to put legislation in place to liberalise immigration policy from the start of 2002. His difficulty will be gaining cross-party support. His Social Democratic Party's coalition partners, the Greens, think the proposals do not go nearly far enough; the (conservative) opposition Christian Democrats think they go much too far. But even the Christian Democrats realise that something has changed. These days, when their politicians intone that well-worn mantra, they use a subtly different version: Germany is not a *classical* immigration country. □

---

with a shockingly low 0.9%. Most forecasters insist that 2002 will be better, with growth of 2% or more. Inflation, too, which in 2001 had been pushed up by higher oil and food prices, is due to return to more normal levels.

Mr Schröder's government has blamed the problems on the economic slowdown elsewhere. And to be fair, members of the euro zone now have limited scope to combat a domestic downturn on their own. In the old days, the obvious remedy would have been to cut interest rates. But these days interest rates for euro-zone members are set by the European Central Bank. Go-it-alone fiscal relaxation has also become more difficult. In Germany, the opposition has suggested bringing forward some of the tax cuts due to be implemented over the next few years. That might well provide an early stimulus, but it would also play havoc with the country's budget consolidation plans.

But even if Mr Schröder cannot pull an economic rabbit out of the hat, he may still win the election. His poll ratings have come down but those of his opponents have not shot up. The Christian Democratic camp is in disarray. The damage done by the party-finance scandal that felled ex-chancellor Helmut Kohl still rumbles on. The current party leader, Angela Merkel, although squeaky clean, is perceived as lacking the authority and experience required of a chancellor. Edmund Stoiber, the boss of the Christian Democrats' sister party in Bavaria and another possible candidate, has both qualities in abundance, but he may be too Bavarian to appeal to Germans outside his home state. To complicate matters, Mr Schröder is having to fight on several fronts. Even his own Social Democrats have shown signs of disunity, not least over sending German troops to Macedonia. And his Green coalition partners have also proved difficult of late, especially over immigration. They may gain less than 5% of votes, below which a party gets no seats.

But Mr Schröder is not known as a *Macher* for nothing. He may try to form a coalition with the small, liberal Free Democratic Party, which for many years was the Christian Democrats' partner in government, but in the more distant past has also governed with the Social Democrats. If that doesn't work, he might consider forming a minority government, or even a grand coalition with the Christian Democrats. One way or another, he is determined to remain in office. He may well succeed. □

Geared up Schröder

Which one will have the last laugh?

The French state stays static

Alan Riding *Paris*

Alan Riding: Paris correspondent, *New York Times*

The French are readying themselves for presidential and parliamentary elections in the spring with remarkably little interest in the result. This could be a sign that they are contented. More probably it means they expect little change, no matter the outcome. What does seem clear is that most will be no more than spectators as power and its privileges are once again carved up among a small circle of all too familiar faces.

There is no state in Europe whose leaders have been longer in politics. The Gaullist president, Jaques Chirac, first held elective office when Tony Blair was a teenager. The Socialist prime minister, Lionel Jospin, started in politics when George Bush was at school. Politics in

France is a lifelong profession. And in 2002 the old warhorses will again do battle.

After four years of a surprisingly civil cohabitation, things have now soured between Mr Chirac and Mr Jospin. Both men are presumed presidential candidates and are expected to face each other in a run-off election (as they did in 1995) after a dozen or so other candidates are eliminated in the first round. Both men are also suddenly looking vulnerable, less to candidates like Jean-Pierre Chevènement on the left and François Bayrou on the right, but to their own records. With polls suggesting a tight race, they have turned their guns on each other.

Mr Chirac, plagued by scandals dating back to his long reign as mayor of Paris between 1977 and 1995, has an obvious weak flank. Investigating magistrates have named him as a suspect in illegal financing of his Gaullist party and even in dubious use of public funds to finance family holidays. Claiming constitutional immunity, the president refuses to testify, but this has persuaded many French that he has something to hide.

Mr Jospin has also been tripped up by his past. His belated admission of ties to a tiny Trotskyite faction until 1982 (when he was already secretary-general of the Socialist Party) revealed he had long lied about the connection. His real problems, though, are more immediate. An economic slowdown is threatening his government's main achievement—that of lowering unemployment and priming the fastest growth in a decade—and is already undermining the shaky leftist coalition that brought him to office in 1997.

As a campaigner, Mr Chirac has the edge, never happier than when he is slapping backs and pressing the flesh. Exercising his right as president to run foreign policy, he was also able to play international statesman after the terrorist attacks in the United States last September: he was the first foreign leader to visit Washington, DC, and New York after the attacks. But if Mr Jospin is often dour and irritable in public, he also comes over as more serious. One leading businessman described the choice: "*Chirac est sympathique, mais incompétent. Jospin est compétent, mais pas sympathique.*"

For 2002, there are further variables. Mr Jospin's move to cut the presidential term from seven to five years was generally applauded. His decision to hold presidential

NORDIC COUNTRIES

FORECAST

The four Nordic countries—Denmark, Norway, Sweden and Finland—have much in common, from traditions of consensus government to prosperity and world-class public services. But one issue divides them all: Europe. The divisions will widen in 2002, as the euro becomes legal tender in Finland, enabling the Finns to go shopping in 11 other European countries without stepping into a bureau de change. But both Denmark and Sweden (which hold parliamentary elections in 2002) have rejected the chance to join the single currency, while Norway has opted to stay outside the European Union altogether.

Might the Danes, at least, change their minds? A new referendum on the euro is not on the agenda, even though Danish opposition may soften slightly once Denmark assumes the EU's rotating presidency in the

second half of 2002. The Swedes seemed to become more positively disposed towards monetary union after the Swedish presidency in the first half of 2001. EU enlargement negotiations with applicants are supposed to be concluded by the end of 2002. Denmark has made achieving a successful outcome one of the main objectives of its presidency.

All four economies are fundamentally sound, with government budgets and current accounts firmly in surplus. They will rebound somewhat. Norway will finally start to spend some of its oil wealth to boost the domestic economy.

An enviable quality of life will just get better. Offices close at 4pm, helping to make the Nordic people the world's second-largest consumers of leisure goods (after Americans). They are also the fittest: the Swedes are the

slimmest people in the OECD.

For a woman, there's no better place to work than in this part of the world. In Denmark women will be granted nine months' paid maternity leave. They will also earn 70% of men's salaries, the highest rate in the world, with Swedish women a close second at 68%. □

GDP GROWTH (%)	2000	2001	2002
Denmark	2.6	1.4	2.0
Finland	5.2	0.8	2.7
Iceland	4.1	1.5	0.5
Norway	2.7	1.8	2.1
Sweden	4.3	1.8	2.0

Economist Intelligence Unit

the EURO.
OUR *money*

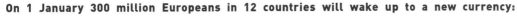

On 1 January 300 million Europeans in 12 countries will wake up to a new currency: the euro. The euro is not new: it's been used in electronic transactions and by banks and international businesses since January 1999. But with the upcoming launch of euro banknotes and coins, anyone who lives, does business or is travelling in any of the 12 countries will benefit from dealing in just one currency.

There are seven euro banknote denominations, which can be recognised easily by their look and feel: the larger the banknote, the higher the value. There are also eight denominations of euro coins, each having a common side and a national side. The common side shows the value of the coin. The national side differs from country to country.

You will be able to use all euro banknotes and coins, in each of the participating countries, from 1 January when – for the first time in the history of Europe – 12 currencies will make way for just one: **the euro. www.euro.ecb.int**

EUROPEAN CENTRAL BANK

power

speed

determination

The survival of the fittest is the driving force
of evolution. The weak, the less well adapted
are destined for extinction.

Similarly today's business environment.

Those with the determination to exploit the power
and speed of the electronic revolution will have
the edge. Communications are at the core of this
revolution, and at the forefront is THUS.

The new THUS national network is now complete.
Its advanced capability effectively integrates the
delivery of voice, image and high speed data
as a stepping stone to convergence.

To get the evolutionary edge, call us now on
0800 027 0570 or email sales@thus.net

www.thus.net

Demon Internet
Contact Centres
Hosting and Broadband Solutions
National Voice and Data Network

Let it be **thus**™

BENELUX

The Netherlands will be the best place in the world to do business, better even than America, according to the Economist Intelligence Unit's ranking of the business environment across 60 countries. The Dutch get high marks for their open culture, their welcoming policy towards foreign investment and their flexible labour markets. A favourable corporation-tax regime and excellent links to the rest of Europe add to the sparkle. To stay competitive, though, the Dutch government will come under increasing pressure to act on a surge in wage costs. Unemployment will start to rise again after a seven-year drop and public finances will be stretched as the economy struggles to pick up steam.

With the highly popular prime minister, Wim Kok, gracefully bowing out of Dutch politics after elections in May 2002, the free-market Liberals will have a chance of edging ahead of Labour, their senior coalition partner in the so-called purple coalition. They could become the largest party in the Netherlands for the first time.

One of Mr Kok's last achievements as prime minister was to smooth the way for the controversial wedding between crown prince Willem Alexander and Maxima, daughter of a member of a former military-junta government in Argentina. Wedding bells will ring in early February.

After the relative glamour of holding the EU's rotating presidency in the second half of 2001, Belgian politicians will have to return to arduous arguments between the six coalition partners. The government has made progress in reforming almost all aspects of public life. However, the range of ideological positions represented in the cabinet could easily lead to a coalition crisis followed by early elections. Legal challenges against a package of institutional reforms passed in 2001, devolving powers to the country's three regions, will also produce new frictions between Dutch-speakers and francophones.

The Belgian economy will recover only slowly along with the rest of the euro area and it will be saddled with a huge debt burden, severe regional imbalances and high unemployment. □

GDP GROWTH (%)	2000	2001	2002
Belgium	4.0	1.4	1.8
The Netherlands	3.9	1.5	2.5
Luxembourg	8.6	4.0	5.0
Economist Intelligence Unit			

elections before those for the National Assembly, however, suggests he believes that, if he beats Mr Chirac, he can keep his party in power. This may prove difficult. The conservative alliance of Gaullists and the centrist Union for French Democracy is profiting from both the implosion of Jean-Marie Le Pen's extreme-right National Front and mounting complaints from Communists, Greens and the small but combative Lutte Ouvrière that Mr Jospin has sold out the left.

If the French have lived under cohabitations for nine of the past 15 years, perhaps it is their preferred way of controlling a political elite notoriously out of touch with the electorate. Indeed, they have dumped the governing party in every parliamentary election since 1981, and they may do so again. Voters look for results and are usually disappointed. Recent economic growth visibly cheered the country. In 2000, the economy expanded by 3.4% and unemployment fell to 9.5%, the lowest in years. Growth slowed in 2001 and fear is again in the air—fear of rising crime and insecurity, fear of globalisation, fear of a resurgence of unemployment. It will be hard for Laurent Fabius, the prudent finance minister, to keep budgetary discipline. Expenditure control in the health-care sector, for example, will be complicated by the introduction of the 35-hour week in public hospitals in 2002.

At least the French have never measured their *gloire* by the value of the franc, so the arrival of the euro is not causing alarm. The European Union as a whole is viewed more suspiciously. Today, few French politicians talk of a federal Europe, while both Mr Chirac and Mr Jospin oppose Germany's promotion of its own federal system as a model for Europe. But long gone are the days when France set the European agenda. And the next stage, expansion of the EU eastwards, will only strengthen Germany's clout.

France's anxiety about its place in Europe mirrors its continuing nostalgia for a prominent place in the world. Here left and right are agreed: France will play it both ways. It will support a European rapid-reaction force to give Europe some military autonomy and, above all, to put teeth into the region's common foreign policy. But France also wants its own voice to be heard in future, whether on Africa, the Balkans and the Middle East, or in questioning America's policies on global warming, a missile shield and globalisation

Globalisation will be a far more divisive domestic issue in France than anywhere else in the West. Many French sense a conspiracy to consolidate Anglo-American hegemony. But French corporations are also actively engaged in globalisation: witness the emergence of Jean-Marie Messier's media and entertainment conglomerate, Vivendi Universal. In the campaign, Mr Chirac and Mr Jospin, both statists at heart, will no doubt warn against excessive globalisation and deregulation.

Immigration will be less of a political issue than some years ago, but the problem has not gone away. It has merely become one of integration, or rather the lack of true integration of the million or more French-born children of immigrants who still feel excluded from French society. North African drug gangs have already turned numerous *banlieues* into "no-go" areas for police.

Still, whatever 2002 holds for the French, they will at least feel confident when their soccer team heads to Korea and Japan for the World Cup in the autumn. *Les Bleus* won the World Cup in France in 1998. If they retain the cup, the French will probably care little which politician receives them in the Elysée Palace on their return home. □

2002

The Netherlands led the way. Now Belgium's parliament votes on a bill allowing gay and lesbian couples to marry.

The Italian job list

Beppe Severgnini   *Rome*

Security, not politics or business, will be Italy's main worry in 2002. National discussion will range from the country's commitment to NATO and the United States, to the attitude towards the Islamic world, to the treatment of immigrants. Italy has always stepped cautiously around these concerns, trying to bring round its southern Arab neighbours, even when they misbehaved. Silvio Berlusconi's government is the most western-oriented for a long time. But the foreign minister, Renato Ruggiero, is his own man. He will use his considerable weight within the administration to prevent any radical or abrupt changes of direction.

Immigrants are going to be a big topic in 2002. There

Beppe Severgnini: columnist for *Corriere della Sera* and Italy correspondent for *The Economist*. His books include "Inglesi" (Rizzoli) and "Ciao America", to be published by Random House/Broadway Books in the spring

We can afford to stand around all day

the centre-left will give Francesco Rutelli, their nominal leader, a hard time. The decline of the post-communist party, Democrats of the Left, will continue. A restless, anti-global and anti-American electorate will prove too much for a sensible, but feeble, leadership.

Italy's job list starts with the need to reform its labour laws, notably the difficulty of firing anyone. The current system revolves around the *Statuto dei Lavoratori*, a law passed in 1970, which states in Article 18 that employees can be dismissed "only for a just cause"; if dismissed unfairly, they must be allowed back into their job. What constitutes a "just cause" is highly debatable but the answer, in practice, is not much. The *Statuto* is the Italian unions' sacred cow: few dare touch it. But Giulio Tremonti and Antonio Marzano—the economy and industry ministers respectively—want to scrap Article 18. The unions hate this. In a country that worships *concertazione* (employers, unions and government deciding economic policy together), seeing through this necessary reform will take much political effort in the coming year.

A star of 2002 will be the education minister, Letizia Moratti. This good-looking, slightly Thatcheresque woman wants to help families to choose between private and public schools. Nowadays nine out of ten Italian children go to public schools (which tend to be fairly good); if families choose private schools—mostly Catholic— they have to pay for them. Public financing of private schooling is forbidden by the constitution. Ms Moratti says that she is ready to change this. The opposition believes that the public-school system will go to the dogs once money is diverted to private schools, and is up in arms. So expect another lively row.

Pensions will also be on the job list. European countries have a big pensions problem but among them, Italy is in particularly dire straits. Pension expenditure costs 14% of GNP (only Austria does worse). Employees of private companies have the equivalent of a third of their salaries earmarked for retirement. Some Italians retire as young as 55. After the reforms of 1995 and 1998, those early pensions should be phased out by 2008. But the Treasury wants them out of the way by 2004. The time to get moving is 2002. The unions, again, are unhappy.

Southern Italy, as always, will be hungry for money in 2002. Mr Berlusconi's grand plan for the poorer south requires much investment: an estimated €97 billion ($88 billion). The government will provide about half this sum, while private investors will come up with a third and the EU a fifth. The priorities will be to build a bridge over the Messina Strait, a pipedream of successive administrations, and to reconstruct the dangerous motorway system. The government also wants to bring water to large parts of the south that are badly in need of it.

Four final pieces of good news. One: flexible Italians will adjust to the euro in no time. Anything will be better than their own inflated currency. Two: Italy's tourism will do better than most countries over the coming year. Europeans, in a troubled world, will want to stay close to home, and a friendly, safe and sunny southern country is what they want. Three: Ferrari will continue to be a dominant force in car racing. Four: the city of Milan will win back its position as the capital of Italian football—after two years in which the league title has gone to Rome. Forget politics and enjoy Italy's real strengths. □

are 1.5m of them in Italy; they live mostly in the north (310,000 in Lombardy alone) and they represent 2.2% of the country's population. The largest communities are from Morocco, Albania, Romania and China. The number of *clandestini*—those who have no legal right to stay—has been estimated at around 400,000. Legislation proposed in 2001 by the government is restrictive: only those who have a job can stay in the country; and those who are caught must leave or risk imprisonment.

But Italy desperately needs workers from abroad. An ageing country, it needs home help (which it draws from Sri Lanka, Russia, Moldova and South America). Manufacturing industries seek workers (mostly Egyptian, Moroccan and West African). A large dairy-products industry in the north relies on Indians.

To exaggerate only slightly, Italians have forgotten to have any children over the past 20 years. (They have the lowest birth-rate in Europe.) The consequence of this is inevitable: the country must take in the young of other nations to fill the gap. So in spite of all the legislation and public anxiety, it is safe to predict that more, not fewer, immigrants will find their way into the country in 2002.

When in Rome...

Politics will be less lively than it has been for a decade. After an overdose of political news in 2001—the year that saw Mr Berlusconi's return to Palazzo Chigi, the prime minister's office—2002 will seem quiet. The ruling right will show occasional differences. The post-fascist National Alliance and once-separatist Northern League do not see eye-to-eye on many subjects, from deregulation to NATO; Forza Italia, Mr Berlusconi's own party, will act as a mediator. The opposition, on the other hand, will just jog along. It will use the prime minister's conflicts of interest to nag the government—whose solution to the problem has been insufficient. Still divided—especially when it comes to foreign policy and loyalty to America—

WHO DO YOU NEED?

**IBM IT Specialist,
Mara Sabisch**

Developed a foreign exchange and money market Internet service for Deutsche Bank, which provides customers with a fast, simple and secure way to trade online – and helps increase transaction volumes.

IBM

PEOPLE WHO THINK. PEOPLE WHO DO.
ibm.com/e-business/uk

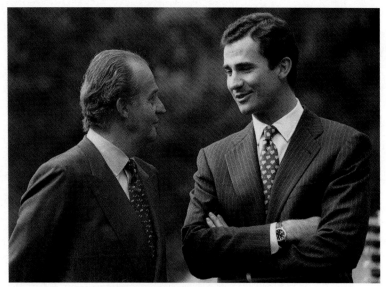

It's reigning men

The flip side of the coin

Juan Luis Cebrián   *Madrid*

Juan Luis Cebrián:
founder and publisher of
El País

What will become of the European monarchies when the dream of a united Europe crystallises into a supranational institution? What role will kings and queens play in their respective native countries? These questions are more or less the same ones that Queen Elizabeth of Britain sprang on Felipe González, then Spanish prime minister, during the period of the Maastricht treaty debate. Apparently, he appeased Her Majesty regarding the immediate future of the royal houses, perhaps without understanding that sovereigns have the vocation of eternity and not the shorter horizons of a politician. Spaniards, however, have not had to wait for the existence of a president of Europe to enter into a heated discussion about the prospects of the crown.

Recent rumours about the possible marriage of the heir to the throne, Felipe of Bourbon, Prince of Asturias, to Eva Sannum, a Norwegian model, have started a debate that will rumble on throughout 2002. Some have let loose a polemic about the advisability of a future head of

state getting married to a woman whose career is on the catwalk, where thousands of people have been able to admire her body. Others worry that the aspiring future queen of Spain was not born a Catholic (though she is doing classes), something that the upper-middle class will find difficult to accept; her mother is divorced and her step-father, not at all a dandy, runs a small family tourist business on the island of Rhodes.

The controversy about the royal marriage would be no more significant than debates about royalty taking place in other European countries such as the Netherlands and Norway—not to mention Britain, which always seems awash with royal sagas—if it were not for the fact that the Spanish monarchic tradition, despite having secular roots, is fairly fragile. Almost half of the past century elapsed under the aegis of either a republic or a dictatorship. Spain's monarchic sentiment is more an identification with the persona of the present king, Juan Carlos, main architect of the restoration of democracy following Franco's death, than with the institution itself. The king knows this himself.

Hence, the nuptial polemic has, for the first time in a quarter of a century and since the signing of the current constitution, opened a discussion on the future role of the crown. This has encompassed the desirability of certain constitutional reforms, such as the current precedence of a male heir over a female one, the only discrimination on the basis of sex that exists in the Spanish legal code. For the past 25 years, the monarchy has benefited from a pact of silence on the part of the media; it has been considered necessary to refrain from questioning the royal family so as not to threaten the stability of an infant democracy.

Conscious of the situation, and a staunch champion of the democratic regime, Juan Carlos has never cultivated Spain's traditional monarchist circles, who reproach him for his lack of commitment to them. He has demonstrated exceeding restraint in the concession of noble titles. He has often followed the example of the Nordic monarchies in his rapport with the people. But Spaniards have hotter blood than Norwegians, and some believe that a mistake by Prince Felipe regarding his future wife could open a debate that could shake the monarchy and threaten its continuity.

A debate about the throne is a novelty in a country

The Irish are not normally known as party-poopers. Yet to the surprise (and horror) of many in Europe, it was Irish voters in 2001 who rejected the latest changes to the European Union's constitution designed to allow a raft of new members to join the club. True, the majority in the referendum was slim and the turnout was only one-third of the electorate. But the treaty changes will lapse—and the EU's enlargement eastwards will be at risk—if voters in the Union's second-smallest member state do not change their minds in another referendum in 2002.

The outcome will depend on the timing of the poll. If held at the same time as the general election, due by mid-year, the referendum will probably approve the treaty changes, as a high turnout would ensure a more

representative sample of one of the most pro-Europe electorates among the EU-15. But in a stand-alone vote, with another low turnout, voters would almost certainly say "No" once again. The result would be that Ireland's standing in the EU, and with those waiting to get in, would be gravely undermined.

The general election itself will bring change, though not much. The centrist Fianna Fail, the senior coalition partner, is likely to remain in power, but its current partner, the tiny, liberal Progressive Democrats, is expected to be replaced by the larger, centre-left Labour Party. This will barely affect the direction of policy, such is the consensus among the mainstream parties on everything from economic management to Northern Ireland—where the shaky peace process will reach

firmer ground.

Might Ireland's economy falter in 2002, after a decade of explosive growth? Certainly, the Celtic tiger is vulnerable to a recession in America, because of its dependence on the world's largest economy for exports and investment. But the chances are that, for the ninth consecutive year, Ireland's economy will be the fastest-growing in the EU. □

KEY INDICATORS	2000	2001	2002
GDP growth (%)	11.5	5.7	5.3
Inflation (%)	5.3	4.3	3.5
Current account (% of GDP)	-0.6	-1.6	-1.8

Economist Intelligence Unit

WHO DO YOU NEED?

IBM CRM Consultant, Emmanuel Calmes

Implemented an e-CRM solution that helped ChateauOnline cut costs, and gain a competitive edge in the online wine market by offering more personalised products and services to their customers.

IBM

PEOPLE WHO THINK. PEOPLE WHO DO.
ibm.com/e-business/uk

where the primary issues of concern are terrorism, the economy, massive clandestine immigration and the introduction of the euro. The arrival of the common European currency coincides with the turn of Spain to assume the presidency of the Union. The prime minister, José Maria Aznar, only converted to the new monetary faith a few months before his election in 1996. The hopes of the government to use the European presidency to its advantage will be much weakened by the position of the minister for foreign affairs, who is surrounded by accusations of business shenanigans before entering the cabinet. And there will be more to run in 2002 on the financial scandal in which government bureaucrats have found themselves mixed up with Catholic bishops, the Civil Guard and police officials. Mr Aznar will have more

problems managing his absolute majority in this parliament than when he was in coalition with the Basque and Catalonian nationalists during the last one. But the polls still show a significant lead by his party, the People's Party, over the Socialist Party. He will need that as economic growth slows slightly from some 2.6% in 2001. The government might find itself short of cash in 2002 if expenditure cannot be trimmed; its budget might slip back into deficit. Cash would also be an issue for Spain's banks if Argentinian companies default on their debts.

But a different cash question will occupy Spaniards: will the Spanish euro shine with the effigy of a new queen raised to the throne, as in children's stories, by love? If the marriage takes place, Eva's face will some day be, together with the prince's, on the flip side of the coin. □

Europe's eastern troubles

Jonathan Ledgard   *Prague*

Rich man, poor man
Comparisons between the EU and the candidate countries

| Unemployment, % | Agriculture's contribution to GDP, % | % of population with mobile phones | % of population with PCs | GDP growth in 2002, % |

Sources: Eurostat, CMT mobile communication, EU World Bank

Jonathan Ledgard:
Central and Eastern Europe correspondent, *The Economist*

It will be a bad year for Central and Eastern Europe. Corruption and incompetence will pitch Moldova, Ukraine and Belarus further into the third world. Homegrown political and economic problems, a wobbly euro and a downturn in foreign investment will knock the rest of the region off its stride, if not quite off its feet.

The year will have its good points. NATO will invite Lithuania, Latvia, Estonia, and probably Slovenia and Slovakia, to join the alliance at its summit in Prague in the second half of the year. If the Americans listen to Slav statesmen such as the Czech president, Vaclav Havel, Romania and Bulgaria could also be made members. In 2002, the European Union will move further along the road to accepting former communist countries as new members of the Union. A rough timetable for entry will be drawn up. The EU may decide on a "big bang" method of enlargement in which all the applicants, except for Romania, Bulgaria and Turkey, will be accepted in one go. The lucky countries will get to vote in the European parliamentary elections in the summer of 2004 and formally join in 2005. A big-bang enlargement will annoy countries such as Slovenia and Hungary which have met the objective criteria laid down by Brussels only to see less-prepared countries, Poland for instance, hurried into the Union for political reasons.

But then Poland could do with a break. It is in for a particularly rotten year. A new left-of-centre government

will have the advantage of a large majority in parliament. Much will depend on the performance of its prime minister, Leszek Miller. The jury is out on this silvery haired, bluff ex-communist. Polish rightwingers deem Mr Miller to be a self-serving primitive. They never tire of pointing out that he served in Poland's last politburo. A fairer view, which most Poles hold, has him as an obedient modern Social Democrat, a self-educated man who has travelled a long road from socialism. Mr Miller will want to act decisively. He will find it hard going. The healthcare system will get worse before it gets better. The massive hole in the budget left by the outgoing Solidarity government will be hard to fill. Unemployment will rise, worryingly so among the young. Foreign investment will fall. Football will be one of the only bright spots for Poland in 2002. Its national team will perform strongly in the World Cup. Leading the team will be an African-Pole, Emmanuel Olisadebe. Nigerian-born Mr Olisadebe will score goals and cement himself as a national hero, changing Poles' sense of themselves and their country for the better.

2002 will be a busy political year in the rest of Central Europe. Slovenia will have a presidential election which the country's long-serving prime minister, Janez Drnovsek, will win, if he decides to stand. The Czechs and the Hungarians will both have general elections, electing centrist variations of the governments already in office. Vaclav Klaus, a Thatcherite former prime minister, will return to power in the Czech Republic. That will mean a rise in anti-EU rhetoric. But 2002 will be a better year for the Czech economy, helped by booming exports of Skoda cars and beer.

The most gripping election will take place in Slovakia where a populist former prime minister, Vladimir Meciar, could be returned for another spell in office. Mr Meciar was a boxer in his youth and like most boxers cannot resist an ill-advised return to the ring. As a politician he resembles the fighter Sonny Liston: inelegant, lumbering, forever popping off ferocious punches. The legacy of his administration is still being uncovered: misuse of the secret service, widespread financial corruption, even the mysterious kidnapping of a president's son. Mr Meciar claims to have mended his ways. He now says that membership of the EU and NATO would be a good thing. But his return to the ring would be bad for the country and the region as a whole.

Romania and Bulgaria are resigned to being left out of the EU's big-bang enlargement. Instead, they will spend 2002 working hard to be accepted by NATO. The Romanian prime minister, Adrian Nastase, wants to do the right things at home. He is frank about his country's shortcomings. If he gets his way, loss-making state industries will be sold off and pensions overhauled. Is he hard enough to face down mass protesters? Alas, probably not. In Bulgaria the former king turned prime minister, Simeon Saxe-Coburg, will have a similarly tough time pushing through reforms. Lacking Mr Nastase's political skills, Mr Saxe-Coburg will find it hard to keep his technocratic but rootless cabinet together. The Bulgarian economy will grow by 4%. Not bad. But not enough to satisfy the unrealistically high expectations of voters.

Parts of the region will leapfrog ahead technologically. Mobile-phone penetration in Central European countries will exceed that of most EU countries. It will remain a challenge to peck out an amorous text message in Czech (not to mention Hungarian) on a mobile-phone keypad but youth in the region will send more text messages than anywhere else in the world. In some countries, as already in Slovenia, government ministers will start getting some of their cabinet business in the form of text messages on their phone. □

The new old Russia

Edward Lucas *Moscow*

Does Putin reflect Russia?

Russia will reap the benefits of a growing international reputation for friendliness and reliability in 2002, although most of the country's underlying problems will remain unsolved. The new polish will pay off best in foreign policy, where President Vladimir Putin will strongly support the international coalition against terrorism. In return for giving up lucrative old friendships with countries like Iraq, Russia will be well placed to bargain hard with the West about its interests closer to home.

Assuming Mr Putin delivers effectively on anti-terrorism and does not irritate by haggling too hard, the payback will be a new willingness in Brussels to listen to Russian fears about expansion of NATO and the European Union. In particular, Russia will be well set to drive a harder bargain on the future of Kaliningrad, an impoverished province sandwiched between Lithuania and Poland. There will be a grand-sounding agreement, perhaps even a treaty, between NATO and Russia. At its summit in November, the alliance will take a low-key approach to membership talks with the Baltic republics of Estonia, Latvia and Lithuania and with other Eastern European states. Russian influence in the Caucasus will grow in 2002, as the Kremlin takes advantage of likely leadership changes in Georgia and Azerbaijan.

At home, politics will be quiet. The main event of the year will be elections in March to a new body: the parliament of the Russian-Belarussian Union. There will be plenty of hype surrounding this, both positive and negative. Other former Soviet republics, including Moldova and maybe Armenia, may want to join this vaguely de-

Edward Lucas: Russia correspondent, *The Economist*.

TURKEY *FORECAST*

After its worst financial crisis since the second world war, it is tempting to believe that Turkey can only improve. But there is still plenty of scope for things to go wrong—alarmingly so for such an important place: positioned between Europe, Central Asia and the Middle East, a big emerging market, NATO's only Muslim member and pivotal in the war against terrorism.

The economy will struggle to live up to its reputation for bouncing back from adversity. A sluggish recovery in the EU, Turkey's main export market, will not be enough to restore economic momentum. To tame the country's chronic inflation the central bank will introduce inflation targeting. But no country has ever used this policy formula to bring down inflation from Turkey's high levels. A few brave investors will be on the lookout for

bargains. Most will stay away, though, put off by concerns that Turkey will find it difficult to pay back previous investors.

At least the governing three-way coalition managed to beat the odds and stay together in 2001. It may not be so lucky in 2002. All three parties know that they would be heavily defeated in an early election. Disillusionment with the present leadership will encourage defections to rivals. They will push for fresh elections and hope to win.

Any number of prickly issues could trigger the poll. The government is deeply divided over whether to execute the convicted leader of the Kurdistan Workers' Party, Abdullah Ocalan, who has taken his case to the European Court of Human Rights. If the court rules in Mr

Ocalan's favour, and Turkey chooses to defy it, EU-Turkish relations will suffer. The EU will also be considering whether to admit into its ranks the divided island of Cyprus. A decision to allow only the Greek Cypriots and not the Turkish Cypriots into the EU would provide further ammunition for a full-scale EU-Turkey diplomatic bust-up. In 2002, Turkey could be worrying not just the West's financiers, but its politicians as well. □

KEY INDICATORS	2000	2001	2002
GDP growth (%)	7.1	-8.0	2.0
Inflation (%)	54.9	54.2	53.1
Current account (% of GDP)	-4.8	2.1	-0.8

Economist Intelligence Unit

Russia goes clubbing

Russia is fed up with being left out of world affairs. In 2002 it will be doing its level best to become a member of more international clubs. Some of its ambitions are pipedreams; others will reshape the way the world does politics.

For an example of the former, look no further than attempts in 2002 to pass laws to enable Russia to join the European Union. As if. Membership is not on the agenda in Brussels; it would push the EU's eastern border all the way to the Pacific. More seriously, it would shift power in the same direction, something that no EU member would accept.

A warmer welcome will come from the WTO. Russia certainly needs to do something about the paltry amounts of foreign investment it attracts, worth only $2 billion in 2002. Before the terrorist attacks on America, the feeling in Geneva was that after exhausting negotiations with China, Russia could wait. The polite way of saying this was to ask Moscow to revise huge swathes of legislation before negotiations could take place. In 2002, however, thanks to his efforts to support America's war, Vladimir Putin could find his application fast-tracked. Membership in 2002 would be miraculous; but entry before 2005 looks possible.

In the summer, Mr Putin hosts a meeting of the Shanghai Co-operation Organisation in Moscow, one of the few international organisations in which he wields influence. The leaders of China and four of the Central Asian republics will discuss trade, fighting Islamic terrorists, and Afghanistan. Pakistan may be invited along. The original idea behind the organisation was to provide a counterweight to America in regional, as well as in world, affairs. In 2002, however, club members will be too busy helping America to crush terrorists in the region to remember such lofty ideals. But all will not be sweetness and light in Moscow; China and Russia have very different ideas of what a post-Taliban regime should look like. □

fined outfit, seeing it as a ticket to cheap energy and preferential access to the (relatively) prosperous Russian market. Some see a new Soviet Union in the making. Neither the hopes nor the fears will prove justified, in 2002 at least. New bodies like this add costs but not clout, for the simple reason that Russia already has its own way in most of the former captive nations.

Mr Putin will spend much time and effort worrying about his huge but increasingly fragile popularity. Most Russians trust him to do his best to make things better, but real reform—for example, of the incompetently run and wasteful domestic utility companies—will be painfully slow. The reaction to bad news will remain a strong desire to silence the messenger: Russia's media will stay under tight, but discreet, control in 2002.

Russia's stronger international reputation should give the security services more leeway in dealing with opposition at home. There will be no return to Soviet-style repression, but fewer worries about criticism abroad when they harass independently minded people and organisations through the courts, tax inspectorate and other bits of the government bureaucracy. Independent trade unions will find life very difficult in 2002, squeezed between angry members and a new labour code that sharply restricts their ability to protest.

The big change, surprisingly, may be Chechnya. Sooner or later the Kremlin will have to start some sort of peace talks with the rebel leadership. No military solution is in sight, as the Kremlin privately admits. Informal contacts in third countries are already underway. The most likely solution involves both the rebel and Russian-backed leaders stepping aside, and elections taking place under international supervision. To push that through, however, Mr Putin will have some tough battles with the military. They promised a quick victory two years ago, delivered a disaster, but will be unwilling to admit that the war is unwinnable.

Relations with other bits of the Russian state will become trickier, as Russia's barons get over the initial shock of having someone tough and competent in the Kremlin. The new leadership's main attempt to deal with the regions has been to set up seven presidential representatives to oversee the uppity locals. This will prove little more than a layer of useless bureaucracy. If Mr Putin is feeling confident, he may declare their mission accomplished and hope no one will ask what they really achieved.

If the oil price stays over $20 a barrel, Russia's economy will chug along. Some Russian businesses are genuinely competitive now, and more will join their ranks in 2002. Most, however, are still sheltered from real competition by a web of unseen and informal relationships.

Russia has created considerable wealth in the past two years. It is undoubtedly capitalist and western. It will have an enviously low marginal top rate of corporate tax of 24% and people will finally pay their tax bills. Much foreign capital will stay away, however, as the country will still seem an inherently hostile market. Russian capital, by contrast, will return from its hidden exile throughout Europe and America. The more promising big businesses will start selling out to foreign investors: 2002 will be the year when a western oil company buys a Russian one for cash. That will create billionaires from some of the lucky young Communist Party hacks who seized chunks of the country's oil industry in the 1990s, sucked in and ripped off western shareholders, and then smartened up their act enough to make their companies sellable.

But even worse than this, and the fact that the banking system is a mess, Russia's huge underlying problem will remain reform of the bureaucracy: a nightmare in a vast country that has never known good government. And that, unfortunately, may be too tough a challenge even for a man of Mr Putin's considerable abilities. □

2002

He was elected on the promise of delivering a "dictatorship of the law". Vladimir Putin introduces jury trials throughout Russia.

Frits Bolkestein, European commissioner for the internal market, predicts much kicking and screaming in the cause of reform

It's the single market, stupid!

"We must move closer to the tougher conditions of Anglo-Saxon capitalism"

When people consider how best to improve Europe's economic performance, they often concentrate on short-term considerations such as the level of interest rates or governments' budget deficits. These are of course important. But the real economic challenge facing the European Union concerns the longer term. In particular, Europe has to improve substantially the efficiency of its markets for products, services and capital.

The best way for Europe to meet this challenge is by developing the full potential of its single market. This was recognised by the European Summit in Lisbon in March 2000. Europe's leaders set themselves the aim of making Europe the most competitive economy in the world by 2010 and agreed on an ambitious programme of measures to meet that target. This programme includes creating optimal conditions for innovation and e-commerce, fully integrated financial markets by 2005 and an accelerated programme of liberalisation of markets for energy, postal services and transport.

It is a daunting challenge, but achievable. Only ten years ago, America's main ambition was to become more competitive than Japan, the competitive doyen of the late 1980s. America realised its ambition and we can realise ours.

Some of our targets have been met. For example, the EU has agreed on important legislation to establish ground rules for e-commerce based on supervision by the country of origin and to adapt copyright rules for the digital age. However, there has been a deplorable gap between the declarations of good intent by leaders of the EU and their willingness to agree on the measures outlined in the Lisbon agenda.

The Community Patent is one example. To encourage innovation we have to make it easier and cheaper to protect inventions with a single patent valid across the Union. In particular, we must simplify procedures and cut translation costs to a minimum. But some member states have lost sight of the overall objective in their determination to defend their own language and protect the interests of their national patent office and courts.

Liberalisation of markets for energy and postal services is another area where progress has been too slow. Opponents tend to argue that market liberalisation puts the quality and provision of services to remote areas at risk. But such arguments often serve as a smokescreen to protect the vested interests of existing service providers. In fact, the commission is always scrupulously careful to include in its proposals strong assurances to improve the quality of service. Clients will thus be well-served in areas where it might not be commercially viable to provide services. Among other things, we require member states to establish independent regulators to make sure operators stick to the rules on provision and quality of services. It is not as if we promote the law of the jungle!

There have also been problems with initiatives on financial services such as pan-EU rules on takeovers and extending the scope of safeguards against money laundering.

Obviously, measures to improve the functioning of the EU's single market can and should take account of all interests affected by these measures. Indeed, it is in our interest to go to great lengths to consult all those who are affected by particular proposals. We must take account of their views so that the measures are adapted to the realities of the marketplace.

One of the fundamental problems is that interest groups may wield a disproportionate influence on the EU's open and democratic decision-making process. The efforts of interests to defend their corners are neither new nor surprising. What is new is that Europe has declared to the rest of the world that it wants to become more competitive than the United States, Japan or anywhere else. The need to make Europe more competitive should take precedence over the interests of particular companies, social groups, sectors, regions or countries.

Are we a sedentary society?

In some cases, the effort required implies some painful structural adjustments. That is why the necessary measures may be politically unpopular and thus difficult to carry out. We must remember that no one is forcing the EU to become more competitive than the United States in eight years' time. But if that is what we really want, we must move away from the comfortable "Rhineland model" of capitalism, in which managers and employees play the primary role.

We must move closer to the tougher conditions and colder climate of Anglo-Saxon capitalism, based on the primacy of shareholders' interests, where the rewards are greater but the risks are also. Capitalism is indeed revolutionary. It respects neither habit nor tradition, neither gender nor class. It is the enemy of any sedentary society. If Europe really does want to become the most competitive economy in the world, it cannot afford to remain sedentary.

The governments of the member states, the European Parliament and indeed the European Commission itself have got to work hard in 2002 to make progress. The Barcelona European Council in March will be a good opportunity to demonstrate that the EU does mean business.

If we fail, the credibility of the whole Lisbon process will be undermined. Europe will project a fuzzy image to the outside world. It cannot on the one hand loudly proclaim a magnificent ambition and on the other, shy away from biting the bullet. This is not merely a problem of losing face with the rest of the world. It would also result in Europe, and more particularly Europe's citizens, having to pay the price in terms of lost jobs and prosperity foregone. □

Why is the world so difficult?

Sebastian Mallaby

Washington, DC

Off to work I go

America's declared war on terrorists will undergo a subtle redefinition in 2002. The nation will come to realise that the war metaphor itself is flawed; terrorism is not an absolute but rests, in part, in the eye of the beholder. Unlike conventional wars, this is not the sort of conflict that can end definitively with the signing of surrender papers. And unlike the cold war, which itself stretched the usual definitions of war, this is not the sort of conflict that can serve as an organising principle for international relations. In times of crisis, simplicity works. But as, in 2002, that crisis mercifully fades, tortuous difficulties will force their way back into foreign policy.

During most phases of the cold war, the United States subordinated all other foreign-policy objectives to the containment of Soviet communism. The promotion of democracy, human rights and economic development was possible only if it supported this central struggle; America was happy to make allies out of dictators as long as they were "our sons of bitches", in the motto of the time. Equally, the United States willingly made accommodations with powers that in the long term might threaten its own interests. China comes most readily to mind.

After the terrorist attacks of September 11th, the Bush administration suggested that the fight against terrorism would become a similarly central struggle around which all foreign policy could be organised. The attacks had killed more than twice as many Americans as Japan's raid on Pearl Harbour, so it seemed reasonable to view terrorism as meriting the sort of single-minded response that requires putting other priorities to one side.

President Bush declared that other countries would henceforth have to decide whether they were with the United States or with the terrorists. And for a while this talk did seem to be reordering geopolitics. Pakistan went from pariah to valued ally, as its intelligence services assisted American agents to operate inside Afghanistan. The former Soviet states of Uzbekistan and Tajikistan underwent similar transformations in next to no time.

In 2002, however, the United States will discover that this reordering of international relations is less profound than it appears. It will discover that it is simply not possible to require states to be for or against terrorism; too many will insist on occupying the ambiguous middle ground. Pakistan, for instance, will be against Arab terrorists who threaten western targets but in favour of Pakistani terrorists who blow things up in Kashmir. Saudi Arabia will be willing to share intelligence on terrorists when the United States demands it, but will be simultaneously channelling state money to terrorist-linked foundations in the hope of appeasing the firebrands. As Americans confront these ambiguities, they will be reminded that the United States itself has a history of allowing fund raising for Irish terrorists to carry on openly within its borders. The clear us-versus-them paradigm that Mr Bush offered will break down.

Moreover, the United States will discover that even unambiguously pro-terrorist governments present foreign-policy choices that are more complex than they seem at first. Iran, for example, will persist in sheltering terrorist groups suspected of killing Americans in Saudi Arabia. It will refuse even to go through the motions of siding with America in the war against terrorism. But the

---

2002

Watch out for the silos being built at Fort Greely, Alaska. Since they could house missiles, this would qualify as a deployment site under the Anti-Ballistic Missile treaty, thereby violating it.

Sebastian Mallaby: member of the *Washington Post's* editorial page

United States will be unsure how or whether to respond. If it applies the us-versus-them rhetoric literally, it would threaten the Iranian government with military reprisals. But even the hawks in the administration would resist this, preferring to go after Iran's chief regional rival, Iraq. Meanwhile, the diplomats in the State Department will point out what else is at stake in the Iranian relationship: access to oil, co-operation in enforcing Iraqi sanctions and the hope of dialogue on the question of Palestine.

The arguments over Iran and Iraq will show why the war against terrorism is not like the cold war after all. The singular focus on containing the Soviet Union was possible because no other threat to American interests even began to match it: no other nation had a comparable nuclear arsenal, a comparably expansionist ideology, or a comparably reckless ambition to recruit proxies like Cuba in America's backyard.

Nowadays, by contrast, terrorism is only one among several threats to American interests. The development of weapons of mass destruction by rogue states is arguably more alarming. So are the nuclear programmes of states such as Pakistan or India, which are not rogues for the moment but whose stability is fragile. And perhaps the greatest threat to American security still comes from Russia's creaky nuclear arsenal, which remains capable of inflicting horrible damage on American civilians by design or by accident. There are other threats to American interests that could flare up at any moment, starting with China's hegemonic ambitions in Asia.

As the memory of the assault on the World Trade Centre fades, these other foreign-policy challenges will resume their natural prominence. To most Americans, this will seem uncomplicated, a sort of foreign-policy parallel to the process by which civilians resume habits of travel and leisure on the home front. But the Bush administration may find itself out of step with most Americans on this question. Even though his advisers will point out the other threats to American interests that deserve attention, the president will stay focused on terrorism. □

A 21st-century recession

Zanny Minton-Beddoes   *Washington, DC*

It is not hard to predict how America will begin the year. The country will be at war and the economy will be in recession. Economic output will have fallen in both the third and fourth quarters of 2001—thus fulfilling the technical definition of a recession—and the sharp slide will continue in the first few months of 2002. Unemployment will be on the rise—close to 5.5% by the start of the year. The winter will be punctuated by painfully high numbers of layoffs.

How the year ends is less certain, and depends on more than economics alone. More terrorist attacks or a protracted and ineffective war would have dire consequences on already jittery businesses and consumers. With Europe and, especially, Japan, looking wobbly at the same time, a dramatic global slump is not inconceivable. But barring such calamities, the American economy will bounce back by the end of 2002. America will seem to have come off lightly, with a classic "V" shaped reces-

Zanny Minton-Beddoes:
Washington correspondent,
The Economist

sion—rather than the elongated "L" of protracted slow growth that many had feared. Unfortunately, this "V" will be built on very shaky foundations.

Sharp downturns spawn dramatic recoveries: the 2001-02 recession should be no exception. The two other sharp recessions of the post-war era—in the mid-1970s and the early 1980s—saw an average economic contraction of 3.2% followed by spectacular 7% GDP growth in the first year of recovery. Part of this recovery is a natural cyclical rebound. Consumers begin to make the purchases they had put off when the outlook was gloomy; firms begin rebuilding scarce inventories as they sense prospects improving.

Massive monetary and fiscal stimulus will also play a role. The Federal Reserve, America's central bank, reacted forcefully in 2001. The federal-funds rate, the key short-term interest rate, began 2001 at 6.5%. By the beginning of September it had fallen to 3.5%. A month after the terrorist attacks it was at 2.5%. That aggressive response will continue. The federal-funds rate will begin 2002 at 2%. It could fall even lower in the early months of the year, pushing real interest rates firmly negative, as the inflation rate hovers around 2%.

Where's the fizz gone?

GDP growth, %

Though inflation hawks will begin to mutter about the risks of such dramatic easing, there will be scant signs of inflationary pressure. Commodity prices will remain weak while the world economy is in recession. As long as military action is confined to Afghanistan, oil prices—which reacted so dramatically to the 1991 Gulf war—will barely budge. Any supply concerns will be far outweighed by the collapse in demand from less air travel and stagnant economies. More surprisingly, the dollar will not fall dramatically. America's huge current-account deficit suggests that at some point the dollar must drop. The country's heightened security risks suggest that drop could come soon. But in 2002 these concerns will be outweighed by the meagre economic prospects in both Europe and Japan. The dollar will barely move.

The dramatic monetary easing should probably be enough to turn around the economy by itself. But there will be other stimulants. And with them comes the danger. America's politicians, terrified by the spectre of slump after a decade of prosperity, will loosen the fiscal pursestrings. Immediately after the September 11th attacks, Congress agreed to spend $40 billion as a down payment on reconstruction and increased security in New York and Washington. They gave $5 billion in aid (plus $10 billion of loan guarantees) to the beleaguered airlines. Weeks later, another $75 billion "stimulus" package of tax cuts and spending (largely for the unemployed) was on the cards. Add in the tax cuts already due to take effect in 2002, and America could see a fiscal loosening of

How to fight in the future

Mark Mazzetti *Washington, DC*

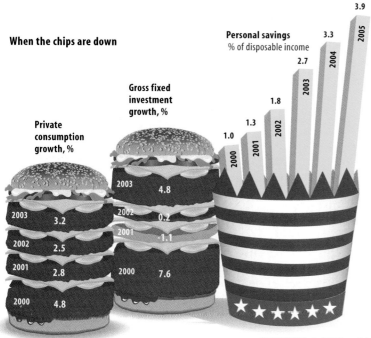

When the chips are down

Private consumption growth, %

2003	3.2
2002	2.5
2001	2.8
2000	4.8

Gross fixed investment growth, %

2003	4.8
2002	0.2
2001	-1.1
2000	7.6

Personal savings
% of disposable income

2000	1.0
2001	1.3
2002	1.8
2003	2.7
2004	3.3
2005	3.9

Sources: IMF, IOTF, Economist Intelligence Unit

$200 billion or 2% of GDP in 2002. In theory that would provide a massive short-term boost. With generous defence and security spending, the budget will put even more stimulus in the pipeline.

In fact, the impact is likely to be modest. Many of the tax cuts will be politically rather than economically motivated and thus will not work well as a quick fix. For instance, the decision to accelerate income-tax cuts previously slated for 2004 and 2006 will benefit mostly richer Americans, who will stash away the extra cash in 2002 rather than spend it.

Though it will be widely heralded as an important political response to the downturn, this budget loosening will end up causing more problems than it solves. For during 2002 the dramatic deterioration of America's long-term fiscal health will become ever more clear. In May 2001 congressional number-crunchers reckoned America's ten-year budget surplus was $5.6 trillion (4% of GDP). By October 2001 the forecast had been cut to $2.6 trillion (2% of GDP) as the Bush tax cut, a slower economy and higher spending took their toll. That estimate will fall further in 2002. This loss of long-term fiscal discipline—and the resulting higher long-term interest rates—will be the Achilles' heel of the American economy in 2002 and beyond.

The current recession will not remove America's long-standing imbalances. The current-account deficit will remain unsustainably large. Personal saving rates will rise as consumers lose confidence, but will still be pitifully low. America's economy boomed in the late 1990s despite these weaknesses. Whether it can do so again in 2002 and 2003 is less clear. In the late 1990s, American productivity growth was the wonder that made up for all other problems. Statistical revisions from before September 11th made it clear that part of this was illusory. But if productivity growth does slow, then America's various imbalances will surely come to haunt it, and the strong recovery of 2002 will be short-lived. □

> **2002**
>
> Senators Jesse Helms, 81, and Strom Thurmond, 99, finally go. Washington will be a wiser place without them.

Mark Mazzetti: national defence correspondent, *US News & World Report*

For the revolutionaries, the rallying cry came on September 8th 1999. At a stump speech during the presidential campaign, George Bush articulated a vision for the American armed forces that abandoned cold-war rhetoric about traditional military might. Taking a page from the "Revolution in Military Affairs" gospel, Mr Bush called for greater emphasis on stealth technology, precision strike weapons and defences against cyberwarfare—not for the tanks and ships once needed to defend against Soviet attack. "The best way to keep the peace is to redefine war on our terms," he argued, and promised to equip the Pentagon to fight the battles of the future.

The future arrived early, on September 11th. The terrorist attacks on New York and Washington roused the Pentagon from abstract debates over the shape and mission of the American military. Arcane discussions quickly became grounded in reality. Most important for the Pentagon, the political battles over defence spending gave way to consensus in both parties to open up the purse for a greater military budget.

As America learned the hard way, a mighty arsenal costing one-third of a trillion dollars annually is of little use against enemies who eschew the traditional battlefield and exploit a nation's weaknesses—employing so-called asymmetrical warfare. "Nobody has an incentive to build an air force that can out dogfight the American air force," explains Andrew Krepinevich of the Centre for Strategic and Budgetary Assessments, a defence think-tank. "You could spend 20 or 30 years and you still wouldn't get there. But you can spend ten years buying lots of missiles and holding those air bases at risk. It's an easy solution for nations that don't have a lot of money." Asymmetrical warfare, of course, is a strategy as old as David and Goliath, but increasingly it will become the new face of battle.

In 2002, America's secretary of defence, Donald Rumsfeld, will try to carry out Mr Bush's revolutionary rhetoric and equip the military for the new battlefield. In his "Quadrennial Defense Review", issued in October 2001, Mr Rumsfeld laid the groundwork for the transformation, yet he will have difficult decisions to make. He must also do battle with the "Iron Triangle"—advocates in the military, in Congress and in the defence industry who protect their own pet programmes from being cut.

Mr Rumsfeld got a taste of the forthcoming fight when he decided to scale back America's fleet of B-1 bombers, cold-war-era aeroplanes built to attack the Soviet Union. Most in the military agree that the B-1's lack of stealth technology makes it ill-equipped for future battles, yet Mr Rumsfeld's decision drew fire from congressmen whose districts house B-1 bases. In place of the B-1, the Pentagon is expected to endorse next-generation planes such as the F-22 and the joint strike fighter, a $35m aircraft that could be shared by the air force, navy and marines.

The new defence strategy also places greater strategic emphasis on Asia, and the Pentagon will accordingly bulk up its military presence in the region. Mr Rumsfeld intends to relocate naval forces from the Mediterranean to the Western Pacific to be closer to countries such as China and North Korea. Although the defence secretary ignored proposals to cut as many as two aircraft-carrier groups to pay for more technologically advanced vessels, the navy is converting submarines and designing new surface ships that can attack an enemy's coastline with up to 150 cruise missiles.

Of all the services, however, it is the army that is undergoing the most robust transformation. The fall of the Berlin wall brought about an existential crisis for the army, which for 40 years had been structured to fight a major land battle on the plains of Europe. Over a decade later, it is just now moving towards lighter, more mobile brigades that can be deployed anywhere in the world within 96 hours, and entire divisions that can relocate within 30 days. The army's transformation efforts will be accelerated in 2002, with the first mobile brigade ready for action by the following year.

Cruising up and down
America's defence budget
$bn (constant 2002 dollars)

310
464
408
315
322
344

1980
1985
1990
1995
2000
2002

Source CBA

Yet all the Pentagon's new toys will take a back seat to the Bush administration's most ambitious, and costly, proposal: to deploy a missile-defence system. Mr Bush's National Missile Defence is proposed to counter a limited strike from a "rogue" nation such as North Korea or Iraq. Bush aides have yet to provide details of what the system might look like, yet it is likely to involve interceptors launched from ground sites, naval vessels and aircraft circling high above enemy territory. All of this will come with a hefty price tag: some estimates put the cost of a fully deployed system at $200 billion. America's entire defence budget for 2002 will be only $344 billion.

What remains to be seen, of course, is whether the system will even work. The Pentagon has thus far conducted rudimentary attempts to "hit a bullet with a bullet", but the successful intercepts have come only with the aid of a homing device on the missile guiding the interceptor to its target. Presumably, North Korea or Iraq would not be so considerate. In 2002, the Pentagon will begin construction on a ground interceptor site in Alaska and accelerate the testing schedule.

Yet in its push to build a missile shield, the Bush administration faces two formidable opponents: the Russians and the Democrats. The 1972 Anti-Ballistic Missile treaty prohibits national missile defence. The government will have to strike a delicate balance in order to get out of the treaty without alienating Russia. As for domestic politics, congressional Democrats will take every opportunity in 2002 to starve funds for the system many dismiss as a "shield of dreams". The Bush administration has the stated goal of deploying a rudimentary missile defence system by 2004. Conveniently, this would be just in time for the president's re-election bid. □

Linda Greenhouse:
Supreme Court correspondent,
New York Times

Shaking up the Supreme Court

Linda Greenhouse   *New York*

A remarkable era of stability in the membership of the United States Supreme Court is likely to come to an end in 2002, with the only question being the ferocity of the fight that will ensue to appoint and confirm new justices.

The seven-plus years since Justice Stephen G. Breyer took his seat in August 1994 is the longest period without turnover in the court since the early 19th century. Rumours of imminent retirements were so intense last June that much of political Washington was left in a state of disbelief when the term ended with all nine justices still in their seats. But the adrenaline is still flowing: the battle was not avoided but merely deferred.

The most likely candidates for retirement are Chief Justice William H. Rehnquist and his fellow Arizonan, Justice Sandra Day O'Connor. At 77, the chief justice has one of the longest tenures in the court's history: 30 years as of January 2nd 2002. As a loyal Republican he would like a Republican president to be able to name his successor. Now that former president, Bill Clinton is enjoying retirement, the chief justice will feel much happier about arranging his own. Justice O'Connor, his ally on many conservative issues, is 71 and passed her 20th anniversary on the court in September 2001. Justice John Paul Stevens, the court's most liberal member, although a nominal Republican, has shown no inclination to retire; he is 81.

To fill a vacancy, expect President George Bush to play a bit of ethnic politics and choose someone of impeccable conservative credentials and Hispanic background. In the past ten years, Hispanics have drawn even with blacks as the country's largest minority, with Mexicans by far the fastest-growing group with a population above 20m. For both political parties, laying claim to the loyalty of Hispanic voters is an urgent priority, and naming the first Hispanic Supreme Court justice would serve that goal nicely.

Mr Bush has a plausible candidate close at hand in Alberto R. Gonzales, his White House counsel and formerly a justice on the Texas Supreme Court. A 46-year-old Mexican-American graduate of Harvard Law School, Mr Gonzales has an appealing personal story. He is one of eight children brought up in a two-bedroom house in Houston by parents who never graduated from elementary school. Mr Bush could go far to disarm Democratic opposition by nominating his personable adviser.

On the court's docket for its new term, there is nothing to compete with the case of Bush v Gore, but then it isn't every term that the Supreme Court gets to pick the president. One important statutory case requires the justices to address a basic issue under the sweeping disability-rights law that Congress passed in 1990: whether an impairment that limits a person's ability to perform a particular job-related task—in this instance, gripping and holding tools on an assembly line—qualifies as a disability. The stakes are high in *Toyota Motor Manufactur-*

LINDE. Ideas that create markets.

The easier the access to suppliers worldwide, the more important professional logistics solutions become. In this global growth market we enjoy international leadership positions with the forklift and warehousing products of our Linde, STILL and FIAT OM brands. Our innovation potential and the rapid

expansion of market positions in Asia and the Americas – combined with the certainty that every online order increases international trade – assure excellent prospects and dynamic growth.

For further information: +49 611 770 317

www.linde.com

Electronic supply chain management.
Logistics by Linde.

We know how.

Engineering and Contracting
Material Handling
Refrigeration
Industrial Gases

What do you want from a business airline?

 Frequent flights between UK airports and major business cities

Aberdeen	Amsterdam	Belfast	Edinburgh	Geneva
Glasgow	Liverpool	London*	Madrid	Zurich

* London Luton and Gatwick

 Great value flexible fares
You can change **every** flight for just £10 plus any difference in fare.

 No rip-off day returns
No ridiculous minimum two night stay for our lowest fares.

 Good punctuality
Best punctuality record of all Low Cost Airlines.

(CAA data - July 2001)

 A long term relationship
FTSE250 public company, growing capacity 25% year on year.

easyJet – good business sense!

 **easyJet**.com
the web's favourite airline

Fat or fit?

Expect your neighbour to get fatter. Obesity is on the rise everywhere. In America and Britain a full 30% of adults in 2002 will qualify as obese—50% will be merely overweight. The causes in the great majority of cases, not all, are twofold: too much food and too little exercise. Personal unhappiness, often springing from the belief that people have lost control of their lives, is also a trigger. Obesity is concentrated among the poor and minorities: the inactive.

In 2002, there will be the first attempts to nail the blame for obesity—and the medical problems that attend it—not on personal responsibility but on the food companies, notably those such as

McDonald's that serve good, cheap but highly calorific food in huge quantities. Expect much absurdity in the American courts as sets of suing lawyers see the prospect of large, punitive damages awards. This will help lawyers but do nothing to prevent obesity. It is certain that this is a long-term problem that will only get worse over the coming years.

The proportion of obese school-

children has doubled in America in the past 15 years. Why? One reason is that schools, bowing to pressure from the teachers' unions, have steadily reduced the amount of sports and physical activity during the school day. And once a child is seriously overweight, the overwhelming likelihood is that he or she will remain that way throughout life, with all the attendant problems of heart disease, diabetes, immobility and premature death.

Obesity, therefore, will become one of the major public-health problems in wealthy societies. These, of course, are the very societies that have come to abandon the concept of personal responsibility for a less useful and more pernicious belief that blame can always be shifted elsewhere. Western countries, in particular, will pay dearly for this misconception in the years ahead.

It is an interesting paradox that those societies that will have the highest rates of obesity will also be those that take exercise most seriously. It is not the obese, of course, who will be exercising. One imbalance gives birth to another. In the United States 13% of the population will belong to a gym and will have regular work-out sessions. In less obese Britain the figure is 7%. In slimmer France and Italy just 4% feel the need for vigorous exercise in an artificial climate. Yet these societies, on balance, will stay healthier. □

Obesity
% of population

1991 — 22
2002 — 30
2025 — 42

Source: IOTF

---

ing v Williams because the very definition of disability, which employers must take concrete steps to accommodate, remains surprisingly undefined under the Americans With Disabilities Act. The court is likely to agree with the employer in this case that a person is not disabled unless the impairment precludes an entire range or broad class of jobs.

In a case that will help define the rules for free speech in the Internet age, the court will hear the government's defence of a law that criminalises the distribution and possession of "virtual" child pornography: material that either depicts real adults who appear to be children or that uses computer-generated images rather than real people of any age. A federal appeals court found the Child Pornography Prevention Act in violation of the First Amendment's free-speech guarantee.

The Bush administration is arguing in *Ashcroft v Free Speech Coalition* that even without using real children, such material causes harm by sustaining the market for real child pornography that exploits real children. The appeal, and the law, are probably doomed before a Supreme Court highly protective of freedom of speech. The court is likely to find that however commendable its purpose, the law goes too far by potentially sweeping away too much constitutionally protected expression.

Developments outside the court will affect law practice in 2002, though not at the pace many expected.

While Mr Bush ran on an anti-lawyer platform of "tort reform", Congress has little appetite for imposing limits on civil liability. The American Trial Lawyers Association, the powerful lawyers' lobby, refers to any moves to dampen the public's enthusiasm for suing corporate America as "tort restriction". The new House Judiciary Committee chairman, James Sensenbrenner of Wisconsin, backed off once the Democrats regained control of the Senate, saying he did not want his committee wasting its time on bills the Senate would kill. Instead, the legislative battle will be played out in the struggle over how to define and channel patients' rights to sue their health-care providers.

The American Bar Association, meanwhile, will relax the traditional ban on revealing client confidences. The proposal likely to receive final approval will permit lawyers to breach confidentiality in order to prevent "reasonably certain death or substantial bodily harm", such as corporate behaviour that threatens public health through defective products. Individual states will then decide whether to make the new rules binding.

There will be more signs in 2002 that the American public's infatuation with the death penalty is cooling, but few politicians will be sufficiently farsighted to take the hint. The number of states using the death penalty will remain at 38, but many more of them will bar execution of the retarded. □

Robert B. Zoellick, United States trade representative, foresees a world made more prosperous and secure by trade

Trading is good for you

"It will be the first year since 1982 that America's foreign trade will fall"

The events of the past century demonstrate how trade can deliver tremendous benefits to countries that open their markets to foreign competition and challenge businesses to sell their goods and services around the world. The past century also reveals that there is a high price— economic and political— when support for free trade withers. This experience points to the importance of moving forward with trade liberalisation in 2002 and beyond.

By opening markets, we can strengthen forces that will help bind nations and peoples together through the peaceful exchange of goods, services, capital and ideas. This is one reason why Albania, China, Croatia, Georgia, Jordan, Lithuania, Moldova, Oman and Taiwan have joined the World Trade Organisation in the past two years.

Building support for free trade and investment—with developed and developing nations— is a top priority for the Bush administration. Our strategy serves five principal purposes.

1. By moving forward with trade liberalisation we signal that there is an international coalition for openness and growth that respects core values. The tragic events of September 11th have given our work a renewed urgency. America and the world have been attacked by a network of terrorists who are masters of destruction but failures at construction. The international market economy—of which the trading system is a vital part—offers an antidote. Trade is about more than economic efficiency. It reflects a system of values: openness, appreciation of differences, opportunity, integration, freedom of choice, governance through agreed rules and a hope for the improvement of life for all peoples.

2. Free trade will help our friends in need, and this will help to sustain coalitions against terrorism. Many democratic governments in developing nations, already struggling with economic challenges before September 11th, now face staggering difficulties. Many depend on trade with G8 nations for growth. The dollar value of trade by the United States, Japan and Canada declined 3.6% in August 2001 compared with a year earlier. If this trend continues for the United States, as I expect it will, 2001 will have been the first year since 1982 that America's foreign trade falls.

3. Trade liberalisation presents the greatest opportunity for developing nations. They will find that it facilitates greater economic integration and political co-operation with the developed world. It will provide them with new investments, production methods and technologies.

A recent World Bank study examined developing countries that opened themselves up to global competition, and those that did not. It concluded that income per person in globalising, developing countries grew more than three-and-a-half times faster. The absolute poverty rates for globalising, developing countries has fallen sharply over the past 20 years, while the income levels of the lowest-income households grew in line with the overall economy. In the six years following completion of the Uruguay round, exports from developing nations grew by nearly $1 trillion, to a level of $2.4 trillion.

Trade's benefits are not denominated in dollars alone. Open trade advances political reform. It swells the ranks of businesses and can reduce the degree of costly government intervention. Furthermore, as the United States pursues free trade, it will do so in a way that is consistent with our values and draws on our compassion. For example, the Bush administration is implementing a flexible policy on intellectual property as it relates to medicines to treat HIV/AIDS. This flexibility, afforded by the major international trade agreement on intellectual property, enables countries and companies to help deal with this tragic epidemic by encouraging low-cost access to critical medicines.

4. Open markets will engender economic recovery in the short term and sustainable economic growth over time. A signal that the world's trading nations are committed to open markets—and that they will resist protectionism—would inject much-needed confidence into financial markets.

After all, there is a bicycle theory for trade: if the trade liberalisation process does not move forward it will, like a bicycle, be pulled down by the political gravity of special interests. By seeking to promote open markets on multiple fronts—globally, regionally and with individual countries—the United States hopes to create a competition in liberalisation that counters the political gravity of protectionism. Additional trade liberalisation will also enhance productivity and efficiency, while helping to keep inflation in check.

5. Trade liberalisation will benefit families around the world. In America, the market openings implemented as part of the Uruguay round and the North American Free Trade Agreement generate annual benefits of $1,300-$2,000 for the average family of four. The numbers may differ in other nations, but it is clear that opening markets can deliver hefty tax cuts for families. And the biggest beneficiaries are those with lower incomes, as they are least able to afford higher prices for food or clothes or appliances.

At the dawn of this new century, we have a choice of ideas. Which ones will triumph: those of fear, destruction and dwindling dreams, or those of humankind's untapped potential and the creative energy of free peoples seeking better lives? While the question is open, the choice is obvious: we must build on the past 50 years, championing ideas that lead to opportunity and growth. With the prospect of freer trade ahead, we will be setting a course for increased peace and prosperity in the world—not just for 2002, but for decades to come. □

The race to end race

Gregory Rodriguez   *Los Angeles*

There is always something new out of California. Watch out for an initiative on the state ballot in March 2002 that will take the first step towards barring the identification of Americans by race. It could overturn, in time, the whole apparatus by which government delivers social policy. It could mark the start of the end of "hyphenated Americans": those who call themselves African-American, native-American, Chinese-American and so on. A new generation is arriving that may spurn the definitions their parents sought.

Ward Connerly, a black Sacramento businessman who sponsored a successful anti-affirmative action measure in 1996, promises to produce a "Racial Privacy Initiative". This, says Mr Connerly, would "protect a person from disclosing his identity to the government". Except for medical or law enforcement purposes, racial identification would stop altogether. Citing his own marriage to a white woman and their multiracial children, Mr Connerly argues that intermarriage, which is several times more common in California than in any other state, is making the concept of race irrelevant.

"At this point," says Tamar Jacoby, a fellow at the Manhattan Institute, "those of us who think that the government's need for race data has become intrusive have to ask ourselves whether we should be patient as racial mixture renders the categories meaningless, or do we attack the system head on, thereby risking the possibility of a backlash."

Political observers fear that the Racial Privacy Initiative could also prove to be as emotionally charged and socially wrenching as were Propositions 187 and 209, the anti-illegal immigrant and anti-affirmative action ballot measures that shook California in the 1990s. Wary of yet another potentially divisive political measure, many Californians are likely to ask themselves whether the end of this initiative is worth the means.

Over the past several decades, an increasing number of multiracial Americans have demanded the right to identify themselves outside of the four racial—and one ethnic—categories normally provided by government agencies. Finally recognising this, the 2000 Census became the first to allow people to mark more than one racial box on their questionnaire.

"Race in America is increasingly becoming a matter of subjectivity," says Peter Skerry, a fellow at the Brookings Institution. Before 1960, when race was considered an objective characteristic, census enumerators were entrusted with selecting the race of American citizens. But since then, the federal government has deemed racial self-identification one more individual right to which Americans are entitled. "Self-identification is sacrosanct now," says Mr Skerry. "But we're beginning to wonder whether these government categories make sense."

Although relatively few respondents—2.4%—took advantage of the multiracial option in 2000, the 7m, largely youthful, generation of multiracial Americans (half are under 18) who did, have opened the door to a whole new era. "Over time, people will begin to answer the race question in more complex ways," says a Harvard sociologist, Mary C. Waters.

The government's growing dependence on this morass of racial data to make public policy is on a collision course with the public's growing desire to resist the questions. For example, in 1998, the first year the University of California abolished affirmative action in admissions, the number of applicants who declined to state their race shot up by 213%. Citing the need to get a full picture of the impact of race-blind policies, admissions directors at the University of California at Los Angeles and the University of California at San Diego later admitted they peeked into SAT exam results in an attempt to ascertain those students' racial backgrounds.

Over the past few years, in an attempt to root out

Any colour is the new black

racial profiling by police, roughly 400 local law-enforcement agencies around the country have begun collecting data on the racial and ethnic backgrounds of all drivers stopped. Because departments generally discourage officers from directly asking a citizen's race—for fear of inviting even greater distrust—they are essentially obliged to guess each driver's heritage before recording it.

Despite the noble purposes of this monitoring, the prospect of the government prying into or guessing the racial backgrounds of citizens will cause increasing concern in American society. "We paint ourselves into a corner," says Ruben G. Rumbaut, a sociology professor at Michigan State University. "In order to combat discrimination, we monitor race, which, in turn, only solidifies and hardens these racial categories."

In 1978, when Supreme Court justice, Harry A. Blackmun wrote his famous dictum, that to go beyond racism, we first must consider race, most Americans could grasp his logic. A generation later, however, racial data collection efforts that make the public even more race-conscious than it already is may strike many Americans as a vicious circle. □

Gregory Rodriguez: senior fellow at the New America Foundation, a non-partisan public-policy institute

Too much stuff

John Quelch   *Cambridge, MA*

2002
President George Bush receives trade promotion authority from Congress. This will boost efforts to get the Free Trade Area of the Americas launched in 2006. Caribbean leaders want a single market in 2003.

Watch out for a new brand of consumer in 2002: the middle-aged person of wealth who, finding himself surrounded by too much stuff acquired over the years, decides to simplify life. Out will go luxury purchases, conspicuous consumption and a trophy culture. Tomorrow's trend-setting consumer will buy more ephemeral, less cluttering stuff: fleeting, but expensive, experiences, not heavy goods for the home.

The economic boom of the 1990s fuelled consumption and democratised access to luxury goods. Millions played the lotteries or aspired to what they viewed on "Lifestyles of the Rich and Famous". As the wealthy grew richer, pressure increased on those below to trade up. And, as they traded up, pressure increased in turn on the wealthy to buy even more—the second home, the big screen TV and the latest sport-utility vehicle. Enter the big houses that measured success in thousands of square feet

COULD I JUST SKIP THE EXPERIENCE AND HAVE DIAMONDS INSTEAD PLEASE?

of floor space, topped by the 40,000 square feet, $50m palace that Bill Gates has built outside Seattle. In 2000, 30% of new homes exceeded 2,400 square feet in floor space compared with 18% in 1986. Ironically, these mansions, owned by business people on the road half the time, grew in number as the size of the average American household declined.

These huge houses had to be filled with more stuff, good news for the home-appliance and home-furnishing industries. Even grocery manufacturers benefited. Larger homes with bigger refrigerators can absorb more inventory. Flat birth rates in developed economies have put pressure on durable consumer-goods companies desperate for top-line growth. Product quality improvements mean these goods break down less often. So durable-goods sales depend on two things: the launch of new, higher-priced, higher-featured, often customised products that persuade consumers to trade in their existing appliances before they break down, as well as household penetration of products such as fax machines and print-

ers previously used only by businesses.

As the world economy slumps, a new segment is emerging in the consumer marketplace. I call this group the Shedders. They have four characteristics. First, they perceive that they have more stuff than they need. Sure, they may collect something specific like porcelain figurines as a hobby, but they are the opposite of the pack rats who fill their attics and basements with "you-never-know-when-you-might-need-it" stuff.

Second, they want to collect experiences, not possessions. And they give experiences rather than goods as gifts to friends and relatives. Experiences may seem ephemeral. They cannot be inventoried except in the form of "Kodak" moments; but they do not tie you down, require no maintenance and permit variety-seeking instincts to be quickly satisfied. Dining out, foreign travel, learning a new sport—are all on the rise.

Third, their stuff embarrasses them. Their Range Rovers no longer tell the world that they are sophisticated town and country socialites. There are simply too many of them on the road to offer much social status. Worse, they now signal the irresponsible selection of a gas-guzzler.

Fourth, Shedders have wealth that is so assured that it no longer requires conspicuous display. They lease their cars, rent other people's holiday homes and would happily outsource other aspects of their lifestyles. The Shedders reject the marketer's continual pressure to spend more money on possessions rather than on education, health care and other social goods.

Shedders are the consumers who are trading in their sport-utility vehicles. They are the empty-nester baby-boomers who are tiring of heating unused spaces in cavernous mansions, now preferring smaller houses with architectural character and intimate spaces, more charm and less maintenance. Their families are scattered, unable to share conveniently the family holiday home and often unwilling to inherit the burden of something they will never use. They do not put their wealth into goods but into mutual funds, and the wealthiest are now setting up small family foundations.

The new economy has made it even easier for Shedders to get rid of their stuff. The high-tech equivalents of the yard sale, electronic auction sites, bring Shedders and those who are yet to catch the Shedding habit together.

This emerging segment—the Shedders—presents a challenge to marketers. These are well-off people who value quality over quantity and do not buy proportionately more goods as their net worth increases. More so than perhaps the protesters on the streets of Seattle and Genoa, the Shedders will dampen expected demand growth in developed economies and require consumer-goods multinationals to focus their efforts on emerging markets where stuff is still king. □

John Quelch: Lincoln Filene professor and senior associate dean at Harvard Business School

Moby, an American star, believes that the music industry and music itself will soon change beyond recognition

Sounds different

"Just say, 'Play me Led Zeppelin's greatest hits but eliminate the slow songs from 1975 to 1977' and your music system will obey"

Not to indulge in hyperbole, it is fairly safe to say that over the next ten years the ways in which music is created, marketed, distributed, sold and even listened to, are going to change drastically. It is almost as safe to say that 25 years from now people will look at a fixed "read only" music medium (that is, a compact disc or a cassette) as a quaint anachronism from the 20th century. The catalyst that is precipitating this monumental change in music creation and distribution is, of course, the "digital revolution". Music can easily be converted into simple binary code and distributed virtually, thus rendering CDs and cassettes and LPs obsolete.

A large part of how we think about music is influenced by the methods by with which it has conventionally been distributed. We think of pop songs as being three or four minutes long because 40 years ago that was all that could fit on one side of a vinyl single. And we think of albums as being around 70 minutes long because that is all that can fit on to a CD.

But if people use hard-disks and RAM as storage media, then there is no limit to the length of a piece of music or to the length of a collection of songs. You could have every Led Zeppelin album on the hard-disk of your laptop and you would not even notice it in terms of memory usage. And with a high-speed modem you could download every Led Zeppelin album in an evening and it would not cost you a thing.

And that is where technology is today. Imagine what the sale and distribution of music will be like when people have speed-of-light modem connections. Within a few years you will be able to walk into your living room and say, "Play me Led Zeppelin's greatest hits, but eliminate the slow songs from 1975 to 1977" and your music system will obey. Instantly.

Whether this music arrives via downloads on to your hard-drive or via an Internet server that you would access through a high-speed modem or via satellite or via some technology that has yet to be developed is, of course, still to be determined. But it is safe to say that, with every piece of music ever recorded at your instantaneous disposal, you will not be buying too many compact discs at $25 each.

Which raises the question of how record companies will be able to justify their existence. At present, record companies exist because they develop the artists, and manufacture and distribute the CDs. But if there are no CDs being manufactured and distributed, then what role will record companies serve?

There is, traditionally, a great deal of antipathy between artists and record companies, so if in the future a musician is able to distribute music directly over the Internet you can be sure that he or she will not feel altruistically committed to the record companies. There will be no need for them to be involved—and they won't be.

One role that record companies have also traditionally served is that of marketing and promotion. But over the past few years a lot of these skills have been outsourced from record companies to stand-alone companies who only do marketing and promotion. So in a world without the traditional manufacturing and distribution of compact discs, how will record companies survive? The big media companies will in theory be able to generate revenue by virtually distributing their old stock of music: hits from the past. But this same back catalogue could easily be illegally distributed by people who engage in "file sharing". Because, in practice, why would music fans want to pay a major media company to listen to a piece of music when they can download it for free from a private site?

The laptop performer

The way in which music is created is also changing drastically, thanks to the digital revolution. In the past, in order to make a successful song, a musician had to spend a lot of time in an expensive recording studio filled with racks and racks of high-tech audio gear. Now the vast majority of recordings are made on computers.

The technology is progressing at such a pace that it is now possible to make a great sounding, commercially and artistically viable piece of music on a laptop. And not a fancy, expensive laptop with all the bells and whistles, either. A musician can easily create a playable and successful piece of music on a cheap laptop using $500-worth of software (if they even choose to pay for the software).

The implications of this are staggering. For why would someone pay money for a new dance record if they can make a better dance record themselves on their lunch break? And why would an up-and-coming musician want to get involved with a record company when they can make a piece of music on their laptop and minutes later have it on their website for anyone to hear?

The recording, manufacturing, marketing and distribution of a piece of music has traditionally been a long and extremely expensive process. With today's technology, all this can cost nothing and can be accomplished, start to finish, in an afternoon. The one requirement for success is talent. If a recording can be made relatively easily with present-day technology, just imagine what the music world will be like in, say, ten years.

One thing is certain. And that is that people have been in love with music for the length of human history regardless of how it has been created and distributed. And I cannot see humanity's love of music disappearing just because the technology changes. But things are going to be a lot different musically from a commercial standpoint as the technology gets better and faster. Music and musicians, audiences and appreciation will remain. All else will change beyond recognition. □

With the AcuLaser C2000, your first 12,000 colour print-outs are free. Use them wisely.

Until 31st December, we're giving away an additional set of colour consumables (RRP £448) with every AcuLaser C2000 colour laser printer. In effect, your first 12,000 colour print-outs are free.* So you'll be sure to get your biro back.

For more details call **0800 220 546** or visit **www.epson.co.uk**

*Assumes 20% coverage per page (5% Cyan + 5% Magenta + 5% Yellow + 5% Black).
Terms and conditions apply.

EPSON. See what you're missing.

EPSON®

Try not to tread on too many toes

China goes for gold

James Kynge

Beijing

China will change more in 2002 than most countries change in a decade. While there will be no revolution, few of the country's 1.3 billion people will avoid the fall-out. A new leader will take the helm of the ruling Communist Party in October. Of all the challenges that will confront Hu Jintao, none will be trickier than coping with his country's membership of the World Trade Organisation (WTO). Tariff barriers on foreign goods will start falling; unemployment will go the other way. China's banks will become even more indebted and rural incomes will fall. Such a huge set of challenges would dwarf any other leadership. But, for reasons of national pride, China's has chosen to add another item to its burgeoning agenda: 2008. The world will then turn to watch as the Olympic torch arrives in Beijing. In preparation, a massive $22 billion building and clean-up operation kicks off in 2002.

But the real challenge for Mr Hu and his colleagues has nothing to do with tall buildings or fibre-optic cables; it is whether they can create a country that by 2008 will live up to such world-class facilities. The answer will be: almost. The things that will not change in 2002—authoritarian habits and a failure to sort out loss-making state enterprises—will be the things that disappoint.

The success of the Olympic bid was seen by many Chinese not only as a token of acceptance into the international community but also an affirmation that the blistering pace of China's economic transformation over the past 22 years has been worth the effort. But now the glow of triumph will fade. China's leaders, its corporations and

policy advisers face a challenging journey ahead.

China is on track formally to join the WTO some time in the first half of the year. Entry will mark the first time in thousands of years of Chinese statehood that the "middle kingdom" has voluntarily agreed to push through far-reaching economic reforms according to the ordinances of an authority beyond its borders. It will mean that almost every sector of the economy will eventually be opened to international competition. For foreign business people operating in China, it will provide a level of comfort—and a form of legal redress within the WTO dispute settlement system—that has hitherto been absent.

Although the full extent of the opening up of the market will not be known until five years after entry, the potential for dislocations—even convulsions—will be all too real in 2002. If the shockwaves from the terrorist attacks in New York and Washington throw the world into recession, the upsurge in foreign direct investment that Beijing hoped for may fail to materialise. Trade, meanwhile, also looks set to disappoint. Exports started to stumble in 2001 and a considerable shrinkage in China's trade surplus is forecast for 2002, reviving the vexed debate—last heard back in 1999—over whether the currency should be devalued.

These difficulties will combine to form a volatile mix. Trade and foreign investment have formed an increasingly important component of GDP in recent years, suggesting that a global recession could be keenly felt. Yet WTO membership commits China to a thorough restructuring of its financial, manufacturing and agricultural in-

2002

75km of new subway, 700km of new highway, a new airport terminal, cleaner air and a new opera house. Beijing prepares for 2008.

James Kynge: China correspondent in Beijing for the *Financial Times*

Jiang applauds himself

dustries. About 5m people in 2002 will face joblessness for the first time. This spectre haunts not only China's workers; it petrifies the political leadership. "Friends, you clap," Zhu Rongji, the premier, told a recent audience. "But we don't yet know how much of a competitive challenge we'll face. My heart is not yet settled."

Mr Zhu, who will run economic policy for at least another year, is aware that if he is to ward off social upheaval he must keep growth above 6%. Huge government spending will, once again, be used in 2002 to deliver this. About 150 billion yuan ($18 billion) of public money is to be spent on infrastructure projects primarily intended to provide jobs and to encourage consumer spending. Economists believe, however, that as much as 250 billion yuan may be required. The more that is spent, the larger the public debt grows. China's government is probably already more indebted, relative to its GDP, than Japan: a headache that will get more painful in 2002.

Domestic pressures may well strain China's external relations. This coming year will show how durable the government's support for America's war against terrorism will be. Is it actually a matter of supporting America or is it that China has a particular dislike of Islamic fundamentalism, particularly in its own western provinces? China wants Islamic fundamentalists in Afghanistan crushed as much as the United States. But conflict could come when the regime that is installed after the Taliban, fragile and fractious, looks abroad for friends. China, as well as Russia and the United States, will want influence. China's implacable opposition to America's plans for national missile defence will also put a strain on relations.

Such concerns will fall on younger shoulders in 2002,

at least officially. Mr Hu will take over from Jiang Zemin as Communist Party general secretary at the 16th Congress in the autumn. A career party official, Mr Hu made friends while he ran Tibet during the 1980s, and more recently at the Party School. This is where senior members go for regular doses of Mao Zedong Thought and Deng Xiaoping Theory. New on the syllabus in 2002 will be Jiang Zemin Thought. Mr Jiang will remain in charge of the military in 2002, and beyond. With the army at his beck and call, he hopes he can continue to call the shots.

There are signs, however, that he will not be allowed to. When he announced in early 2001 that private business people should be encouraged to join the party, many party stalwarts criticised his failure to consult them. The policy went through, and will be enshrined at the Congress in 2002, but the commotion revealed the limits of Mr Jiang's authority. Mr Hu is popular, if not charismatic, and he looks like a safe bet. Other posts will be more hotly contested. Look out for jostling to succeed Premier Zhu in 2003. Vice-Premier Wen Jiabao is a favourite, but Mr Jiang's friend, Li Changchun, currently running Guangdong province, might just sneak in. Dozens of other senior jobs will change hands during 2002-03, setting the shape of policy for years to come.

This new generation faces a host of problems, but none is more delicate than how to pursue political reform. The issue is pressing. High-profile corruption cases have shocked the Chinese public. In one, it emerged that Shenyang, China's fifth biggest city, was in thrall to ruthless mafia bosses who commanded the loyalty of the mayor, his office, the local tax bureau, the chief prosecutor and several other officials. The leadership has tried to come down hard; senior people are now regularly executed or imprisoned. Expect more of the same in 2002. But the party's refusal to accept the simple truth that absolute power corrupts absolutely means that real success will remain unattainable.

Corruption, a huge public debt, and an authoritarian government: China will have all these things in 2002. But the changes that take place will, crucially, all point in the right direction, towards making China a prosperous country, more content with its place in the world. If Mr Hu and company can manage this difficult transition until 2008, they will have deserved an Olympic medal. □

HONG KONG

Hong Kong is losing its lustre. China, not Hong Kong, now makes clothing, plastic toys and radios for the world. Since the summer of 1997, when tourists and journalists flocked to see the territory's colourful handover to China, the place has lost much of its appeal and economic buzz. In 2002, even visitors from mainland China—to whom anywhere else is colourful—will prefer to spend their time and money in genuinely foreign places like Thailand and Tuscany.

To make Hong Kong interesting again, the government is spending a fortune on a Disneyland with Chinese characteristics, next to the shiny new airport bequeathed by the departing British (like everything to do with transport in Britain, it was a year late). But Disneyland will not open until 2005. Until then, the economy will have to be kept going with intravenous

injections of deficit financing, a recently acquired habit the government is promising to kick.

Hong Kong remains deliciously different from the rest of the Chinese motherland. Its people can still lampoon their leaders in vicious cartoons and they can light candles and sing democratic songs in Victoria Park to commemorate the Beijing massacre on June 4th 1989—an activity that still earns severe punishment across the border. But it shares one time-tested political institution with the mainland: rigged elections. In 2002, the unpopular chief executive, Tung Chee-hwa, will almost certainly be "re-elected" by a committee whose members have been selected by the seven old men in the Politburo of the Chinese Communist Party in Beijing.

Another bad habit Hong Kong is acquiring from the

mainland is the publication of implausible economic numbers. In 2000, for example, the Hong Kong government reported, bogusly, that the economy grew by 10.5%. This was not evidence of a roaring economy but of an errant statistic that usually lurks unnoticed in the bowels of the bureaucracy: the GDP deflator. Government officials have promised that the deflator will behave itself in 2002. That will mean duller economic data, too. □

KEY INDICATORS	2000	2001	2002
GDP growth (%)	-0.2	2.6	2.6
Inflation (%)	-3.8	-1.4	1.2
Current account (% of GDP)	5.4	2.2	2.1

Economist Intelligence Unit

Japan updated

Peter Tasker   *Tokyo*

Peter Tasker: partner in Arcus, a money-management firm specialising in Japanese securities. Author of "Japan in Play" and "Samurai Boogie", a novel

A comprehensive industrial restructuring such as Japan has embarked on is a protracted and messy affair. Success is never obvious until well after the event. Such was the case with the transformation of the Anglo-Saxon economies which began in the early 1980s but received due acclaim only in the late 1990s. The restructuring of Japan is a larger task undertaken in less propitious circumstances. Even so there will be clear signs of progress in 2002. Beneath the apparent stagnation dramatic changes have been taking place.

A sticky situation
Over 65-year-olds
% of population, 2020

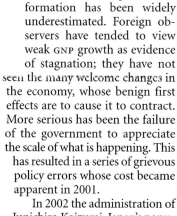

Sources: Japan's Statistics Bureau, United Nations Secretariat

The extent of Japan's transformation has been widely underestimated. Foreign observers have tended to view weak GNP growth as evidence of stagnation; they have not seen the many welcome changes in the economy, whose benign first effects are to cause it to contract. More serious has been the failure of the government to appreciate the scale of what is happening. This has resulted in a series of grievous policy errors whose cost became apparent in 2001.

In 2002 the administration of Junichiro Koizumi, Japan's popular prime minister, will wake up to the perils of deflation. It will shift to an explicitly reflationary policy. Key features will include an inflation target, an injection of public funds into the banking system, a weaker yen, and a revitalisation of the housing market. Meanwhile Japan's best companies will accelerate their restructuring programmes, leading to a wave of mergers, spin-offs, and buy-outs. Asset prices will finally bottom out. Playing host to the soccer World Cup will help to restore the nation's battered self confidence.

The metamorphosis of Japan from a manufacturing-oriented, high-savings, high-investment economy into a service-oriented consumer economy is being driven not by politicians but by the private sector. One of the clearest signs of progress has been the shift in employment from manufacturing to services. As Japan's large manufacturers have restructured their operations—moving production overseas, slimming down supplier networks, rationalising distribution—the heartland of industrial Japan has endured a ferocious shake-out. In a classic case of creative destruction, bankruptcies have soared at the same time as corporate margins have rebounded.

It is not only manufacturing that is bearing the brunt. The construction sector, once the Japanese equivalent of America's military-industrial complex in terms of political clout, has been hit by weak private demand and a squeeze on public works. As a result the order book of the largest 50 construction companies is at its lowest ratio to GNP for 30 years.

For many decades the big electric power utilities were, like the construction companies, instruments of economic management. The purpose of their massive investment programmes was to boost regional economies and keep orders flowing to capital-goods producers. But here too there has been a move to asset efficiency and profits. Since 1993, the major utilities have cut capital investment by a third and have been overtaken as Japan's biggest spenders by the telecoms firms.

As in western countries, the rise of the service economy has profound cultural implications. The era of the samurai salaryman, who gave absolute loyalty in return for permanent job security, is over. Middle-aged males are finding themselves on the scrap-heap, often without the skills to find new opportunities. Service employment is concentrated in smaller companies, and demands flexibility and specialist skills. The proportion of part-time workers has risen dramatically from 12% in 1988 to 24% in 2000. The unemployment rate for men between 45 and 54 has been rising, while the rate for women between 25 and 34 has been falling. Not surprisingly Ginza and Akasaka, the traditional watering holes of the "lords of the expense account", are in crisis while Odaiba, Harajuku and other areas favoured by trendy young "freeters" (freelance workers) are seething with life.

Changing consumer behaviour is symbolised by the staggering success of the Uniqlo apparel chain, which has risen in three years from obscurity to the status of Japan's most successful retailer. Its recurring profits of ¥100 billion ($830m) are greater than the profits of the top ten department-store chains put together. Uniqlo is the most visible of a large group of fast-growing chains, covering everything from toiletries to furniture, from spectacles to Buddhist reliquaries. Foreign retail groups, such as The Gap, Carrefour and Starbucks, are building a major presence in Japan, and luxury-goods merchants such as Gucci and Bulgari, whose target market is young women rather than middle-aged men, are hardly noticing the supposedly weak state of consumption. Both foreign and new-breed Japanese retailers have a high proclivity to source from overseas. This has helped to drive the remarkable growth in imports, up 60% in the past eight years against a 25% rise in exports.

With so many positive changes, why the persistent

The raw data

Construction investment % of GDP

Number of workers in the service sector, m

Number of workers in manufacturing, m

GDP growth %

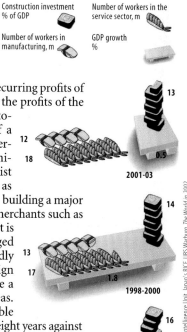

2001-03: 13, 12, 18, 0.5

1998-2000: 14, 13, 17, 1.8

1995-97: 16, 15, 16, 6.3

Sources: Economist Intelligence Unit, Japan's RICE; UBS Warburg, *The World in 2002*

Will soccer settle old scores?

Matthew Glendinning

More than 400,000 soccer fans will travel to Japan and Korea for the 2002 World Cup, the world's biggest sporting event. Each of the two countries, which have a history of rivalry and strained relations, had fought determined campaigns to be the sole host. Instead, FIFA, the soccer world's governing body, opted for this co-hosting arrangement. Matches will be held in 20 cities. Seoul in South Korea will stage the opening match on May 31st. Yokohama in Japan will host the final on June 30th. One billion viewers will tune in.

There is no better sign of Japan's changing self-image than its new generation of sporting heroes. Back in the high-growth era fans flocked to see baseball stars like Shigeo Nagashima and the home-run king Sadaharu Oh, both loyal members of the Yomiuri Gi-

ants squad for their entire careers and model citizens on and off the field. No more would it have occurred to these stalwarts to ply their trade overseas than it would have to dye their hair yellow.

Now Japan has a hero who has done both these things. Soccer play-maker Hidetoshi Nakata took big risks in quitting the pampered life of a domestic superstar in order to try his luck at the sport's highest level. His success in the gladiatorial atmosphere of Italy's Serie A, playing for Parma, sparked off an exodus of other talented players. Meanwhile, Japanese baseball has its own overseas hero to cheer. Ichiro—as Ichiro Suzuki is known in both Japan and the United States—had a phenomenal first season in the major leagues, setting batting records for the Seattle Mariners and winning selection

to the All Star game. Both Ichiro and Nakata are prickly, uncompromising personalities, truer to their own talent than to the ideals of teamwork and self-sacrifice that animated their illustrious predecessors. Both have become icons of the New Japan.

World Cup officials on both sides of the Sea of Japan will be kept busy smoothing the logistical—and diplomatic—operation. Take this example. The World Cup's official title and trademark, printed in English, is "2002 FIFA World Cup Korea/Japan". That was cause enough for a row over which country's name should come first on official Japanese World Cup documents and websites. This was only resolved when it was decided to leave out both.

Korea has proposed that North Korea should host one of the games in a gesture of cross-border unity. But since North Korea is not a member of FIFA (and one of the few nations that did not so much as enter the qualifying rounds for the 2002 finals) the move is unlikely to be sanctioned.

Fans can expect a hi-tech spectacular from their Asian hosts. Each country has invested well over $1 billion in excellent state-of-the-art stadiums and the event should be carried on a wave of public enthusiasm. For travelling fans some unexpected cultural differences should be noted. South Korea is planning to ban smoking inside stadiums and has proposed a five-minute clean-up time immediately after matches when spectators will be urged to pick up their litter. European fans will take some persuading. But the tournament is unlikely to be the scene of hooliganism. Trouble-makers tend to limit their activities to Europe.

The biggest shocks will come on the field of play. European teams have never won a World Cup outside their own continent. With Brazil's star in temporary decline, the tournament is wide open. But don't expect an Asian winner. □

You should see them when they score

Matthew Glendinning: finance editor, SportBusiness Group

sense of malaise? The answer is that the private sector's new emphasis on profitability, flexibility and efficiency has deflationary implications. In particular, the downsizing of capital investment from 22% of GNP in 1990 to 14% in 2001 has worsened Japan's chronic capital glut. Put together worsening deflation, a highly leveraged corporate sector, and a poorly supervised and under-capitalised banking system, and you have a recipe for semi-permanent financial crisis.

When the global economy was booming and big manufacturers were earning good profits overseas, Japanese policymakers deluded themselves into thinking that radical counter-measures were unnecessary. It took a

global slowdown and a collapse in exports to shatter the policymakers' complacency.

The Koizumi administration came to power on a "pain before gain" agenda, wildly popular with a disillusioned electorate. In 2002 it will stick to the key themes of ending public-works boondoggles and clamping down on bank bail-outs of politically important borrowers. However, as the pain intensifies the government will stimulate the economy. Take all these factors together and 2002 will be a constructive year for Japan. As usual, the conventional wisdom about the country makes a poor pointer to the future. A leaner, tougher and once again dynamic Japan stands, surprisingly, on the threshold. □

Back in plaster

Simon Long

It recalls the plight of a man recovering from a broken leg, who has no sooner got back on his feet than some big bully kicks his crutches away. For much of developing East Asia, potential recessions in America and Europe mean that 2002 will be another year of painful economic physiotherapy. Countries still coming to terms with the after-effects of the financial crisis of 1997-98 have found their chosen cure—rapid increases in exports to the West—suddenly rendered ineffective. This has thrown into sharp relief the incomplete nature of the reforms forced on them by the last disaster. It has also placed new strains on political systems making uncertain strides towards pluralism and accountability.

Not that 2002 will see a re-run of the sort of financial meltdown that began five years ago. Of the five countries worst-affected then—Thailand, Malaysia, Indonesia, the Philippines and South Korea—only Malaysia now pegs its currency, the ringgit, rigidly to the dollar. If the dollar depreciates in 2002, there will be sharp downward pres-

necessity will force the North into renewed dialogue. But little will come of it, assuming, as seems likely, that the creaky Stalinist machine of North Korean repression manages to stave off total breakdown for another year (if not much longer). Although Mr Kim has presided over the most impressive of all recoveries from the 1997-98 collapse, in 2002 he will be a lame duck. His popularity has plummeted, the opposition Grand National Party's Lim Hoi Chang is best-placed to win presidential elections at the end of 2002, and Mr Kim has to cope with a strong parliamentary opposition likely to block dramatic end-of-term gestures towards Pyongyang.

In South-East Asia, as in South Korea, the downturn in America, Japan and Europe has highlighted the failure to see through the reforms compelled by the last crisis. In Thailand, Indonesia and Malaysia, banking systems remain hamstrung by the weight of bad loans on the banks' books. Liquidating the underlying assets was always a political nightmare; and while there seemed a prospect of a relatively swift return to rapid economic growth, it did not seem a necessity. But, as Japan has shown, one year's financial crisis can turn into a wound that festers for a decade or more.

In 2002, economic difficulties will further undermine

2002

The world's largest savings institution, Japan's Post Office, will be turned into an independent company. Junichiro Koizumi would like to privatise it.

Asia walks to market

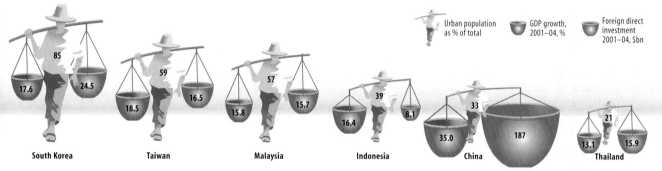

Urban population as % of total · GDP growth, 2001–04, % · Foreign direct investment 2001–04, $bn

South Korea 85 — 17.6 / 24.5
Taiwan 59 — 18.5 / 16.5
Malaysia 57 — 15.8 / 15.7
Indonesia 39 — 16.4 / 8.1
China 33 — 35.0 / 187
Thailand 21 — 13.1 / 15.9

Sources: Economist Intelligence Unit, World Bank, Xinhua

sure on Asian currencies too. But since most are far less dependent than they were on short-term inflows of foreign capital, the consequences should be less drastic.

Two places that weathered the last crisis most successfully—Taiwan and Singapore—were first into recession this time around. Both suffer from what proved a source of strength in the 1990s: their success in manufacturing electronic components. When America's information-technology bubble burst, their exports slumped. Both economies are protected by decades of economic policies that have taken prudence to the point of paranoia, and left foreign-exchange reserves big enough to withstand all but the rudest external shocks. Taiwan, however, will have a rocky 2002. Nerves will be rattled by mainland China's efforts to use Taiwan's economic weakness as a means to extort political concessions. Singapore will, as always, be casting a nervous eye around its neighbourhood, and will worry about instability in Indonesia. The People's Action Party will have easily won an election in November 2001. When times are tough, voters see even less reason than usual for irritating the government.

South Korea has reason to worry about what is happening next door. The arrival of the Bush administration has cast a shadow over President Kim Dae Jung's "sunshine policy" towards North Korea. In 2002, economic

the power-base of the Malaysian prime minister, Mahathir Mohamad, as well as that of Thaksin Shinawatra, a telecoms tycoon who became Thai prime minister in 2001 with a huge electoral mandate. The popularity of both leaders is based on their credibility as economic managers, and as nationalists, who stand up to the buffeting of globalisation. Both qualities would be severely tested by a worldwide recession.

Economics is not all, however. The region will face a challenge in dealing with what Lee Kuan Yew, Singapore's senior minister, called, even before the September 11th attacks on America, "a kind of Islamic globalisation". Some governments, notably Malaysia's, may be exaggerating the danger they face from Islamic terrorist groups. But it is certainly true that Islamic parties in Malaysia and Indonesia now represent perhaps the most important opposition groups, and that in the Philippines, Thailand and parts of Indonesia, Islam is linked with separatist forces that will certainly gain strength in an economic downturn. That in turn may provide an excuse for a revival of military influence. For different reasons, in Indonesia, the Philippines and Thailand, the army has in the past year increased its sway over the government. In 2002, it will try to make sure that it is not forced into another retreat. □

Simon Long: writes for Global agenda at *Economist.com*

Chen Shui-bian, president of Taiwan and recipient of the 2001 Prize for Freedom, predicts that his island's style of democracy will be a model for elsewhere in Asia

Learning about democracy

"Chinese history is full of violent power struggles. Will these energies be channelled into the rule of law?"

Democracies can be awkward things. And young democracies, like young people, can be more awkward still. Consider Taiwan in 2002. It will attract the envy and animosity of Asia as the only truly democratic Chinese state.

Taiwan's first presidential election took place in 1996, and it was not until May 2000 that we experienced our first democratic change of government. As a novice in the ways of democracy, 2002 will be a difficult year. The global slowdown has hit Asia hard and, as a small island heavily dependent on high-tech exports, it has hit us harder than most.

Domestic political disagreements have exacerbated these problems. The shape of the new constitution is not ideal. For example, a winning presidential candidate does not need to gain the majority of the popular vote. The president is allowed to appoint the prime minister without the agreement of the Legislative Yuan, our parliament. This is not satisfactory.

But despite being painful at times, the development of a young democracy can also be exciting. Look at our attempts to end the influence of money and crime in Taiwanese politics. The Legislative Yuan is considering a series of "sunshine laws" which attempt to end corruption in public life. Together with my party, the Democratic Progressive Party, I am committed to cleaning up politics and will work with members of all political parties to achieve this aim.

Democratic politics is competitive, and that is a good thing. But sometimes it is too competitive. One of the things that we are learning, slowly, is the art of achieving consensus between political opponents in order to achieve common goals. In the past, we have missed opportunities to do this, particularly when it comes to economic policy. I believe that we should co-operate more not only in economic policy, but also in more general public policies too.

Economic hardship is not accepted readily in Taiwan. Since records began in 1952, we have not experienced a single recession. In fact, we are accustomed to an average of 8% annual growth. In August 2001, together with the island's business leaders, I called a conference for us to consider how we should respond to the worsening economic conditions. Strengthening our economic links with mainland China was one of the options forwarded. There were proposals to end the ban on direct commerce, communications and transport across the Taiwan Straits. I am keen to pursue these ideas. Our economists predict that in 2002 our economy will grow at around 4%, although that would be dependent on worldwide conditions picking up too.

Here in Taiwan, we host the first ethnic Chinese democracy that promotes the fundamental values of human rights and freedom. I view our experience as the product of a long historical search for true emancipation from the vicious cycle of dynastic and authoritarian rule. Chinese history has been full of violent power struggles, corruption, inequality, war and collapse. Will these energies be channelled into the rule of law? Our hope is that democracy, although not perfect in every way, will help prevent us returning to these old ways.

The Chinese way

The people of Taiwan are so proud of their democracy that they reflect on the previous authoritarian government only to avoid it. We will share our experience of democratisation with other countries throughout Asia. Taiwan can, and will, prove to be the best model for a non-western democracy, a society where local cultural values are mixed with the universal values of free votes and free speech. I believe that only when people are free to express their ideas, and to choose their leaders through regular elections will their country be strong and prosperous.

Comparison with what is happening across the Taiwan Straits in mainland China is inevitable. The harsh treatment of the Falun Gong spiritual group symbolised the authoritarian character of the leadership there. The widening income gap between urban and rural areas, and between people in the east and west of the country, is causing social stress. There is widespread corruption and crime. We are concerned about the rise of nationalism, often characterised by xenophobic tendencies. And the rest of the region worries about what China's rising military spending augurs for the future of regional peace and security. Countries throughout the world, particularly Taiwan, need to encourage China to look within to solve its problems. We need to do everything in our power to prevent the use of military action to divert attention from these pressing internal problems.

I believe that peaceful negotiations are the best solution to head off conflict. War brings only death and destruction, breeds hatred, and rarely solves the underlying problems. We must accurately identify the intentions of mainland leaders and discourage the use of force by showing sincere goodwill. Only by offering the mainland a real hope for the future can we play our part in avoiding conflict.

We live in a world where national boundaries and sovereignty are becoming secondary to the higher values of human rights, peace and prosperity. Taiwan is ready to pursue these higher values for all, including the people on the Chinese mainland. This may seem unrealistic for people who read news about Taiwan only when there is tension in the Straits. But the reality of co-operative development may not be that far away. After both Taiwan and the mainland are admitted to the World Trade Organisation, we will have many opportunities in 2002 for talks on trade and related issues. □

India's curse

Swaminathan S. Anklesaria Aiyar   *New Delhi*

India will enter the new year sullen and depressed. Politics will be divisive and gridlocked, and the economy will go nowhere. In short, another wasted year. Whilst the 20m people of the Indian diaspora flourish in their adopted countries, the one billion at home will remain bogged down in political corruption and chaos. The only things that could go well will be in areas without government interference, notably the information-technology sector. But the software bust in the West will also mean little prosperity of this sort in the East in 2002. In areas where India's cheap labour force might theoretically flourish, such as manufacturing for the international market, it will be comprehensively beaten, yet again, by the Chinese.

Politics remains the villain. Expect the ruling coalition, headed by the Bharatiya Janata Party (BJP), to flounder in 2002. It has two major problems. One is its lack of a majority in the Rajya Sabha, the upper house of Parliament. The other is the feuding between liberals, headed by Prime Minister Atal Behar Vajpayee, and Hindu nationalists within the party. Hindu nationalism shares many of the unattractive traits of other fundamentalist groups: it is essentially anti-modern and, therefore, anti-western. Take an absurd example: expect riots next February 14th, with windows broken in shops that dare sell Valentine cards. Or a serious one: the nationalists strongly oppose economic reforms as a sell-out to multinationals. They criticise the reduction of subsidies and tougher labour laws as anti-worker.

Lack of a majority in the Rajya Sabha explains why the government keeps promising without delivering. In his budget speech in 2001, the finance minister promised a raft of painful but necessary economic reforms and declared that tough labour legislation would be introduced in the budget session itself. Nothing of the sort happened.

New legislation requires Congress, the main opposition party, to co-operate in the upper house. So, the BJP depends on its main political foe to get anything done. This is not a happy position, and looks like getting un-

Putting a gloss on India

happier. In 2002, expect the BJP to lose further ground in the Rajya Sabha. This body is indirectly elected by state assemblies, and Congress has done much better than the BJP in recent state elections.

India's biggest state, Uttar Pradesh, goes to the polls in March 2002. Opinion polls suggest that the BJP, which rules there today, will lose. The most seats in a hung legislature may go to the Bahujan Samaj Party (BSP), which represents the *dalits* (once called untouchables) and some other lower castes. The BSP battles upper castes, and has little time for economic ideology. One of its leaders declares baldly that the party is neither leftist nor rightist, simply opportunist. It will join hands with any party to push its agenda of uplifting untouchables.

To improve the BJP's poll prospects, Hindu nationalists want to start construction of a temple at the site where they destroyed a mosque in 1992. The target date is March, to coincide with the poll. This will violate court orders and, of course, inflame Hindu-Muslim passions. That, claim Hindu militants, is exactly what will yield

Swaminathan Aiyar: consulting editor, India's *Economic Times*

THE PHILIPPINES

FORECAST

Nasty business, kidnapping, especially when some of the hostages turn up headless. The southern Philippines has been terrorised for more than a year by a brutal Islamic militant group, the Abu Sayyaf, which claims to be fighting for Muslim solidarity.

Mainly, though, it seems interested in stealing loot, and in butchering some of its victims. The Philippines' feisty president, Gloria Macapagal Arroyo, has used the army to beat them. She has had some success but she won't catch them all: the jungles are too deep and the local population too sympathetic.

Ms Macapagal Arroyo—Gloria to almost everyone— will have an easier time dealing with Joseph Estrada, the former president ousted in a velvet coup in January 2001. The trial of the still-popular "president of the poor" on charges of economic plunder will drag on.

Wisely, prosecutors will not seek the death penalty; no need for a martyr, although the government will be keen that Mr Estrada pays some sort of price for his misdeeds and that some of the loot is recovered.

The trial, in any case, will be dramatic. If the government could charge admission, it probably would: the budget deficit will be huge again in 2002, though better than the year before. This, too, is the legacy of Mr Estrada and his cronies. More ominously, politics in the Philippines will be awash with nastier stuff: allegations of murder and narco-terrorism by present and former political figures, though not it seems those closest to the current president. This is a violent country and there will be plenty of causes for unrest ahead.

Like most East Asian economies, the Philippines will be marking time in 2002: an exporter of

electronics, especially to the United States, the economy will not rebound strongly until the rest of the world does, in 2003. But the Philippines will handle the global technology slump better than most: old-fashioned agriculture will do rather well. Despite the lacklustre economy, and the left-over political scandals, President Arroyo cuts a strong figure as head of government. Slowly, an air of confidence will return and with it foreign investment. □

KEY INDICATORS	2000	2001	2002
GDP growth (%)	4	2.3	2.5
Budget deficit (% of GDP)	4.1	3.9	3.3
Trade balance ($ billion)	6.9	3.3	3.3

Economist Intelligence Unit

more votes. However, the liberal wing of the party points out that most voters dislike excessive militancy: the BJP lost the Uttar Pradesh state election called after the mosque's destruction. In the 2002 election campaign, Mr Vajpayee will aim to limit militancy to rhetoric. He would be fortunate to succeed.

The prime minister likes summits. In 2002, he is likely to hold a productive one with President George Bush and an unproductive one with President Pervez Musharraf of Pakistan. Mr Vajpayee has carefully cultivated the United States since exploding a nuclear device in 1998 and will stress that the two face a common enemy in terrorism. He has gleefully supported American moves to replace the Taliban in Afghanistan with the Northern Alliance, which has always been friendly to India. A new government in Kabul could help to crack down on Islamic militants who support the insurrection in Kashmir. In 2002, Mr Vajpayee will keep asking the United States to strong-arm Pakistan into closing training camps for Kashmiri militants there.

President Musharraf will insist that there are no terrorists in Kashmir, only freedom fighters. Under pressure from the American administration, he has reluctantly abandoned the Taliban, but will find it practically impossible to abandon Kashmiri insurgents. Mr Vajpayee earlier showed signs of flexibility on Kashmir, but in 2002 will play hardball. He will remind Mr Bush that those bearing guns against India today may turn them against America tomorrow.

The Indian economy has slowed down with the global one. Like many other Asian businessmen, Indian manufacturers have lost confidence in their ability to compete with China. Even if the global economy recovers, they will hesitate to step up investment in 2002. Long-term prospects look better in industries relying on intellectual property rights: computer software, pharmaceuticals and entertainment. Software exports have been rising by 50% annually for many years, but slowed to a crawl in 2001. Yet their long-term prospects are excellent.

Unlike software, pharmaceuticals and entertainment exports have soared despite the global slowdown. Indian companies like Ranbaxy, Cipla and Dr Reddy's Laboratories have emerged as strong exporters of generic drugs. They have become major exporters of drugs to combat AIDS and have also made impressive progress in discovering new molecules.

Many countries fear they cannot compete with Hollywood, but India's entertainment industry—Bollywood—will always beat Hollywood in the local market because of the language barrier. Bollywood's foreign sales are also expanding fast with the growing numbers and prosperity of the Indian diaspora, and Indian films and music have an increasing audience in many developing countries too. "Lagaan", a Hindi film about an imaginary cricket match between British colonialists and Indian villagers, made it to the top ten at the British box office, showing that subtitled Indian films can attract white audiences too.

A decade ago, India's economic reforms were expected to launch the country on the path of export-led manufacturing pioneered by the Asian tigers. That has not happened: China beats India hands down in manufacturing. But, unusually for a developing country, India has risen fast in IT, pharmaceuticals and entertainment. These happen to be the three leading industries of the United States too. Just possibly, India might leapfrog the traditional stage of labour-intensive manufacturing that developing countries usually trudge through, and bound straight into creating intellectual property: an industry blissfully free from politicians. □

The new nation

Simon Long

In the first half of 2002, the world will be joined by a new independent nation, East Timor. It will be ruled by a parliament dominated by Fretilin, the party that led its first, ill-fated experiment with independence in 1975. Its president, Xanana Gusmao, made his name as a guerrilla fighter and political prisoner during the Indonesian occupation that followed. Tiny, dirt-poor and still bearing the charred scars of the arson that marked Indonesia's withdrawal in 1999, East Timor will not be much of a threat to anybody. But in Indonesia, Timorese independence was always feared for the example it might set other restive parts of the country: tug on this thread too hard, argued the generals, and the whole archipelagic tapestry might unravel.

Megawati's wave of unrest

It will not. No other part of Indonesia had as unanswerable a claim to independence as did East Timor, where, throughout Indonesian rule, the United Nations continued to regard the colonial ruler, Portugal, as the administering power. But, perhaps even more than the economic worries that face her, separatism will be the biggest headache in 2002 for Indonesia's new president, Megawati Sukarnoputri. Daughter of the country's founding president, she does not want to preside over her country's disintegration.

Her biggest immediate challenge is in Aceh, at the country's western tip. As in East Timor, years of brutal repression by the army have bred a total distrust of Indonesian rule. Some soldiers may have hoped Miss Megawati would back them in an even more thorough sweep against independence activists. That would be a disaster. The best hope is that her good relations with the generals enable her to persuade them to curb abuses, stand back and make "autonomy" seem credible to the Acehnese.

That would also send a strong signal to other places, notably Irian Jaya, or West Papua, at the far eastern end of the country, where the raising of the flag of independent East Timor will evoke envy, as well as intensifying local resentment of the government in Jakarta. □

Australia: up under

Michelle Grattan   *Canberra*

After coming down from a two-year high—celebrating first the Olympic Games in Sydney and then the centenary of its federation—Australia will have to get through 2002 without a party. But it will have a new national government with something to celebrate: a country that is in surprisingly good economic shape and social heart. The economy has defied international trends, from the Asian crisis of 1997 on, to remain buoyant. This is tipped to continue.

The Australian Treasury estimates growth for the 2001-02 financial year will be 3%. A fall of one percentage point is predicted in business investment, but a 20% rise in residential-property investment, reflecting a housing boom. Australia's current-account deficit will worsen from $A18 billion ($12 billion) to $A26 billion in 2002—a result of the international slowdown squeezing exports and a still-healthy local economy sucking in imports. Expect consumer spending to stay fairly steady, headline inflation to drop from 6% in 2001 to nearly 3%, and unemployment to hover around 7%.

The mood in rural and regional Australia, alienated by years of squeeze on services, has lightened a little. Good prices for beef and wool, a weak Australian dollar, reasonable seasons and plenty of funds from the federal government have resulted in higher incomes and improved amenities.

After years of debate about tax and labour-market reforms, Australia is starting to turn to other issues including, like many of the wealthy countries, worrying about an ageing population. A report to the government by Access Economics, a consultancy, has warned that over the next 20 years new sources of labour "will dry up". Australia has a low birth rate and faces an inevitable baby-boomer retirement bubble. Some politicians have suggested "gold collar"' workers should be encouraged to stay in the workforce until they are 70. The Labor Party wants a population inquiry. Both sides of politics flag the need for changes to superannuation but have left the detail for the new parliamentary term.

One partial counter-measure to Australia's ageing problem would be to boost the immigration programme, a course which has support from certain business sectors. But there is no public backing for a large increase in the number of immigrants.

Australia will slowly re-establish its relationship with Indonesia, which was fractured by the East Timor crisis. The former president, Abdurrahman Wahid, visited Australia before being pushed from office; the Australian prime minister, John Howard, was the first foreign leader to call on his successor, Megawati Sukarnoputri. But Australia has neither the opportunity nor the desire to return to the intimacy of the 1990s, when a ground-breaking security agreement was reached between the two countries. The complicated relations have been further strained

by Indonesia being a transit post for boat people, mostly middle-eastern and west-Asian asylum-seekers. Australia complains of Indonesian slackness in combatting people-smugglers and their cargo. Indonesia has declined Australia's offer to build a detention centre. The boat people, though they run into only a few thousand, have once again become a highly emotional issue in a society quick to feel any "threat from the north". The entry into Australian waters of a Norwegian freighter, Tampa, which had rescued a sinking boat, sparked sharp exchanges between Australia and Norway. Australia is determined to board and divert boats in order to deter asylum-seekers.

Australia has failed to achieve a long sought-after reconciliation with its indigenous people. Black-white relations are intensely strained. Within the aboriginal community argument rages about whether welfare benefits are helping or harming. The push for a formal treaty between indigenous and non-indigenous Australians has gained pace among some aboriginal leaders, but even the

Australia has the world by the tail

left-of-centre Labor Party proceeds with high caution. Expect little progress on this issue in 2002, though it is an important one. A cloud hangs over the elected head of the nation's governmental indigenous body, Geoff Clark. Several women have claimed he raped them many years ago. Before these allegations, Mr Clark had forged a good rapport with Mr Howard, despite their differences, including organising a cricket match between a government team and an aboriginal one.

There is another piece of unfinished business that will rumble on through 2002 and beyond: Australia's constitution and its desire to become a republic, independent of the British crown. It is still as far away from this goal as ever, although a Labor government would put the issue back on the agenda, after the defeat of a referendum in 1999. The earliest a republic could be achieved is in the middle of this decade. But Australians are so suspicious of politicians that it is doubtful they would accept anything other than a directly-elected president, a model favoured by few among the political elite. It would probably require an extensive rewrite of the constitution if it were not to introduce the danger of an over-powerful head of state. □

Michelle Grattan: political editor, *Sydney Morning Herald*

2002

Traffic jams in Bangkok are the stuff of legend. A new metro system will sort out some of the mess. Trains start running in 2002.

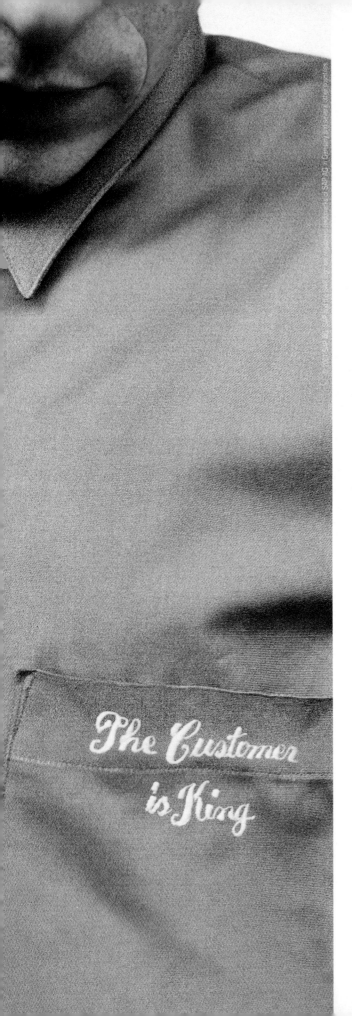

ANNOUNCING A RADICAL IDEA IN CONNECTED INTEGRATED CRM: CONNECTED INTEGRATED CRM.

Putting your customer on a pedestal is a nice concept. Putting your customer at the center of your entire operation is a breakthrough. And at the center of it all is mySAP™ CRM. The first and only CRM solution that integrates seamlessly in real time with all of your existing business processes — from inventory control to data warehousing to marketing to product development to finance to…well, you decide. It all leads to increased customer value and back-end efficiency. But then, we said this was radical, didn't we? Visit sap.com for details.

SAP™

THE BEST-RUN E-BUSINESSES RUN SAP

I'd rather have a job

An unhappy 1423

Roula Khalaf

The Middle East enters 2002, the year of the Prophet 1423, as a more dangerous and more unhappy place than it has been at any time in the past decade. The Palestinian *intifada,* or uprising against Israel, will not end, at least not entirely. Israel will turn alternatively from revenge killings to policies of restraint during the course of the year. America will step up its efforts to find an end to the bloodshed and even attempt a lasting solution to the conflict. America's alliance with Israel will come under strain, but not enough to undo 50 years of friendship. There will be economic stagnation across the region, including in Israel. All of the things that the Middle East most urgently needs—education, foreign investment, political pluralism and jobs—will be put on hold. Political nervousness combined with a low price for oil will make this part of the world one of the hardest hit by the events of September 11th.

Not all is lost. The West has long relied on quiescent, reactionary and decidedly non-democratic governments to serve its perceived interests. It will increasingly discover that these governments are the very ones that stand in the way of progress. The international mood could give a boost to a liberal Islamist movement that will battle harder to find a voice. But even the liberals will have trouble building links with the West so long as the war on terrorism is in its military stage and the Arab-Israeli con-

flict is raging.

All eyes will be on Saudi Arabia. It would be reckless to predict the demise of the Al-Sauds, rulers who have proved resilient to many a difficult crisis in the past. In Riyadh, as in Washington, debate will emerge as to how sustainable is the mutual dependency and whether it is time to define a more distant but more productive alliance. The tug of war in the kingdom between modernists and Islamists will continue.

Almost all of the Arab world's governments know their domestic shortcomings. In some cases, these include overly religious education systems; in most cases, there is unemployment, which ranges up to 20%, and everywhere there are authoritarian attitudes that leave little room for political expression. They realise fully, if belatedly, that these things are key contributors to the general malaise, especially as the majority of the Arab population is under 30. This extraordinary population bubble is about to burst into Arab adulthood: one more reason why the present state of things is not sustainable.

But while the aftermath of September 11th may provoke a revived emphasis on the need for economic reforms, it is unlikely to breed more political tolerance. In North Africa, in particular, there is a danger that the lesson to be drawn from the recent wave of terrorism is that governments should have a free hand to repress Islamist

Roula Khalaf:
Middle East editor,
Financial Times

movements and disregard human rights.

Iraq's attitude will be important. Saddam Hussein has been warned not to take advantage of the crisis but he is known to overplay his hand at critical times. Arab popular opinion is mightily opposed to any military move by America against Iraq. From Cairo to Riyadh repeated warnings will be issued by officials against American action. None of these states loves Mr Saddam. They all know, however, that an attack on Iraq would be seen as an attack on Arabs as much as on Islam; and their societies could not sustain the strain.

Iran, on the other hand, may stand to benefit from the campaign against global terrorism. Tehran's concerns are likely to be taken into account in the building of a new regime in Afghanistan and there is a sense in both Iran and America that common interests in Afghanistan could produce better relations. Iran has a traditional middle class that, having been through a dire period of

Islamic fundamentalism, is starting to enjoy new-found liberties. In 2002 expect Iran to nudge its way back into the international community.

How the American-Iranian relationship progresses will depend, as everything else in the Middle East, on the Arab-Israeli conflict. The United States will want to see evidence that Iran has curtailed its support for Palestinian and Lebanese groups fighting Israel. These are movements that the American government regards as terrorist organisations. The more America works to solve the Palestinian-Israeli crisis, the more productive will be its efforts to maintain Arabs in the coalition against terrorism. Syria and Lebanon, for example, can be easily put under pressure from America but they are unlikely to dismantle Hizbollah, the Islamist movement that drove Israeli troops out of southern Lebanon in May 2000, without a peace agreement with Israel. An agreement there may be in 2002, though not one that can last. □

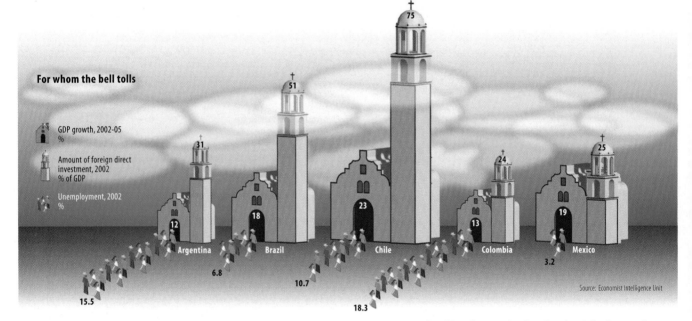

For whom the bell tolls

GDP growth, 2002-05
%

Amount of foreign direct investment, 2002
% of GDP

Unemployment, 2002
%

Argentina 12 · 31 · 15.5
Brazil 18 · 51 · 6.8
Chile 23 · 75 · 10.7
Colombia 13 · 24 · 18.3
Mexico 19 · 25 · 3.2

Source: Economist Intelligence Unit

Latin America's bad luck

Michael Reid

Michael Reid: Americas editor, *The Economist*

It will be a year of foreboding in Latin America, the most difficult period since the wave of liberal reform was launched in the region in the mid-1980s. Two things will dominate: one is the spectre of a region-wide recession and the continuing threat of an Argentine financial collapse; the other is Brazil's presidential election in October, which could see a shift to the left in the region's largest country. There will not be a wholesale retreat from democracy or the market. But there will be a nudge towards economic nationalism and greater reliance on industrial policy.

That will be a reaction of self-defence: Latin America's chronic vulnerability to outside events will punish the region once again. A slowing world economy and continuing fragility in emerging-market finance hit the region hard in 2001, stopping Mexico's impressive growth in its tracks and choking a promising recovery in

much of South America barely after it had got going.

On an optimistic view, Latin America could see economic growth of 1-2% in 2002, barely up on the previous year's 1%. That would imply a quickening recovery in 2003. But it might still be much worse.

Whether it is depends on outsiders. A world recession would mean lower prices for Latin America's commodity exports, including the oil which kept countries such as Venezuela and Ecuador fairly buoyant in 2001. Mexico would be especially hard hit, since the United States takes almost nine-tenths of its exports.

And then there is Argentina. The question is when and how, rather than whether, the country reschedules its debt. The president, Fernando de la Rua, will struggle on despite a poor showing for his Alliance party in a congressional election in October 2001, but he will be dependent on the opposition Peronists. Domingo Cavallo will survive as economy minister only as long as his policy of balancing the budget. The big test for both will be when Mr Cavallo seeks congressional support for reforming the finances of provincial government. Success might open the way to an effort, backed by the IMF, to buy back some of Argentina's debt.

Even so, there is little prospect of Argentina returning to growth in 2002. Political opposition to austerity will grow. It could trigger a unilateral debt default. That could be followed by the abandoning of the fixed exchange rate that pegs the peso to the dollar or, more likely, by Argentina adopting the dollar. An Argentine default would hit Brazil's already weakened currency, risking a return of inflation.

That is only one of the many uncertainties surrounding Brazil's election campaign. During eight years of liberal reform under Fernando Henrique Cardoso, Brazil overcame inflation, and made progress in education and land distribution. But sustained economic growth remains elusive, poverty remains widespread, and botched privatisation recently led to electricity rationing. A slowdown in foreign investment will translate into a credit squeeze for consumers. So Mr Cardoso is far from certain of being succeeded by his chosen candidate.

It will be a wide-open election, and could be won by any of three candidates. Luiz Inacio Lula da Silva of the left-wing Workers' Party, making his fourth attempt on the presidency, will run his strongest campaign since 1990, and could win. Lula, a former car worker and trade-union leader, is more moderate than in the past, and anyway would have to find allies in the centre to gain a congressional majority. He would not try to implement full-blooded socialism. But his talk of debt re-negotiation makes investors nervous.

The same goes for Ciro Gomes, a maverick populist. The third possible winner is Mr Cardoso's candidate. But who will he be? Not she: Roseanna Sarney, a state governor from the north-east and daughter of a former president might fill the vice-presidential slot. The nomination looks to lie between two men. Jose Serra, the health minister, is a social democrat, but a poor campaigner. Then there is Tasso Jereissati; thrice the state governor of Ceara in the north-east, he has connections among Sao Paulo's business elite. And he might take Mr Gomes, also from Ceara, out of the race, since the two are personal friends.

The election may come down to a run-off between Lula and the government candidate. The government

Colombia goes to the polls

Michael Reid

In May, Colombia will hold a presidential election that will be closely watched not just by the voters but also by the country's left-wing guerrillas, right-wing paramilitary vigilantes—and by the United States. At stake is the future of peace talks with the FARC guerrillas launched by Andres Pastrana, who on August 7th 2002 steps down as president after four years.

The election will be closely fought. The likeliest winner is Horacio Serpa, an experienced social-democrat who is the official candidate of the Liberal Party. But he will be pressed hard by Alvaro Uribe, an ambitious, independent Liberal standing on a hardline law-and-order platform. Broadly speaking, Mr Serpa would continue with Mr Pastrana's peace effort with the FARC, and would also try to strike a peace deal with the ELN, its smaller guerrilla cousin. But Mr Uribe has said he would make continuation of the peace talks conditional on the FARC agreeing to a cessation of hostilities and kidnapping, and on its acceptance of international verification of the "demilitarised" zone, a huge swathe of jungle granted to it by Mr Pastrana in order to get talks going.

The presence of two more significant candidates means the election is likely to go to a run-off. Noemi Sanin, an independent conservative, is campaigning against corruption, while Lucho Garzon, a trade-union leader, will try to show that there is space in Colombia for a peaceful and democratic left-wing movement.

The FARC are likely to try to influence the result, both through attacks in the run-up to the vote, and perhaps by well-publicised

Will it be handed to Serpa?

meetings with individual candidates. A separate election for Congress in March may see the paramilitaries try to elect representatives. The Liberal Party however, should retain its dominant position.

Whoever wins will have to reach an understanding with the United States about what is to replace Plan Colombia, the American-backed scheme to fight drugs and guerrillas. Mr Serpa has had difficult relations with the United States in the past, though both sides now say they would work together. Mr Uribe would face other problems: human-rights activists see him as favouring the paramilitaries. The Americans will want the new president to carry on with their project to wipe out cocaine production by spraying coca fields with weedkiller.

Will 2002 be the year that estimates of cocaine production in the Andean countries go down significantly for the first time in a decade or more? Or will it be the year that the United States Congress finally draws some rational conclusions from the failed war on drugs and legalises cocaine? Probably neither. That would be depressing enough. The greatest worry, however, is that Colombia's battle against drugs and guerrillas spreads violence and instability beyond its borders. □

may be helped if a mild El Niño current brings heavy rain to central Brazil, filling the dams and allowing electricity rationing to be lifted.

Democrats all

Four other countries hold presidential elections in 2002. All will signify that this region of the world, for all its considerable problems, is entrenching its democracy, free speech and relatively open economics. It will be all the more frustrating in 2002 that these achievements, which still elude many other parts of the emerging world, will not bring home the economic bacon. The people of Latin America will not be richer. Colombia's campaign will be the most closely watched. Having adopted the dollar, Ecuador was the region's surprise economic star in 2001, with growth of 4% as it bounced back from hyperinflation. President Gustavo Noboa, an independent law professor, may be followed by an old-guard politician, either Rodrigo Borja, a social democrat from Quito, the highland capital, or Leon Febres Cordero, a conservative populist from the port of Guyaquil. Both are former presidents. A third contender is Alvaro Noboa, a banana magnate, who may slip up.

In Bolivia, another two former presidents will vie to return to power. Jaime Paz Zamora has the support of Bolivia's young interim president, Jorge Quiroga. Gonzalo Sanchez de Losada is one of Latin America's most innovative reformers. He might benefit from the memory of economic growth during his presidency. But since neither man will win a majority, the election will be decided in Congress, where Mr Paz has more allies.

In Costa Rica, a small but successful country, voters are likely to choose Abel Pacheco, a popular television personality. He is from the governing Social Christian Party, but won its nomination by campaigning against the party hierarchy. He would abandon the current timid efforts at privatisation and structural reform. He will face a tough fight against Rolando Araya, of the opposition Social Democrats.

Jamaica will hold its election in the first half of the year. The campaign is likely to be scarred by violence. The opposition Jamaica Labour Party, led by Eddie Seaga, a veteran former prime minister, should win. But in a close race, the governing Peoples' National Party might just squeak back, thanks to a reviving economy and the campaigning skills of P.J. Patterson, the prime minister.

Elsewhere, governments will try to ride out the economic storm. In Mexico, the popularity of President Vicente Fox will dwindle, especially if he fails to get key legislation through a Congress controlled by his opponents. In Venezuela, President Hugo Chavez will become increasingly unpopular as the economy slows, but will not face serious challenges. In Chile, in an election in December 2001, the right-wing opposition is likely to win a majority in Congress for the first time since democracy was restored in 1990. That will make governing harder for President Ricardo Lagos.

Latin Americans will press for free trade—and complain about agricultural protectionism—at a summit between the region's leaders and those of the European Union, in Madrid in May. Mr Fox will start to fill the role of Latin America's weightiest leader, a title previously held by Brazil's Mr Cardoso. ☐

Africa needs all the entrepreneurs it can get

Winter in Africa

Patrick Smith

The rebound from the terrorist attacks in America will hit Africa hard in 2002. Its exporters will lose markets while campaigns for debt relief and cheaper HIV/AIDS and malaria drugs will be sidelined. Africa's few winners from America's war on terrorism will be the authoritarian Muslim states in the north, and perhaps Sudan and Tanzania. Intelligence swaps and military muscle, as well as more aid and trade deals, will shore up helpful regimes.

The British prime minister, Tony Blair, will struggle to keep his new Africa enthusiasms on the international agenda. French interest in Africa will wane further if Lionel Jospin becomes president. Another casualty will be the New African Initiative, a development plan led by South Africa's president, Thabo Mbeki. Western investors will be distracted, and Mr Mbeki will face opposition at home to his policies on HIV/AIDS and market economics. The American administration's new foreign-policy principle will operate like the anti-communist loyalty test of the cold war. American covert operations will return to the continent after a brief hiatus. African states supporting a free press, pluralist politics and market economics won favour in the new world order; now loyalty to the war on terrorism will trump all that.

In Kenya and Zimbabwe, the septuagenarian big men—Daniel arap Moi and Robert Mugabe—will see their parties win the elections in 2002 by hook and by crook, confident that international attention will be elsewhere. President Moi will anoint his nephew, Musalia Mudavadi, as successor at the last minute; Mr Mugabe will choose his spymaster, Emmerson Mnangagwa.

Western backing for United Nations peacemaking in the wars of Congo-Kinshasa, Sierra Leone-Liberia and Angola is at risk, as military planners and diplomats concentrate on Central Asia and the Middle East. Sierra

2002

The World, a cruise ship, goes to sea with its 200 residents. They will have paid between $2m and $7m for their permanent berths. Expect a wave of megacruise ships to follow in its wake.

Patrick Smith: editor, *Africa Confidential*

Leone's President Ahmed Tejan Kabbah will win another election. Liberia's warlord, President Charles Taylor, will turn his attention to the unravelling Côte d'Ivoire. There will also be less western carping about the Algerian and Egyptian security services. President Abdelaziz Bouteflika will be boosted against the shadowy Groupe Islamique Armé, the Front Islamique Salut and Berber oppositionists. President Hosni Mubarak will extract more aid dollars and a lead role in fresh Middle East negotiations.

Morocco's King Mohammed VI, claiming lineage from the Prophet, faces a dangerous year. He has not managed to consolidate power after his father's death in 1999: rowdy politicians, an incipient movement of militant Islamists and the uncertain fate of Western Sahara all threaten his throne. Farther along the littoral, Tunisian President Zine el Abidine Ben Ali's plans for an unconstitutional fourth term after 2003 will be politely approved by western diplomats. Flinging open business doors, Libya's Colonel Muammar Qaddafi will be another winner; stamping on Islamist opposition groups will suit him well. In Sudan, General Bashir, who hosted Osama bin Laden in the 1990s, risks provoking more hostility. Under military threat the country handed over militants and intelligence to Washington, but it will remain on the United States' watch list. The 35-year civil war, the world's longest, will drag on.

Other African states on the watch list are wracked by war, or just recovering from war. The latest war between Ethiopia and Eritrea ended in 2000 but both regimes will face growing internal dissent in 2002. Chad's President Idriss Deby is keen to keep foreign investors on board a $2.5 billion oil pipeline while battling with southern secessionists and northern Islamists.

Nigeria has 60m Muslims and provides about 10% of the West's oil. President Olusegun Obasanjo believes this will make his country key to western strategy. He wants creditors to slash Nigeria's $35 billion foreign debt as opposition grows ahead of the 2003 elections. Secessionist movements are winning support, and Christian-Muslim confrontations have already cost thousands of lives. Angola's planned election in 2002, at which President Eduardo dos Santos had promised to step down, will, of course, not take place.

African states without oil and unthreatened by Islamist subversion will get little help. Global aid to Africa dropped from $18 billion in 1990 to $11 billion in 1998, and it will fall again in 2002. Africa's terms of trade will worsen. The global recession means that commodity-export prices will hit the floor. The World Bank reckons another 10m Africans will be thrown into poverty by the slowdown. Coffee prices have fallen by more than 60% since 1997, and prices for cotton, tobacco, copper and aluminium will all drop again.

Tourism, which has brought an annual income of $10 billion to Africa over the past few years, will slump, and with it the continent's airlines. African leaders will step up demands for rich countries to open their markets and slash the $300 billion subsidies they pay their farmers. Expect more tough talking at the UN conference on development finance scheduled for March 2002 in Mexico.

Economic growth in North Africa in 2002 will edge up by 5%; for the rest of Africa it will be closer to 4%. The brightest hopes will be: Botswana, whose average annual GDP growth of 9.2% made it the world's fastest growing economy from 1966 to 1997; Mozambique, buoyed by gas and mining development; Tanzania, whose mining boom will push growth above 6%; and Ghana, where a more business-minded government is bringing in investment. For once, however, in 2002 Africa's isolation from the global economy will help: tens of millions of farmers, bankers and taxi drivers will ply their trade, unaffected by the storms beyond. □

2002

Kasparov and Kramnik face each other over the chess board again in October. But only if Kasparov wins his qualifying matches. He insisted on a qualifying round for the loser of the last World Chess Championship match. However, he lost.

Living day to day

Life on $2 a day or below
Numbers of people, m

South Asia
1,091   1,074

East Asia
753

Sub-Saharan Africa
638
524

323

Europe and Central Asia
86
47

Latin America
153   133

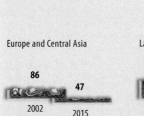

2002 2015   2002 2015   2002 2015   2002 2015   2002 2015

Sources: World Bank, *The World in 2002*

With the world economy treading water, or worse, an important lesson will be learnt in 2002: when economies stagnate, the poor suffer. The past decade saw the greatest reductions in poverty in those countries with fast growth. China's shift to capitalism greatly reduced poverty. Brazil and Bangladesh also made progress. Getting inflation under control helped. Inflation hurts the poor more than the rich; their money cannot be tied up in property or escape overseas.

Economic growth is important. It is the only way long-term poverty can be reduced. But ensuring that the benefits of growth are distributed equitably is also important. In many developing countries, boosting agriculture is crucial to achieving both goals. Europe and America's protection of their agricultural markets does not help. Education is vital too. Without it the poor miss out on the opportunities created by growth.

East Asia's prospects are bright. According to the World Bank, the number of people living on less than $2 a day there will halve to 323m by 2015, given decent growth rates. In contrast, the outlook for Africa is dark. If high infant-mortality rates, terrible education and health services, and rotten governments were not enough, the HIV/AIDS epidemic will pile on unbearable misery. Over 26m people will have HIV/AIDS in sub-Saharan Africa in 2002. □

Surprise, surprise

A year ago, *The World in 2001* asked the country analysts at the Economist Intelligence Unit to pick where would be the worst place to be a citizen in 2001. Their depressingly prescient answer was Afghanistan. So this time we put a less gloomy question: which will be the most surprising country in 2002?

Surprises are particularly tricky to predict because, almost by definition, most of them are unlikely to happen. A new Palestinian state (anything is possible in the Middle East)? A settlement in divided Cyprus (a slim chance, though looming decisions on EU enlargement will put the pressure on)? Miracle growth in Ukraine (actually quite likely, despite lamentable government)?

After careful consideration the choice is certainly surprising: the Democratic Republic of Congo, a place that only last year was runner-up for the title of the world's worst country of which to be a citizen. Congo then was the centre of a war involving seven countries and ten rebel movements. Living conditions (too often, dying conditions) were abysmal.

The partition of Congo's sprawling territory of jungles and rivers by warring parties and the collapse of basic services had caused an estimated 3m deaths since the war began in 1997. Prospects for a UN-backed peace plan were poor under the dreadful leadership of Laurent Kabila, who openly obstructed international mediation. Even by Africa's lowly standards, Mr Kabila's rule had degenerated to a tragi-comic level of incompetence, capriciousness and violence.

But recent events have laid the basis for an extraordinary turnaround. Mr Kabila was assassinated. He was replaced as president by

Kabila's thoughts could be uplifting

his 30-year-old son, Joseph. The young president has exceeded expectations—dropping, at a stroke, the objections to deployment of UN forces, and broadly accepting many (though not all) of his obligations under the peace agreement. Although the process will be long and complicated, and could easily come unstuck, for the first time in three years there is now a reasonable chance for peace in Congo.

The economic turnaround promises to be even more remarkable. Until recently, Congo had some of the most obtuse economic policies imaginable. Government

costs were covered by treating the central bank as little more than a gigantic money-printing machine; soldiers were sent into the markets to force traders to sell at prices below cost; contracts with foreign investors, lured to the potential riches of the mining industry, were routinely torn up without notice. The consequences were predictable: hyperinflation, an economy which contracted at a rate of 10% a year, and living standards in free-fall.

All this is changing. The previous cabinet of cronies, know-nothings and hangers-on responsible for the mess has been replaced by a new one of technocrats, many of them expatriate Congolese lured back home by the hope of seeing economic reason prevail. The exchange rate has been floated, the budget brought into surplus and monetary growth strictly controlled. The central bank has been granted independence and a new, investor-friendly mining code drafted. Projects to help atrophied government services to resume are getting under way. Foreigners are responding by opening their pockets. The World Bank and IMF have re-engaged with the new government while other donors, scared away by the previous chaos, are resuming assistance.

As stabilisation takes effect and the resource-rich economy begins to emerge from the corruption and inefficiency which have held it back for years, growth will resume for the first time since 1995.

The Congolese people, who are far more sophisticated and resourceful than the shambles of their country may imply, will in 2002 at last have the chance to take advantage of these abilities. A surprise, indeed, and a ray of hope for Africa. □

A world court for world criminals

Adam Roberts

T rials for crimes against humanity, heard in an international court, may soon become a permanent feature of world politics, and a good one too. As an indication of this you will find the white-haired Slobodan Milosevic on your television during much of 2002. Yugoslavia's ex-president goes on trial in The Hague for war crimes and genocide in the Balkans, probably in April. He is the biggest fish ever hooked by the International Criminal Tribunal for the former Yugoslavia, and only the second head of state (after a Rwandan prime minister) to face genocide charges in an international court. So expect wide interest.

Mr Milosevic calls it a show trial and he, or his lawyer, if he agrees to have one, will throw any spare spanners into the legal works to disturb the judges and earn media

attention. The big challenge for his duelling partner, Carla Del Ponte, the Swiss chief prosecutor, is to make her case watertight in good time. Too often indictments are ill-focused and late. She must also decide between a "super trial", charging Mr Milosevic over the wars in Croatia and Bosnia, and one that focuses alone on murders of Albanians in Kosovo in 1999.

The latter should be easier, and quicker, to prove: a clearer paper trail leads to the top, and more gruesome evidence will be unearthed from mass graves in the next year. If so, a judgment (the prosecution has a good rate of convictions) is likely by the end of 2002. A super trial would take longer.

The rest of the tribunal will be kickstarted too. By January, The Hague will have six trials ongoing each day,

Adam Roberts: Africa correspondent, *The Economist*

The Fletcher School
Tufts University

Learn Globally. Study Locally.
The Global Master of Arts Program (GMAP)

Are you an experienced international affairs professional who wants to further your education without taking a year off? If so, consider the GMAP offered by The Fletcher School at Tufts University. This one-of-a-kind, one-year master's program in international relations combines three (3) two-week residency sessions with 33 weeks of computer-mediated instruction.

As a GMAP student, you perform your professional duties while pursuing your education. You work closely with our highly respected faculty and receive a top quality Fletcher education. Plus, you become part of our active and influential international community. Classes begin July 2002. Contact us today to learn more about this challenging program.

THE GMAP INTERNATIONAL CURRICULUM INCLUDES:
Crisis Management & Complex Emergencies • International Finance
International Business & Economic Law • Leadership & Management
International Negotiation • International Technology Policy
International Trade Economics & Investment
Transnational Social Issues

The Fletcher School | Cabot Intercultural Center | 160 Packard Avenue
Medford, Massachusetts, USA 02155
TEL: 617 627 2429 **WEB:** www.fletcher.tufts.edu/gmap
E-MAIL: fletcher-gmap@tufts.edu

WHY CHOOSE BETWEEN A EUROPEAN AND AN AMERICAN MBA? IMM GIVES YOU BOTH!
www.mostinternationalmba.com

IMM, the International Master's in Management, is a joint venture of four top schools: Purdue University, USA; Tilburg University, The Netherlands; Budapest University of Economic Sciences and Public Administration, Hungary; and ESCP-EAP, Paris.

IMM represents the most international executive MBA. Indeed, every aspect of the program is international: participants, campuses, faculty, curriculum, and degrees. It is designed to accommodate the needs of executives with demanding schedules. Participants attend six two-week residencies interspersed over a two-year period, with state-of-the-art Internet support year-round. The residencies rotate among the campuses of the four schools.

This distinctive, cross-cultural program leads to both an American MBA degree (Purdue) and a European MBA degree (Tilburg, Budapest or ESCP-EAP).

How can you become one of the 60 international professionals to join the next IMM entering class? Visit our website and discover the international meaning of success.

THE NEXT PROGRAM STARTS JANUARY 2002

Purdue
+1 765 494 77 00

Tilburg
+31 13 466 86 00

Budapest
+36 1 210 02 12

ESCP-EAP
+33 1 49 23 27 59

tias
BUSINESS SCHOOL

ESCP-EAP

Only the gates close.
Everything else stays open.

We don't just remain open for flights. Every aspect of our airport operates around the clock - which means you can eat, sleep, drink, shop, swim, workout and relax 24 hours a day; 365 days a year. (Just remember when your flight departs.)

If only all airports were like this.

Fly-Buy-Dubai

DUBAI INTERNATIONAL AIRPORT

Where the world connects

as new *ad litem* judges share the caseload. A quicker pace should quieten critics of the court's efficiency, and will mean that the 110 indicted suspects will be tried sooner rather than later. Two men would rival Mr Milosevic for attention if they were arrested in 2002: Radko Mladic and Radavan Karadzic, both senior Bosnian Serbs who got their hands very bloody in Bosnia's civil war. But don't hold your breath.

Rwanda's genocide court in Arusha, Tanzania, will draw less attention. The sister tribunal to The Hague may welcome some calm after allegations of incompetence. But there will be activity there too. It too hopes for extra assistant judges, and to get convicted men faster into African prisons that meet international standards but are not too plush. Kingsley Moghalu, spokesman for the court, is looking forward to trials of some of the military men behind the massacre of more than 800,000 Rwandans in 1994. Theonest Bagosora of the Ministry of Defence is accused of being "the brains behind the genocide" and takes the stand in 2002. Others on trial now, including a group of journalists accused of encouraging others to kill, and a pastor who allegedly oversaw slaughter in his church, face judgments early in the year.

Farther afield in Africa, a sprinkling of new international courts will emerge. A war crimes court for Sierra Leone, part international and part domestic, should get legs in 2002. It has struggled to find funds and political backing, but donors will now be forthcoming as long as the civil war does not flare up again. Even rebel soldiers whose detained leader, Foday Sankoh, is the number-one accused, are cautiously willing to go along with proposals for the tribunal. But any plans to try child soldiers, who were used widely in the brutal war, will be dropped. There will be some talk about two other African courts—a human rights one, and a court of justice—modelled on European Union ones, but do not expect much progress.

Perhaps most significant, a permanent International Criminal Court is likely to come into existence, possibly at the very end of the year, once 60 countries ratify the necessary legislation. By late 2001 nearly 40 had done so. The ICC will eventually replace other international courts, such as The Hague, and will claim universal jurisdiction for any war crimes or crimes against humanity. In future,

The green summit

Just in case you thought big, global conferences were an endangered species, look out for a huge one in Johannesburg, South Africa, in September 2002. Some 50,000 delegates will participate in the World Summit on Sustainable Development; all countries will be represented, more than half by their heads of state; NGOs will also be out in force. Delegates will discuss everything from fresh water to desertification to human rights. Protocols on, among other things, "bio-safety", will be argued over and signed. The Kyoto protocol on climate change will be revived. Progress towards various targets (halting the spread of HIV/AIDS by 2015; eliminating gender disparity in education by 2005) will be reviewed. Not happy with such bread-and-butter issues, some malcontents will want to talk about globalisation too. Expect to hear much about accountability, equity and justice. Activists hope that Jo'burg, coming ten years after a similar conference in Rio de Janeiro, will set the world's green agenda for the next decade. Yet the sheer breadth of topics, and the impossibility of pleasing everyone sitting around the table, may make the whole thing unmanageable. If so, expect calls to make summits like this extinct. □

Cloudy outlook
Global CO₂ emissions, tonnes bn

2002 total 25.3
2010 total 29.6
2020 total 34.1

OECD countries
Developing countries

Sources: World Energy Outlook, *The World in 2002*

for example, individuals behind attacks on civilian targets, such as those on New York and Washington in September 2001, could be tried for crimes against humanity. The United States, a reluctant signatory to the ICC, might then muster more enthusiasm for international law. Without its participation, the permanent court would begin life as a weakling. But as The Hague and Arusha show, even weaklings may grow up strong. □

THE GULF

Although successive OPEC production cuts—not to mention the aftershocks of global terrorism—have propped up oil prices, the Gulf states are all too aware that they cannot rely on oil alone to provide jobs and services for their fast-growing population. Some of the world's most secretive monarchies have thus become reform-minded, opening their economies, and especially their oil sectors, to foreign capital and influence. Saudi Arabia will pass a milepost in November 2002 when, for the first time since it nationalised petroleum in the 1970s, it allows oil majors into its upstream hydrocarbons sector under a $25 billion gas development plan.

The leading example of diversification is Dubai, which will push ahead with developing tourism, trade, IT, retailing and financial services as its oil reserves dwindle. Bahrain, too, will promote its pre-eminence as

a financial centre. Qatar's huge gas-based industrialisation programme will start to pay off, as the first Qatari liquid natural gas displaces Russian and Mediterranean supplies in the coveted European market. The UAE will move forward with its partly private Dolphin gas project, linking Qatar's prolific gas fields with industrial markets in Abu Dhabi, Dubai and Oman; this is the region's first major cross-border natural gas pipeline, a sign of things to come.

As economies start to open, so too—ever so slightly—will autocratic political regimes. In Kuwait, which has the region's only elected parliament, MPs will gain influence in their dealings with the appointed government. The reformist emir of Bahrain will see stop-go progress on his charter granting political freedoms. Qatar will nurture its independent-minded television station, Al Jazeera, while setting an example with the

enfranchisement of women. None of this will seriously challenge the ruling regimes. But political stability may be tested in power struggles, as ageing or ailing leaders in Saudi Arabia, the UAE and Iraq transfer authority to designated successors. □

GDP GROWTH (%)	2000	2001	2002
Bahrain	5.2	4.8	4.6
Kuwait	4	2.1	2.6
Oman	4.7	5.8	4.5
Qatar	4.8	6.3	7.2
Saudi Arabia	4.5	1.3	2.6
UAE	6	3	3.2

Economist Intelligence Unit

Amartya Sen, Master of Trinity College, Cambridge, and winner of the Nobel prize for economics, asserts that the rich world will need to change its attitude to the poor

Addressing global poverty

"Insofar as protesters focus on the huge inequities of the world, they deserve a careful hearing not a roughing up"

The optimist believes that we live in the best of all possible worlds, whereas the pessimist, it is said, fears this is true. Sharp diversities in assessing the consequences of "globalisation" in the world seem to produce a similar unity of radical opposites. The urgent need for economic and political reform to reduce global inequity gets a cold shoulder from two quite different sides. Adoring admirers see globalisation as a great contributor to the enrichment of the world and want to leave well alone (rather than trying to reform something that is "working so very well"). Those irreconcilably hostile to globalisation identify it as the basic source of the main woes of the world (and see no point in trying to reform something that is foundationally "nonreformable and pernicious"). The promotion of gloom and doom, thus, joins hands with impervious complacency.

Major institutional reforms are globally needed, to work against the inequalities and unfairness of the current economic and political order. They are needed not because the defenders of globalisation are wrong to detect the vast scientific, technological, economic and social opportunities that globalisation offers. These opportunities are indeed real and immense. Precisely for that reason, fairness requires that they be shared more equitably, without the monumental disparities that characterise the contemporary world. Insofar as anti-globalisation protesters focus on the huge inequities of the world, they deserve a careful hearing rather than being roughed up by the *Carabinieri*.

Institutional change is possible. If well designed it could also be effective. The market economy quickly responds to different incentives; a deliberate change, for example, in the functioning of trade agreements, the working of patent laws and the operation of credit facilities can help to reduce the imbalance. It would be politically naive to expect that there is a real chance of making major "transfers" of assets and resources across the border of the rich and poor worlds. But the scope for this can be broadened to some extent by the use of innovative arrangements such as the "Tobin tax" on international financial transactions, and by instituting special drawing rights linked to, but independent of, international financial institutions, for expanding "public goods" (as has recently been proposed by George Soros). The opportunities for the poor are restricted not only by antecedent poverty but also by two types of structural faults. First, "global omissions" include the absence of an adequately strong, globally shared effort to combat the lack of educational facilities and health care. And second, "global commissions" can take many different forms, including one-sided institutional arrangements such as the existing patent laws.

These adversities call also for local efforts at rectification in the poor countries themselves. But there is global responsibility as well. Regarding global omission, there is an urgent need for a more comprehensive programme of worldwide co-operation in eradicating illiteracy and untreated illnesses, which exterminate people's ability to help themselves and help others. There is a strong case for strengthening the hands of those who are trying to broaden the reach of international policy within the existing institutional structure (including Kofi Annan of the UN and James Wolfensohn of the World Bank). We should also consider a broadening of the international institutional architecture set up by the Bretton Woods agreement in the 1940s (when the world was a very different place and global disparities were more easily tolerated).

Regarding global commission, there has been discussion recently of the need to change counterproductive institutional arrangements. These include not only trade restrictions that repress exports from poor countries, but also the patent laws which inhibit the use of life-saving drugs—vital for diseases like AIDS.

A trade to stop

There is another—and less discussed—global commission that causes intense misery as well as lasting deprivation: the involvement of the world powers in trade in arms. Local wars and military conflicts draw not only on regional tensions, but also on the global trade in arms and weapons. Indeed, the world leaders who express deep frustration at the irresponsibility of anti-globalisation protesters, lead the countries that make the most money in this terrible trade. The share of G8 countries in the world export of arms was 87% during 1996-2000.

The world establishment is firmly entrenched in this business: the permanent members of the Security Council of the United Nations are together responsible for 81% of conventional arms exports. The share of the United States alone is close to 50% of the total sales in the world. And, furthermore, as much as 68% of the American arms exports go to developing countries.

The arms are used not only with bloody results, but also with devastating effects on the economy and the society. Historically in the genesis of political militarism in Africa, these powers played a big part. During the cold-war decades, when military overlords—Mobuto or Savimbi or whoever—busted social and political arrangements (and ultimately economic order too) in Africa, they could rely on support either from the United States or from the USSR, depending on their military alliances. The world powers bear an awesome responsibility in the subversion of democracy in Africa. Global arms exports continue that evil tradition. The recent refusal of the United States to agree to a joint crackdown even on illicit sales of small arms (as proposed by Kofi Annan) illustrates the difficulties involved. A change in priorities is urgently needed. □

BEFORE EXTRACTING
WHAT'S UNDERGROUND,
WE LISTEN TO
EXPERTS
WHO KNOW HOW
TO RESTORE
WHAT'S ABOVE.

During exploration, problems can arise that we can't solve on our own.

At the Malampaya Deep Water Gas to Power Project in the Philippines, for example, the removal of trees (many small scrub trees) to accommodate a temporary structure proved unavoidable.

Shell asked local botanists to look at the likely impact before felling. And with the structure now gone, specialists then helped us to replant 10 saplings for every tree removed. This is not just replenishing those removed, it's also providing a new habitat for endangered Philippine Giant Fruit and Flying Fox bats.

By enlisting help like this, we're ensuring that the extraction of one natural resource doesn't mean the destruction of another.

For details of this and similar projects, see the Shell Report 'People, Planet and Profits' at www.shell.com

A ramble to Africa

For the second year, Royal Dutch/Shell and *The Economist* together ran an essay competition to encourage thinking and debate about the future, this time in the broad field of transport and travel. The competition was entitled "Going faster—but where?" The judging panel chose eight prizewinners, whose thoughts ranged from the problems of cities to the prospects for tourism, from the role of information technology to the transport troubles of women. They can be found at www.economist.com. The first prize of $20,000 was won by Mari Rhydwen, an Australian. Here is her essay, which is in eloquent praise of the merits of travelling slowly

I had just stopped for a coffee in the Kenyan village where I had walked to do my shopping when I read an advertisement: "Write an essay on how fast we're all travelling these days. No rambling please." Having spent the past two years sailing around the Indian Ocean at a walking pace I was itching to respond: to challenge the assumption that we are all travelling fast, and the implication that rambling, literally or literarily, is undesirable. But I needed to find out more about the competition and this was problematic. "I suppose", I say to my husband as we stroll the couple of miles back to our yacht, "it simply didn't occur to them that we wouldn't be able to access the web." We meander back past the markets where I stop at a stall to try on a cotton frock, past the mud huts and the shambas, past the bunch of cheery children who like to practise their English and shake hands and past the men cutting the roadside grass by hand to feed the cattle. We talk about how we can get to an Internet café. It will take a day.

Sailing to Africa from Western Australia has taken two years but we have met many other cruising people who had spent ten years travelling this far. They did nothing to disguise the fact that they thought we were rushing, impatient, still infected by the hyperactivity we had deliberately tried to leave ashore. This has little to do with speed at sea, but with the amount of time spent puddling along coastlines, lingering at anchor and pondering the sky, as well as days engaged in hauling well-water or walking to market. For many people, cruising has become a permanent lifestyle, financed by portable or casual work, or by retirement pensions. A rare minority have taken time off work, rented out the house and intend to resume their former lives within an allotted timespan. Some of us have loosened our grip on the illusion of security and given up homes and jobs to travel the oceans for a while and just see what happens. It is not a way of getting anywhere. It is a way of being wherever you are. Indeed it is a form of rambling and seems to belong to a whole genre of contemporary sins including loitering, idling and wandering vaguely, that conspicuously fail to get to the point or to get things done. Practitioners of such unambitious, goal-disoriented lives are

Some tourists take tea...

prone to being labelled losers. Curiously though, if done blatantly and wholeheartedly in a little yacht, people express interest, even envy, rather than scorn.

Designer primitives

Increasingly, sailing takes you only to places that can also be reached faster and more comfortably by people who are in more of a hurry to find tranquillity. Since anchoring in commercial ports or near big towns can be unsafe, sheltered bays on remote islands are particularly attractive but it is here that one most often stumbles upon exclusive resorts where guests are delivered from the nearest airport by private planes or motor yachts. At one, famously expensive, we dressed up and went ashore for a reconnoitring coffee, curious to know what you got for $2,000 a day. We found: bamboo-shingled roofs; open-sided buildings furnished with timber, cane and cream linen; coral-rubble paths; tasteful touches of local art; good-looking young staff in sarong-meets-Paris uniforms and iconic views of white sand and palm trees. It was the ubiquitous low-key casual tropical-paradise elegance we observed in posh hotels throughout the Indian Ocean. But would you know if you were staying on Moyo Island or Ari Atoll? Would it matter?

Chagos is the ultimate exclusive retreat, to which no one can buy a ticket. Part of British Indian Ocean territory, it lies mid-ocean, out of the path of cyclones, and is thus strategically significant to the cruising sailor as well as the military sort. Private vessels are permitted to stop for a limited time at some of the atolls and we stayed six weeks waiting for a change of monsoon. Here are picture-book coral atolls where people live out shipwrecked-on-a-tropical-island fantasies, or reality in the case of the couple aboard the sailing yacht *Vespara* which ran aground there a few years ago. Chagos is probably unique in being a group of habitable but uninhabited islands, a consequence of the relocation of the population at the time of British annexation. I was there reluctantly, already jaded with Eden-like beaches, but swimming daily with baby manta rays, snorkelling through reef undamaged by bleaching or dynamite, and being a thousand kilometres from a shop, restaurant, hairdresser or bank, has some charm. Nonetheless, these idyllic uninhabited islands are chimerical, created and maintained through territorial haggling and dispute.

The nearest destination to Chagos to which one may purchase a ticket is the Maldives. Although tourist-processing is a major industry, visitors are kept as separate from local people as possible. There are about 200 inhabited islands and over 80 resort islands. Private yachts, like backpackers, are not made welcome and are permitted to stop only at Male or at some resort islands. Anchoring off what are termed "inhabited islands"—those with a local population—is forbidden. Ironically, we spent thousands of dollars there on essential repairs. Indeed, yachtspeople visiting remote places often spend far more than the average package tourist, doing long-term provisioning at local shops and markets, buying hardware and fuel. Like backpackers, they spend their money at local businesses and not at multinational hotel chains. They spend less but benefit the local economy more.

The Maldives accepts tourists' dollars, but wants their bodies kept at a safe distance. That tropical-island paradise was this traveller's dystopia. Is the point of travel to be cocooned in a fantasy theme-park version of a native village well away from the real thing? The segregation is the result both of the local people's fear of being swamped by an alien culture and the tourists' desire to be able to enjoy the pleasures of an idyllic tropical island, unconstrained by any concerns about offending others' sensibilities. It is an efficient way of managing tourism but I do not travel to be sequestered in a tourist ghetto. If I wanted an uninhabited island, I would sail back to Chagos.

A delightful aspect of travelling slowly is having time to hang around in places and meet people, travelling by foot or on public transport and going to hotels and cafes that local people can afford to patronise. Making connections, sharing breakfast at the top of a volcano with a shockingly impoverished university professor and his family on the island of Flores, collecting eggs and a chicken-filled snake on a Malaysian engineer's hobby farm and attending a time-warped meeting of the East African Women's League in Kenya—these are the highlights but they cannot be bought and cannot be rushed and cannot be organised. Travel must be slow enough to allow such accidents to happen.

But slow travel is trivialised when reduced to a collection of amusing anecdotes and feelgood experiences. It has mainly been about learning again and again that most people are poor, a very few people are exceedingly rich and doing nicely, corruption is normal, clean water is precious and good people everywhere are doing what they can. Tourists are generally shielded from the grosser evidence of this: airport officials do not hassle for baksheesh and even cheap hotels have running water where few of the population do. Entering a country by boat, it is first necessary to deal with customs, immigration, port and health authorities, a host of bureaucracies. These first

delicate encounters with officialdom have proved a remarkably accurate barometer when compared with the Corruption Perception Index published by Transparency International, a Berlin-based pressure group.

Fast and furious

Fast travel enables increasing numbers of people to visit more exotic and remote places, but as tourism becomes a significant factor in strug-

... others take time

gling economies, more and more incredibly fancy resorts are being built in places with the poorest populations and most intractable sociopolitical problems. Instead of bringing people closer and facilitating mutual understanding and awareness of global issues, it is dividing the world more sharply in two, the rich and the poor. Naturally most tourists on their two-week holiday do not want to be confronted by poverty and disease or reminded that the soup they just ordered costs twice the waiter's daily wage. The waiter, here in Kenya's shrivelling economy, may count himself lucky to earn a daily wage. Everywhere I find myself looking for ways to counteract the intensifying polarisation of wealth and the devastation so evidently caused by rampaging greed. I yearn to ask the rapacious, "What is it you really want so badly? Respect? Happiness? Immortality? Don't you know they are not for sale?"

Each night at sea I do the midnight to six o'clock watch. Since having a light on kills night vision I do little except monitor our position regularly, trim the sails and perhaps learn to recognise another constellation or rehearse some little phrases of Bahasa Indonesian, Kiswahili or whatever, ready for landfall. Otherwise it's like being a cat: eyes half-closed but ears twitching.

Each morning the miracle of sunrise, the colour comes back into the world, blueness to the sky first, then a little yellow in the east and the vivid redness of the safety-harness strap that ties me to the earth. After that it will be half an hour till the sun gets up and there is time for a cup of tea while I watch any hitchhiking boobies or terns take off, always flying away after the colours arrive but before the sunshine. Sometimes I am so glad of the company of other living beings through the long night, I even thank them for coming. Travelling fast, but where are you going? Travelling slowly, always at home. □

The judging panel consisted of:

Richard O'Brien, an economic consultant at Outsights;

Peter Warshall, a biologist and environmentalist;

Jusuf Wanandi, a strategic-studies scholar;

Sally Feldman, dean of School of Media, London College of Printing;

Adam Raphael, political correspondent, *The Economist*;

Peter Dickens, professor of economic geography, University of Manchester;

Philip Watts, group managing director, Shell International;

Bill Emmott, editor, *The Economist*.

The world in figures: Countries

Western Europe

AUSTRIA

GDP: $214bn
GDP per head: $26,100
Population: 8.2m
GDP growth: 1.8%
Inflation: 1.6%

Austria's Freedom Party, once headed by the xenophobic Jorge Haider, has performed poorly as the junior partner in the coalition government. Mr Haider therefore may take on a more visible national role in 2002 (though not as a minister: the rest of Europe would not tolerate it). To build momentum, he may stage an early election for the governorship of the state of Carinthia, where he is currently the incumbent.

The government's goal of balancing the budget by 2002, a commitment made under the euro zone's Stability and Growth Pact, will be abandoned. With the economy remaining weak, austerity measures would be needed to meet the target—not likely, as this would make matters worse. Still, the budget deficit will be less than 1% of GDP.

DENMARK

GDP: $185bn
GDP per head: $34,600
Population: 5.4m
GDP growth: 2.0%
Inflation: 2.1%

An election must be called by March 2002. The opposition centre-right Liberals have seen their lead in the polls erode as the centre-left government, led by the Social Democratic Party, has clawed its way back by addressing public services. Despite this, and the fact that no incumbent government has been thrown out of office since 1973, the opposition should lead the next fragile coalition.

Denmark assumes the EU presidency in

All figures are 2002 forecasts unless otherwise indicated.

Inflation: year-on-year annual average.

Dollar GDPs calculated using 2002 forecasts for dollar exchange rates, based on June 2001 rates.

Source:

Economist Intelligence Unit

except where indicated.
london@eiu.com

Budget balance
% of GDP

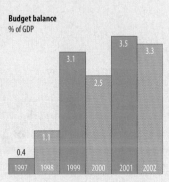

| 1997 | 1998 | 1999 | 2000 | 2001 | 2002 |
| 0.4 | 1.1 | 3.1 | 2.5 | 3.5 | 3.3 |

the second half of 2002. It will have three aims: to complete enlargement talks with applicant countries; to make progress on a common environment policy; and to prepare for the next inter-governmental conference scheduled for 2004.

FINLAND

GDP: $142bn
GDP per head: $27,200
Population: 5.2m
GDP growth: 2.5%
Inflation: 2.0%

After seven years of strong growth, the ruling five-party coalition government led by the prime minister, Paavo Lipponen, will remain in office until the next general election in 2003.

To watch:
Nokia. The telecoms firm accounts for more than 3% of Finnish GDP and nearly a quarter of the total value of Finnish exports. Indeed, its share of output will continue to rise. On the other hand, the company is almost 90% foreign owned, so falling share prices do not hurt Finns very much.

FRANCE

GDP: $1,472bn
GDP per head: $24,600
Population: 59.9m
GDP growth: 1.7%
Inflation: 1.7%

Lionel Jospin has his work cut out ahead of parliamentary elections in 2002: the crime rate is rising, the unemployment rate has stopped falling, relations with the employers' federation remain poor and the planned devolution of power to Corsica has run into problems. His coalition government will look more ragged as the junior partners distance

themselves from his Partie Socialiste. The coalition should just limp through, although the right-of-centre parties are well set to win a parliamentary majority.

Like Europe's other major economies, GDP growth in France will recover modestly in 2002—but will hardly inspire—at no more than 2%. Stronger exports will help, but business investment and consumer spending will both grow more slowly than in 2001.

To watch:
Jacques Chirac. Despite a lengthening shadow of sleaze, France's president is likely to stand for another term in the election, and to defeat Mr Jospin in a second round of voting. Sooner or later, though, he will have to explain his role in illegal fund-raising schemes while mayor of Paris, and why he used government cash to pay for holidays.

Export growth
%

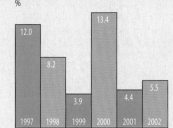

| 1997 | 1998 | 1999 | 2000 | 2001 | 2002 |
| 12.0 | 8.2 | 3.9 | 13.4 | 4.4 | 5.5 |

GERMANY

GDP: $2,128bn
GDP per head: $25,900
Population: 82.0m
GDP growth: 1.5%
Inflation: 1.6%

With the economy in less than robust health, the opposition Christian Democratic Union will put up a good fight in the next parliamentary election, due in September or October 2002. Even so, the governing coalition of Social Democrats and Greens, led by Gerhard Schröder, will finish on top, helped by tax-cuts, a moderate, centrist image and well-honed political skills.

The 2002 budget will be a tricky one. The government will be under pressure from its own side to boost the economy. However, it will need to cut spending if it is not to fall badly short of fiscal targets agreed with other EU countries.

After an unexpectedly dismal

Export growth
%

| 1997 | 1998 | 1999 | 2000 | 2001 | 2002 |
| 11.4 | 6.3 | 4.6 | 14.0 | 3.8 | 5.4 |

performance in 2001, the economy will fare somewhat better in 2002. With inflation declining, taxes coming down and nominal wages rising, consumers will feel more confident. So should exporters, unless the slump in America turns into a fully fledged economic rout.

To watch:
EU enlargement, and rising tension between the elites and the common folk. Germany's best and brightest see the EU's eastward expansion as in the country's interest. Most average Germans see something else: a flood of cheap labour, cross-border crime and higher budgetary contributions.

GREECE

GDP: $135bn
GDP per head: $12,700
Population: 10.6m
GDP growth: 3.3%
Inflation: 2.5%

The prime minister, Costas Simitis, faces growing opposition from within his governing Pasok Party over plans to push ahead with privatisation, liberalisation and, most recently, pension reform. Expect little progress on these fronts in the coming year. If the political environment gets much worse, an early election in 2002 is possible.

Greek firms are watching Macedonia closely, and for good reason. If the violence there spreads, economic activity in the Balkans could be badly disrupted, jeopardising the $5bn of Greek investment in the region.

To watch
The impasse over Cyprus and a lack of progress on territorial disputes in the Aegean could undermine support for the Greek government's rapprochement with Turkey.

ITALY

GDP: $1,234bn
GDP per head: $21,300
Population: 58.0m
GDP growth: 1.9%
Inflation: 2.1%

Gross fixed investment growth
%

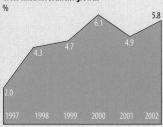

Silvio Berlusconi, Italy's obstinate prime minister, has no intention of selling his vast, mainly family-run, businesses. No surprise, then, that he will face constant accusations of conflict of interest in 2002. If he is convicted of any of the serious charges pending against him, his position will become untenable.

A policy of wage moderation has been in place since 1992. But discontent among workers is growing, concentrated in the main left-wing union. It is making more militant noises and in 2002 is expected to call strikes and bring its members on to the streets.

The economy will revive a bit. Investment will support growth, thanks to an increasingly favourable tax regime for small and medium-sized businesses, lower interest rates, new incentive schemes and brighter export prospects.

To watch:
The public prosecution service. Before the 2001 election, Mr Berlusconi promised to curb the autonomy of public prosecutors, but so far has kept his powder dry. If he decides to press ahead, he would face a storm of protest from the judiciary and centre-left parties, not to mention the international press.

NORWAY

GDP: $175bn
GDP per head: $38,700
Population: 4.5m
GDP growth: 2.1%
Inflation: 2.3%

The new government will continue to reconsider the state's role in the economy, and display a more open-minded attitude towards privatisation and foreign ownership of Norwegian companies. (StatOil has already been part privatised.) The administration will make plans for further sell-offs in the banking and energy sectors.

The economy will perform somewhat better in 2002. Consumer spending should rebound in response to lower interest rates, increases in real disposable household incomes and more investment.

PORTUGAL

GDP: $123bn
GDP per head: $12,200
Population: 10.1m
GDP growth: 1.7%
Inflation: 2.9%

Antonio Guterres, the prime minister, enters 2002 looking more vulnerable than ever. The weak economy and a loss of public confidence means his Socialist Party government could fall in 2002. But the opposition Social Democratic Party won't want to trigger a crisis.

Inflation was well above the EU average in 2001, and the consequences could be felt in 2002: trade unions want higher pay rises to compensate for reduced purchasing power. Given the tightness of the labour market, they may get it.

To watch
The "Lusiads". The 400-year-old epic poem, recounting Vasco da Gama's voyage to India, is a classic normally taught to students in ninth grade. But in 2002, the government wants to push back teaching it to 12th grade. Not relevant enough to the new generation, say proponents, and the language is outdated. Traditionalists will battle to block the change.

Consumer prices
% change

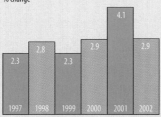

SPAIN

GDP: $659bn
GDP per head: $16,600
Population: 39.6m
GDP growth: 2.4%
Inflation: 2.8%

Radical new leadership at ETA, the separatist paramilitary group, augurs greater violence in 2002. But ETA's growing isolation suggests that it will lose influence and popular support.

Spain will use its presidency of the EU during the first half of 2002 to punch its political weight, while demanding at the same time special recognition as one of the EU's poorest countries.

To watch
Fall-out from Latin America. If Argentina defaults on its debt, Spain, which has invested heavily there, will feel the pain.

SWEDEN

GDP: $255bn
GDP per head: $28,700
Population: 8.9m
GDP growth: 3.0%
Inflation: 1.9%

Even if the three-party parliamentary pact does not survive until the next general election, scheduled for September 2002, the Social Democratic government, led by Goran Persson, will continue as a minority administration.

Sweden is in the EU, but outside the single currency. Most Swedes would prefer to leave the Union altogether: only a third have anything nice to say about it. Mr Persson has promised a referendum on euro-zone membership by 2004.

Sweden's taxes are the highest of any industrialised country, a dubious distinction. They will come down a little in 2002, but not enough to allow Sweden to reap the full benefits of structural reforms to its economy.

SWITZERLAND

GDP: $265bn
GDP per head: $36,500
Population: 7.3m
GDP growth: 1.7%
Inflation: 1.4%

The Swiss will vote on membership of the UN in the first half of 2002. Expect a close result, but the majority will say "No". If financial markets remain volatile, the Swiss franc will be bolstered by its "safe haven" status, hurting competitiveness.

To watch:
Bank secrecy. The EU will press the Swiss to give up their bank secrecy laws as a way of curbing tax evasion. International efforts to crack down on terrorist financing will raise the pressure for more transparency. But the secrecy will remain.

TURKEY

GDP: $146bn
GDP per head: $2,180
Population: 67.2m
GDP growth: 3.5%
Inflation: 53.1%

Tensions within the left-right-centre coalition government will be suppressed as an early election would find all three parties falling below the voter threshold required to enter parliament.

The economy will rebound in 2002 but the recovery will disappoint. The export-

Exchange rate
L'000:$

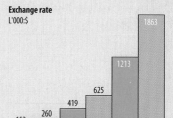

kick resulting from the 2001 devaluation will be undermined by sluggish global growth. Tighter fiscal policy would keep government debt in check, but global risk aversion will jeopardise tourism and foreign investment.

To watch
Turkey's strategic location—bordering with Iraq, Iran and Syria—will ensure it plays a critical role in the American-led effort to flush out terrorism. As a NATO member, Turkey will remain on the side of the Americans. But with its enfeebled economy, it will ask for—and get—more financial support.

UNITED KINGDOM

GDP: $1,525bn
GDP per head: $25,500
Population: 59.8m
GDP growth: 1.8%
Inflation: 1.7%

Tony Blair's Labour Party will turn its attention to fixing Britain's public services in 2002. The task is daunting: the transport system is a shambles, the health service is awful and the crime rate is rising. Mr Blair will spend plenty but little will improve right away.

The economy should pick up in the second half of 2002 as America and Germany revive and a build-up in British inventories is worked off. If America continues to slump, however, all bets are off: the two economies are closely linked through trade and investment, and Britons will feel the pinch more than most other countries in Europe.

Outward direct investment
$bn

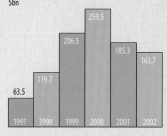

To watch
Membership of the euro zone. Does Mr Blair have a secret plan for bouncing Britain into the single currency? He may start making his case in 2002.

Central and Eastern Europe

BULGARIA

GDP: $15bn
GDP per head: $1,960
Population: 7.9m
GDP growth: 4.4%
Inflation: 5.8%

A former king, Simeon Saxe-Coburg, is now the prime minister, but his powers are anything but absolute. His party rules in coalition with the ethnic Turkish Movement for Rights and Freedoms. The cabinet contains right- and left-leaning elements. Expect clashes.

Taxes will fall across the board in 2002. They will be eliminated for the poor and will come down for everyone else. Capital gains taxes will also be scrapped.

To watch
The IMF. With a high current-account deficit and poor FDI, the IMF will take a harder line over lending as it becomes clear that the government's economic growth projections are over-optimistic.

CZECH REPUBLIC

GDP: $67bn
GDP per head: $6,510
Population: 10.2m
GDP growth: 4.2%
Inflation: 4.3%

Inward direct investment
$bn

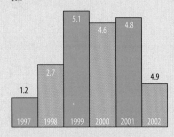

The minority Czech Social Democratic Party (CSSD) government will remain in power until the June 2002 general election. A stable coalition government is likely to emerge, most plausibly between the CSSD and the Quad Coalition.

Expect disagreements with Brussels on the Czech Republic's bid to join the EU. Areas of conflict include movement of labour, tax policy (especially duty-free shops) and financial controls. Even so, membership is likely by 2005.

To watch
Privatisation. The government has an ambitious schedule of sell-offs in 2002—mostly energy companies and telecoms firms. Expect more delays.

HUNGARY

GDP: $63bn
GDP per head: $6,300
Population: 10.0m
GDP growth: 4.4%
Inflation: 7.1%

The 2002 election will be a tight contest between the Federation of Young

Inward direct investment
$m

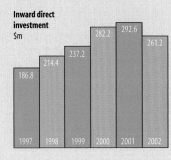

Democrats-Hungarian Civic Party and the opposition Hungarian Socialist Party. Neither will secure a majority. The far-right Hungarian Justice and Life Party might hold the balance of power.

Nationalist rhetoric during the election campaign will raise tensions with Slovakia and Romania. Both countries oppose Hungary's Status Law, which will give preferential access to employment and social services in Hungary to ethnic Hungarians living abroad.

To watch
The forint. The widening of the exchange-rate band in 2001 will help in the fight against inflation. But appreciation could threaten exports.

POLAND

GDP: $202bn
GDP per head: $5,200
Population: 38.7m
GDP growth: 2.7%
Inflation: 5.3%

A close result in the 2001 parliamentary election has left the government vulnerable to attack from a group of populist and Eurosceptic opposition parties. This will make it harder to push through the tough measures needed to speed up negotiations on entry to the EU.

Budget balance
% of GDP

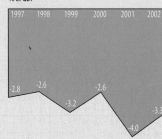

Two main factors will hold back the economy in 2002: uncomfortably high unemployment, which is putting a brake on consumer spending; and interest rates, which will remain high in real terms, curbing corporate investment and spending on consumer durables.

To watch
The budget. The government, elected in 2001, inherited a deficit that will be equal to 3.6% of GDP in 2002. Tighter fiscal policy is likely.

ROMANIA

GDP: $42bn
GDP per head: $1,870
Population: 22.3m
GDP growth: 3.8%
Inflation: 26.0%

The ruling Party of Social Democracy is no longer considering an alliance with one or more of the parliamentary opposition parties. The present grudging co-operation between government and opposition will continue.

Arguing its case for entry into NATO in 2002, Romania will emphasise its strategic location and that membership would increase stability in the Balkans. But NATO will be occupied with reconstructing the alliance to fight the "war against terrorism".

To watch
Dracula Land. A theme park commemorating Romania's favourite son, Vlad the Impaler, is scheduled to open in 2002. But before the garlic-flavoured ice cream goes on sale, the government faces a more determined blood-sucker. Universal, an American film studio, owns the rights to many cinematic Dracula images, and will want hefty copyright fees.

RUSSIA

GDP: $345bn
GDP per head: $2,390
Population: 144.4m
GDP growth: 3.8%
Inflation: 17.0%

President Vladimir Putin will remain popular. He may be authoritarian, but Russians seem willing to accept this in return for political stability. However, if commodity prices fall, Mr Putin will not be immune.

Russians will spend much of 2002 worrying about the "2003 problem": the coincidence of slowing growth, high debt-servicing costs and crumbling infrastructure that will hit soon.

Mr Putin has been a commendable economic reformer, guided by Andrei Illarionov, his chief adviser in such matters. But Mr Illarionov has many enemies. If reforms begin to exact a high

GDP growth
%

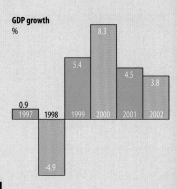

political cost in 2002—a growing risk—he may well be replaced by someone more statist.

To watch
Relations between Vladimir Putin and George Bush. They will get warmer. American missile defence will be an issue, but as Russia will not be able to stop it, scope for a deal may emerge.

SLOVAKIA

GDP: $22bn
GDP per head: $4,160
Population: 5.4m
GDP growth: 3.8%
Inflation: 6.8%

Despite constant feuding within the governing coalition, the ruling parties will hold together until the next parliamentary election, set for September 2002. Another unwieldy coalition government will emerge.

To watch
Budget blues. The deficit will grow even larger as purse strings are loosened ahead of the election. High unemployment, depressed wage growth and tax relief for foreign-owned companies will cut into the government's revenue.

UKRAINE

GDP: $45bn
GDP per head: $909
Population: 49.9m
GDP growth: 5.0%
Inflation: 11.1%

Deeply unpopular and corrupt, Leonid Kuchma will try to ensure that a hostile majority does not win the parliamentary election in March. If he fails, he may be impeached. This means only minimal progress in restructuring the energy sector, and dismantling exemptions and privileges for favoured industries.

To watch
Relations with Russia. Unpopular with EU governments, Mr Kuchma will turn to Russia for support, and will exploit fears of closer links with Moscow to extract concessions from the West.

Asia

AUSTRALIA

GDP: $398bn
GDP per head: $20,400
Population: 19.6m
GDP growth: 3.0%
Inflation: 2.6%

Gross fixed investment
% growth

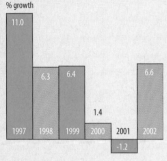

John Howard's incumbent Liberal/National government was set to win a new term in the November 2001 election. This means his landmark tax reforms will not be rolled back, as the opposition had threatened to do.

Australia's economy will enjoy a powerful cyclical recovery, which may make it the fastest-growing industrialised economy in 2002. Business investment is expected to grow by about 8%. The mood in rural areas will lighten.

To watch
Trade policy. The United States is interested in a free-trade agreement with Australia and negotiations could begin in 2002. But talks will not be quick or easy since both countries have large commodity sectors.

CHINA

GDP: $1,309bn
GDP per head: $1,020
Population: 1.3bn
GDP growth: 7.4%
Inflation: 1.9%

The Communist Party will meet for its 16th Congress in the autumn to give its

Trade balance
$bn

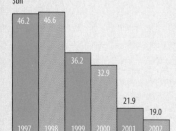

blessing to a new general secretary, Hu Jintao. Mr Hu may add the state presidency to his CV in 2003. However, infighting among current leaders to see their protégés promoted—and so retain influence after retirement—will be rife.

Formal admission to the WTO will be ratified by the National People's Congress in 2002. Opening up to foreign competition will hit many domestic industries. Expect plenty of foot-dragging on implementation, especially in the farming sector.

To watch
Foreign relations. China will have a difficult year internationally. Its roller-coaster relationship with the United States will be mostly down, flaring up over the American government's pro-Taiwan policy and its aggressive anti-terrorism activities. China will also resent Japanese nationalism.

INDIA

GDP: $520bn
GDP per head: $504
Population: 1.0bn
GDP growth: 5.6%
Inflation: 4.8%

The coalition government, the Bhartiya Janata Party (BJP), is looking as frail as its leader, the ageing Atal Behari Vajpayee. Tainted by scandal, the BJP must do well in a critical state election in March 2002 in Uttar Pradesh, its heartland. A poor showing at the polls and its national allies will flee, possibly bringing down the government.

Inward direct investment
$bn

The government is desperate to step up the pace of privatisation; the budget deficit is enormous, curbing the rate of economic growth needed to reduce poverty. Expect some additional sell-offs in 2002, but not many: with a troubled government, the will to push through unpopular privatisations will be weak.

To watch
Kashmir. The threat of war over the disputed territory is ever present. The Indian and Pakistani governments will continue talking, but after their failed summit in 2001, progress will be slow. Expect plenty more killing in 2002.

INDONESIA

GDP: $189bn
GDP per head: $863
Population: 219.5m
GDP growth: 3.6%
Inflation: 9.2%

GDP growth
%

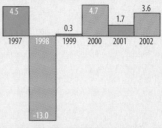

The honeymoon for President Megawati Sukarnoputri will last only into the early months of 2002. Factionalism within the cabinet and opposition from Islamic parties will undermine reforms.

If Ms Megawati can achieve some degree of political stability, the economy will grow at a faster rate than most of its Asian neighbours. Less dependent on electronics exports, Indonesia has not been so badly hurt by the collapse of the IT sector in the West.

To watch
East Timor. No longer a part of Indonesia, East Timor will become a sovereign state in 2002, having been freed from UN stewardship. Ms Megawati will be determined not to let other provinces get away.

JAPAN

GDP: $4,055bn
GDP per head: $31,900
Population: 127.0m
GDP growth: -0.9%
Inflation: -0.6%

The prime minister, Junichiro Koizumi, will look increasingly vulnerable as his domestic popularity declines. He may call a snap lower-house election in 2002 in order to strengthen his hand.

Mr Koizumi has promised tough reform to bring the economy back to life. Though well-intentioned, he will not deliver: the economy is too weak to sustain big budget cuts. He will resort to more pump-priming in 2002. Real reforms will have to wait.

To watch
The yen. Trapped by debt and deflation, the government may engineer a substantial devaluation to restart the economy. This might help domestically, but it would wreak havoc with its export-dependent neighbours. And the United States might see its own overseas sales eroded.

KAZAKHSTAN

GDP: $24bn
GDP per head: $1,630
Population: 14.8m
GDP growth: 6.1%
Inflation: 6.9%

The authoritarian president, Nursultan Nazarbayev, will tighten his grip. He will cite a need for strong central authority and for public security measures to ward off the perceived threat of Islamic extremism. His real goal, though, will be to silence all voices except his own.

The government will get bolder at squeezing concessions from foreign investors in the energy industry. With massive profits to be made in Kazakhstan, multinationals will have to put up with the harassment.

To watch
Caspian oil. Tortuous negotiations over formal ownership of the sea among the littoral states—Russia, Iran, Azerbaijan, Kazakhstan and Turkmenistan—will heat up considerably in 2002.

MALAYSIA

GDP: $95bn
GDP per head: $3,920
Population: 24.2m
GDP growth: 2.1%
Inflation: 1.7%

A weak economy and growing social unrest will present the greatest threat in years to the prime minister, Mahathir Mohamad. He will resort to increasingly repressive measures, only stoking resentment. Although another election is not due for three years, he may even be forced by his party to retire in 2002.

Government pump-priming will help revive the economy in 2002. The Bakun hydroelectric dam "mega-project" in Sarawak state, with a cost of at least $4 billion, will provide ample opportunity for Dr Mahathir to spend money.

Export growth
%

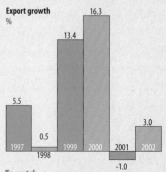

To watch
The ringgit. Fixed to the dollar since 1998, the ringgit could come under pressure in 2002. If the yen drops sharply in value, the government will have no choice but to scrap the peg.

NEW ZEALAND

GDP: $54bn
GDP per head: $13,800
Population: 3.9m
GDP growth: 2.2%
Inflation: 2.2%

The centre-left Labour-Alliance government, led by the prime minister, Helen Clark, will maintain a confident grip on government in 2002 and should survive the election due later in the year.

To watch
Genetic engineering. This will prove divisive for relations between the government and the Greens. The government had imposed a moratorium on most field testing but pressure from farm groups could see this lifted. Unhappy Greens.

PAKISTAN

GDP: $61bn
GDP per head: $425
Population: 143.6m
GDP growth: 4.4%
Inflation: 7.0%

Agricultural production
% change

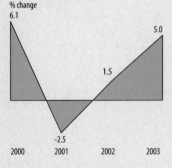

Pakistan's president, General Pervez Musharraf, will be under pressure from religious fundamentalists, and from those in government and intelligence who opposed his co-operation with America in the strikes on Afghanistan. But he is in firm control of the military and should ride out the storm.

Pakistan is back in the good graces of the IMF. It will receive continuing financial support in 2002 after meeting most of the agreed targets in 2001. And the West will want to reward it for its help in the fight against terrorism.

To watch
A return to civilian rule. General and provincial elections will be held in the first half of October 2002, as the military ostensibly gives way to civilian control. But don't believe it. The National Security Council, which will be run by General Musharraf and his appointees, will have the power to dismiss the prime minister. Military rule in all but name.

SINGAPORE

GDP: $88bn
GDP per head: $20,700
Population: 4.2m
GDP growth: 0.5%
Inflation: 1.0%

The ruling People's Action Party won the election in November 2001 under Goh Chok Tong. He will hand over power to the deputy prime minister, Lee Hsien Loong, before the next election, scheduled for 2006. The economy will bounce back from sharp recession.

To watch
Bilateral free-trade agreements. Singapore is determined to complete trade pacts with America and Japan in 2002. Such deals will help the highly trade-dependent state, but will anger neighbours who fear their own trading arrangements will be undermined.

SOUTH KOREA

GDP: $458bn
GDP per head: $9,530
Population: 48.1m
GDP growth: 4.1%
Inflation: 1.8%

President Kim Dae Jung cannot run again when his term ends in December 2002. His Millennium Democratic Party has no one with his charisma, so the presidency is likely to go to the opposition Grand National Party's Lee Hoi Chang.

The chilly American attitude to North Korea could slow progress on President Kim's "sunshine policy". But if the North makes real concessions, especially on security guarantees and economic co-operation, progress may yet be possible.

To watch
The 2002 football World Cup, co-hosted with Japan. An opportunity for old enemies to build up trust?

TAIWAN

GDP: $316bn
GDP per head: $13,900
Population: 22.6m
GDP growth: 2.6%
Inflation: 1.3%

President Chen Shui-bian's Democratic Progressive Party may emerge with a stronger hand in the December 2002 legislative election, if it can ally itself with a new party headed by the former president, Lee Teng-Hui.

Taiwan will emerge from a punishing recession as worldwide inventories of technology goods are run down.

To watch
Cross-Straits relations. Direct trade, transport and telecommunications links between Taiwan and China are

Trade balance
$bn

possible in 2002. Taiwan is committed; China is willing but wants agreement from Taiwan on the "One China" policy. A semantic fudge could bridge the gap.

THAILAND

GDP: $113bn
GDP per head: $1,770
Population: 63.5m
GDP growth: 2.1%
Inflation: 2.7%

The prime minister, Thaksin Shinawatra, is popular. But with firm control of parliament and no tolerance for dissent, he will become increasingly autocratic. A former businessman, he sees this merely as good management.

Mr Thaksin will implement his pump-priming policies to boost the economy. He will have some success, but by the end of the year the rise in public debt will lead to more stringent budget policies.

To watch
Anti-corruption efforts. Mr Thaksin's dubious acquittal on corruption charges in 2001 has undermined the independence of anti-corruption agencies. They will get weaker.

VIETNAM

GDP: $32bn
GDP per head: $403
Population: 80.0m
GDP growth: 5.8%
Inflation: 2.4%

Nong Duc Manh, the new Communist Party general secretary, will promote stability within the party, bridging the divide between its ideological extremes. The government will maintain its cautiously pro-reform stance in 2002.

The new trade agreement with America will finally take effect in 2002. This should lead to more foreign direct investment in Vietnam as western firms look both for new production centres and new export markets.

To watch
Rural discontent. Ethnic and religious tensions, and local government corruption will cause trouble in the highlands. On top of all this, a big new hydro-power project will dislocate 700,000, mostly from ethnic groups.

North America

CANADA

GDP: $778bn
GDP per head: $24,900
Population: 31.2m
GDP growth: 1.6%
Inflation: 1.9%

The Liberals, led by the prime minister, Jean Chrétien, will face little threat to their political dominance in 2002. They will pursue a pro-business agenda while maintaining strong public support.

To watch
Relations with the United States. Canada's reservations about America's plans to build a missile-defence shield could have serious implications for the North American Aerospace Defence Command.

UNITED STATES

GDP: $10,708bn
GDP per head: $37,300
Population: 286.9m
GDP growth: 1.4%
Inflation: 1.6%

The government will maintain a vigorous anti-terrorist campaign, rooted more in intelligence-gathering than in armed attacks. But expect more pre-emptive military strikes in 2002. The broad American coalition will begin to fray, however, forcing the Bush administration to stress diplomatic initiatives.

GDP
% change

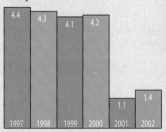

The economy will begin 2002 slowly, held back by concern over the military build-up and job losses that accumulated in the second half of 2001. But the recovery will be delayed, not aborted. A moderate upturn in manufacturing will boost investment and consumer spending.

To watch
Mid-term congressional elections. Partisanship, it is said, stops at the water's edge. But as Democrats look to recapture the House of Representatives, they will become more critical of George Bush and the inevitable mis-steps he will make in the campaign against terrorism.

Latin America

ARGENTINA

Total foreign debt
$bn

| 1997 | 1998 | 1999 | 2000 | 2001 | 2002 |
| 128.4 | 141.5 | 147.9 | 148.6 | 149.7 | 153.6 |

GDP: $286bn
GDP per head: $7,550
Population: 37.9m
GDP growth: 1.4%
Inflation: 1.0%

The disintegration of the ruling Alianza coalition and the weak leadership of President Fernando de la Rua will keep politics in turmoil, and investors on the sidelines. Cuts to stabilise the budget and bring down interest rates will cost jobs.

To watch
Debt default. Unless the government is able to restructure the public sector and agree new revenue arrangements with the provinces, the benefits of IMF loans will be short-lived. Argentina would then have to default on its debt, possibly triggering a full-blown emerging-markets crisis.

BRAZIL

GDP: $514bn
GDP per head: $3,030
Population: 169.6m
GDP growth: 2.0%
Inflation: 4.5%

The government of Fernando Henrique Cardoso will suffer from the effects of a weak economy, power rationing and fiscal austerity. The left-wing opposition will gain ground; the governing alliance will need to unite behind a good candidate in the October elections.

Brazil will remain vulnerable to contagion from a crisis in Argentina, but a new IMF loan programme should restore confidence in the government.

CHILE

GDP: $68bn
GDP per head: $4,370
Population: 15.6m
GDP growth: 2.2%
Inflation: 3.2%

Chile will return to liberal economic policies in 2002 following congressional elections in 2001. The centre-right Alianza opposition is likely to win parity

with the ruling Concertacion in the Senate. This will mean more pro-business policies and political co-operation from March, when the new Congress convenes.

To watch
Constitutional reforms. Major changes will be approved, including several changes to return the military to the apolitical status it held before 1973.

MEXICO

GDP: $625bn
GDP per head: $6,110
Population: 102.3m
GDP growth: 2.0%
Inflation: 4.6%

President Vicente Fox will suffer from political gaffes in 2002; he remains inexperienced, and his PAN party lacks a majority in Congress. Mr Fox needs a better cabinet strategist if he is to advance his legislative agenda.

The government will push for a temporary-worker programme with the United States to legalise migrant flows. George Bush is open to discussion, but an EU-style labour mobility pact is out of the question any time soon.

Export growth
%

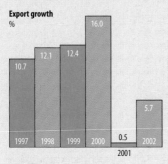

| 1997 | 1998 | 1999 | 2000 | 2001 | 2002 |
| 10.7 | 12.1 | 12.4 | 16.0 | 0.5 | 5.7 |

To watch
The peso. Further volatility in Argentina could prompt a run on the currency, which would probably spark capital flight from Mexico.

VENEZUELA

GDP: $142bn
GDP per head: $5,650
Population: 25.1m
GDP growth: 2.9%
Inflation: 13.6%

The popular president, Hugo Chavez, has accumulated unprecedented political power and will go unchallenged in 2002; the opposition is weak. He will have the clout to make sweeping economic reforms but will not use it.

To watch
Trade pacts. Mr Chavez wants Venezuela to become a member of Mercosur. But he has also signed the Declaration of Carabobo, committing Venezuela to closer integration with the Andean countries. Will he get both?

Africa

KENYA

GDP: $9bn
GDP per head: $301
Population: 30.6m
GDP growth: 2.5%
Inflation: 3.0%

Speculation is growing that the president, Daniel arap Moi, does not intend to relinquish power when his final term ends at the close of 2002. A constitutional review process—which he effectively controls—may give him the means to stand again for election.

Relations with the IMF will remain severely strained, the result of the government's failure to pass an important anti-corruption law in 2001. But Kenya needs financial support from outside donors to fund its budget, and will do just enough to re-start the flow of loans later in the year.

Two international issues will dominate the political scene: efforts to promote greater regional integration through the recently launched East African Community, and the problem of political instability in the Horn of Africa, which is causing bandit activity and an influx of refugees in north-eastern Kenya.

To watch
Elephant herds. The elephant population is rising, but Kenyan officials are not interested in culling, as has been done in southern Africa. Instead officials will begin using a contraceptive vaccine that temporarily sterilises elephants.

NIGERIA

GDP: $37bn
GDP per head: $314
Population: 117.1m
GDP growth: 4.1%
Inflation: 13.3%

Nigeria has nothing close to genuine democracy, a grim thought with elections due between late 2002 and early 2003. Expect plenty of fraud and vote-rigging. The balloting will take place against a

Consumer prices
% change

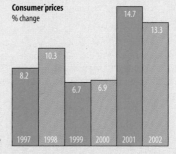

| 1997 | 1998 | 1999 | 2000 | 2001 | 2002 |
| 8.2 | 10.3 | 6.7 | 6.9 | 14.7 | 13.3 |

background of rising criticism of a self-serving political elite, desperately slow reforms and the failure to improve living standards.

Economic growth, as always, will be driven by the oil and gas sector. With increasing energy output in 2002, the economy will do reasonably well. Inflation will fall, but remain in double digits. The value of the naira will drop.

To watch
The military. A political crisis might encourage the more opportunistic junior and middle-ranking officers to seek power. If such a group challenged the established leadership, the military itself might splinter, leading to massive instability.

SOUTH AFRICA

GDP: $117bn
GDP per head: $2,570
Population: 45.5m
GDP growth: 2.9%
Inflation: 5.8%

Exchange rate
Rand:$

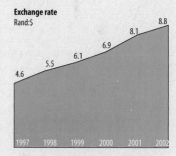

| 1997 | 1998 | 1999 | 2000 | 2001 | 2002 |
| 4.6 | 5.5 | 6.1 | 6.9 | 8.1 | 8.8 |

Thabo Mbeki will remain unchallenged as president in 2002, but his many blunders, including bizarre charges of conspiracy, are worrying the deeply divided African National Congress. He will be re-elected as ANC president in December 2002 but the end of the road is nearing.

Land reform will continue to be an issue. Do not expect a Zimbabwe-style crisis, but the government is keen to make greater progress in 2002 on a more equal distribution of land and housing.

To watch
HIV/AIDS. There is growing concern about the epidemic in South Africa. Owing to the paucity of data, it is difficult to know how badly the economy will be affected. Government efforts to fight back have achieved little; results will be only slightly better in 2002.

Hungarian Economic Review

An information service on business, investment and tourism from leading Hungarian organisations

Economic strategy
Revving up to maintain growth

"This is the winning ticket," enthuses Minister of Economic Affairs György Matolcsy, referring to Hungary's ability to host foreign direct investment (FDI) in the heart of what he notes is a fast-growing rim around the eastern perimeter of the EU, the world's largest market. "Central Europe is on the rise and catching up with the EU," he states.

Indeed, Hungary's recent and projected economic performance continues to defy partly the global downturn. With an FDI stock of more than €24.7 billion as of mid-2001, much of it made by multinational manufacturers, Hungary's average growth of just under 5% since 1997 was led by booming exports, up 30.0% during 2000. While in 2001 the global slowdown will reduce export growth, which was 19.2% during the first half, this decline is being partially offset by increasing domestic investment and consumption. GDP growth of just above 4%, more than twice that of the EU average and among the fastest in Central Europe, is expected this year with up to 4.5% projected for 2002.

Foreign investment by country
Diversified sources

Others 20
Japan 31
Austria 9
US 10
Holland 15
Germany 15

Jan–Jun 2001

Source: National Bank of Hungary

Domestic investment has been significantly boosted by a national redevelopment plan announced in 2000 and named after Count István Széchenyi, whose reforms and projects, ranging from the establishment of the Hungarian Academy of Sciences—endowed with a year's worth of his own earnings—to the launch of steam navigation of the Danube river and Balaton lake to the introduction of horse racing and casinos in Hungary, helped propel a then-kingdom emerging from feudalism to West European development levels by the early 20th century.

The objective of the Széchenyi Plan is to kick-start development projects via government co-funding in branches where the state must take the lead, such as infrastructure; or areas where Hungary has a comparative advantage via natural assets, but which remain under-utilised, such as high scientific literacy and thermal waters; or

endeavours where a modest amount of government support can yield disproportionate returns, such as in fostering small- and medium-sized enterprises (SMEs) or strengthening the housing market.

In many ways the Széchenyi Plan is designed to compensate for lingering distortions caused by more than 40 years of central planning forced on Hungary prior to 1990. And Mr Matolcsy is quick to point out that, as a public-private partnership, the Széchenyi Plan relies foremost on the private sector, including both domestic and international financial and strategic investors, for know-how, management and capital as well as involving local entrepreneurs and municipalities throughout the country.

Take infrastructure. The half of Hungary to the east of the Danube has been underdeveloped relative to the western half dating back to the Ottoman occupation and has suffered from decades of under-investment. More recently, the lion's share of FDI has been concentrated in Budapest and the country's western half, which has better infrastructure, particularly transport links to EU markets. "The Széchenyi Plan's development of motorways and regional airports will improve access for investors to eastern Hungary, which contains some of our best universities and well-educated graduates," says Mr Matolcsy, "and because one out of every four municipalities is involved in local Széchenyi Plan projects, growth will be spread evenly."

Hungary's strong scientific tradition—the nation boasts the world's highest per capita number of Nobel prize winners—includes not only legendary figures such as Eugene Wigner and János von Neumann, who conceived some of the defining technologies of the 20th century, such as the atomic bomb and the computer, but also the likes of those who furthered the latter innovation, such as Intel's Andy Grove and Charles Simonyi, Microsoft's chief software architect, who was responsible for the development of programs such as Word and Excel.

The snag is that while a rigorous education prepares Hungarians for theoretical research, to have serious value such research must be developed into a product and marketed. For that Hungary needs partners with global reach. "This is why the Széchenyi Plan supports investment in R&D," Mr Matolcsy says, citing such operations by Audi, Siemens, Ericsson, Motorola and Bombay-based global IT firm TATA, which recently opened its first European software R&D centre in Budapest. "We would get nowhere alone but have tremendous potential with some of our brilliant global investors," he adds.

Another area in which Hungary has unique assets is tourism. Accounting for about 10% of GDP, the sector is one of the country's most dynamic, with foreign currency revenues in the first half of 2001 up 18.5% versus the same period last year. But the sector remains underdeveloped due to

a dearth of high standard accommodation.

Fortunately, in addition to the unique cultural heritage of a kingdom established one thousand years ago, Hungary also happens to be positioned above a giant natural jacuzzi. Particularly warm thermal waters are found in about 80% of its territories. Part of the Széchenyi Plan is to bolster health and wellness tourism—a hot sector worldwide given ageing populations—by developing spa resorts and other tourism services to the level offered in Austria or Switzerland by 2005, when Hungary is expected to join the EU. Tourism development also offers good prospects for SMEs.

Another development opportunity for SMEs is as suppliers and sub-suppliers to multinational exporters, the enhancement of such relationships is another objective of the Széchenyi Plan. While most SMEs have difficulty tapping export markets directly, they can do so more efficiently by piggybacking on the products, brands and distribution channels of multinationals, which account for a large share of the country's well more than €30 billion of annual exports—75% of which go to the EU—that can help to integrate organically Hungarian SMEs into the global economy.

While inflation has been brought under control (7-8% is forecast for 2001, falling to about 6% in 2002), the introduction of world market prices during the early 1990s fuelled inflation. The accompanying high interest rates retarded the development of a mortgage market and therefore the overall housing sector. The Széchenyi Plan's assistance of the construction industry and, in cooperation with banks, the mortgage market, has helped to increase the country's home loan portfolio by 72% within one year while the number of new flats and homes built has grown from 20,000 in 2000, to a forecast 30,000 in 2001 and a projected 40,000 in 2002.

At the same time rising real income has boosted consumption, increasing retail sales volume by 5.7% during the first half of 2001. Yet there is no sign of overheating as the current account deficit, already well under control, declined to 3% of GDP during the first seven months of 2001 versus 3.3% last year. Unemployment also continues to decline, from an average of 6.6% during the first half of 2000 to 5.8% in the same period of 2001, well below the EU average of 7.5%. Thus, a revival in domestic demand after the spartan years of the mid-1990s has proven a timely stabiliser in light of weakening external economic trends.

The government initially figured that each dollar allocated by the Széchenyi Plan would catalyse an equivalent amount of private capital. In fact, the government's $1 billion commitment during 2001 mobilised $5 billion from the private sector. A bit larger amount has been earmarked by the government for 2002 and thereafter a percentage of GDP for each year up to 2006. EU pre-accession funds may also be tapped in line with

MINISTRY OF ECONOMIC AFFAIRS
www.gm.hu

MINISTRY OF FOREIGN AFFAIRS
www.kum.hu

MAI Central Eastern Europe
Contact: Christopher Gore
1136 Budapest, Pannónia u 11
T/F 361 239 4515 / 239 4514
maihungary@mai-cee.com
www.mai-cee.com

ALLEN & OVERY

Contact: Éva Hegedűs
1075 Budapest, Madách Imre u 13-14
T/F 361 483 2200 / 268 1515
eva.hegedus@allenovery.com
www.allenovery.com

EU regulations.

"The attraction of this level of private capital would have been called wishful thinking just a few months ago," beams Mr Matolcsy, who reckons incremental GDP growth due to the plan will be 1.5% in 2001 (representing €743m)—along with the creation of 22,000 jobs—and 2% in 2002. But, according to Mr Matolcsy, the full impact of projects undertaken so far will only be felt in 2003 and 2004. "The new engines that will drive our economy have only just been started," he says.

Legal issues of FDI
Last minute (Széchenyi) plans

"Get on the next plane to Budapest," replies Ildikó Varga, executive partner at Nagy és Trócsányi, Hungary's largest indigenous law firm, when asked what advice she would have for investors considering establishing operations in Central Europe. Why the rush?

"All foreign direct investors are applying for, and serious proposals are generally receiving, funding from the Széchenyi Plan," says Ms Varga, referring to the country's economic redevelopment plan through which the state is co-financing between a quarter and a third of selected projects in seven prioritised sectors: infrastructure, housing, small- and medium-sized enterprises (SMEs), tourism, regional development, R&D and information society.

While the application procedure for Széchenyi Plan funding is complex—indeed Ms Varga suggests hiring a consulting firm that can navigate potential investors through the maze of paperwork (much of which is only available in Hungarian) and provide valuable practical lobbying at the processing level.

However, once the application is submitted the process tends to flow smoothly and the legal documentation procedure is relatively straightforward. "It goes quickly and the government has been flexible," explains Ms Varga, noting that the actual operation for which the funding would be used need not be up and running at the time of application, the only requirement for which is the establishment of an Hungarian company.

In preparation for EU accession, the country has put in place a comprehensive package of laws that gradually harmonises Hungarian legislation with 80,000 pages of EU law and regulation, the *acquis communautaire*. "We believe that this legislative package, which has been enacted, published and will become effective over time, complies with all EU mandates," states Ms Varga.

As part of this sequential process, on January 1st 2002 the application procedure for Széchenyi Plan funds will be modified in line with EU requirements. This means that applications for certain categories of funding will require (surprise) more documentation. This will support the calculation of economic multipliers, the implementation of a point system to evaluate applications and the establishment of a national body with responsibility for granting funding. Certain bookkeeping requirements and other documentation will enable monitoring the use of state funds.

Ms Varga says that while some investors have pulled back as falling demand has impacted plants supplying EU markets, new foreign direct investment (FDI) continues to flow in, citing current projects among her clients in sectors such as energy, industrial manufacturing and electronics, including Samsung, which is about to open a greenfield plant. Ms Varga also notes that such investors value the housing component of the Széchenyi Plan as it is already improving the availability and mobility of labour, a key decision factor for investors.

The Széchenyi Plan's multiplier effect certainly seems to have increased business at Nagy és Trócsányi, which has 25 lawyers, a total staff of 60 and this year celebrated its 10th anniversary. About half of the firm's work is general corporate while a third is litigation and arbitration and a sixth tax-related.

Interestingly, the firm has carved out a niche of working for law firms that have clients interested in Hungary but may have no local office in the country and generally don't like to use international firms that represent competition in other markets. Such work, which accounts for more than 40% of Nagy és Trócsányi's activity, is mostly for Anglo-Saxon firms, including the likes of Gibson, Dunn & Crutcher; CMS Cameron McKenna; Paul, Hastings, Janofsky & Walker; and Coudert Brothers, and to a lesser extent French, German and other European firms. "We find working with other law firms very efficient, as we speak the same language," Ms Varga says "and of course we speak Hungarian, too."

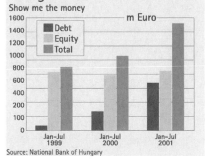

Foreign direct investment flows
Show me the money

Source: National Bank of Hungary

Reinsurance
The price goes up

At their annual gathering in Baden Baden in late October, few reinsurance firms, which insure the risks of insurance firms, were prepared to be specific about rate increases for next year. But the consensus is that they will be substantial as the sector attempts to recoup losses related to the September 11th terrorist attacks, the claims related to which could exceed $40 billion.

And indigenous insurance firms in Central and Eastern Europe (CEE) that are not part of a global network may have it even tougher: General Cologne Re, Munich Re and Swiss Re, the major European reinsurers, indicated that contracts not achieving new profitability targets, which are inversely proportional to plummeting global equity markets, will be particularly scrutinised.

This is a significant change of direction for the largest reinsurers, which have viewed CEE as a development priority. The three firms initially provided reinsurance to former state-owned insurers and later to the region's developing private insurers at relatively favourable terms to grab market share, according to Christopher Gore, boss of MAI Central Eastern Europe, an insurance brokerage active throughout CEE. "While nobody knows exactly how much rates will go up on January 1st, it will clearly impact our region considerably," says Mr Gore.

Reinsurance allows insurance companies to write policies in excess of the amount enabled by their own capital. As a rule of thumb, insurance companies in Central Europe should not expose themselves to a single risk larger than 10% of their capital and reserves, according to Mr Gore. Insurers reinsure the excess exposure by so-called facultative, proportional or non-proportional reinsurance.

Facultative reinsurance, which covers single risks, is most exposed to the new reinsurance market conditions. Prices on the largest industrial risks have increased by up to 2-3 times and 5-10 times on some energy risks.

Proportional reinsurance can be thought of as automatic facultative, in which reinsurers provide capacity annually for which they allow a commission—the rate of which is likely to fall—to the insurer. Proportional reinsurance typically covers mid-sized commercial and motor risks. While reinsurers are reducing the capacity of these agreements, their desire to keep a position in CEE markets means these terms will not harden as much as those of facultative.

Non-proportional reinsurance is overall reinsurance against combined catastrophic, and large single, events. Heavily influenced by the September 11th attacks, prices will increase by 30-100% globally, which is in line with recent renewals by MAI RE, MAI's reinsurance arm.

Indigenous CEE insurers could find themselves particularly exposed in the event that they are unable to renew reinsurance on their outstanding policies, which would force them to increase the premiums they charge. Smaller players may have to consolidate or seek a strategic investor. "Insurance buyers must confirm that their insurance company is properly reinsured," cautions Mr Gore.

Another issue is the link between insurance and corporate finance. Bank loans and lease terms often require the borrower to maintain minimum levels of insurance, which, if withdrawn, as recently happened to airlines, could jeopardise such financing. "This could be terminal in CEE, where firms have fewer financing options," notes Mr Gore.

MAI, which is also active in retail insurance brokerage and offers its own special insurance products, is scrambling to restructure contracts of the 30 CEE insurance firms for which it manages and buys reinsurance. Yet in the midst of such challenges MAI has found new opportunity. The potentially prohibitively high cost of facultative reinsurance has led the firm to roll out a new structure that pools the capital of several of its clients such that the lower-cost proportional reinsurance can be used instead. Necessity, it seems, remains the mother of invention.

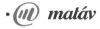
matáv
T/F 361 458 0000 / 458 7176
www.matav.hu

NAGY ÉS TRÓCSÁNYI LAW OFFICE
Contact: Ildikó Varga Ugocsa u 4/b, 1126 Budapest
T/F 361 487 8700 / 487 8701
budapest_office@nagyestrocsanyi.hu

WESTEL Mobile Co.

the Connection
Tel/Fax:
361 265 9200 /
204 4128
www.westel.hu

HUNGARY
THE HUNGARIAN INVESTMENT
AND TRADE DEVELOPMENT AGENCY
1051 Budapest, Dorottya u 4
T/F 361 318 0051 / 318 3732
info@itd.hu, www.itd.hu

Middle East

ALGERIA

GDP: $50bn
GDP per head: $1,550
Population: 32.1m
GDP growth: 5.5%
Inflation: 3.6%

Abdelaziz Bouteflika will survive as president in 2002 but pressure from the military elite is building. Many of the generals are deeply suspicious of his economic agenda, which threatens their cosy business relationships. They also disapprove of his dalliance with Amnesty International, which led to revelations about abuse and murder.

Protests in the Berber-dominated regions, which unnerved the government in 2001, will remain a problem in 2002, but the demonstrations will be less intense. The Berbers want greater democracy, and above all jobs. The generals seem incapable of compromise.

To watch
Unemployment. The rate of joblessness is sky high: 28% for the population at large and more than 50% for those under 30. With strong resistance to economic reforms, it will not fall much.

EGYPT

GDP: $83bn
GDP per head: $1,170
Population: 71.1m
GDP growth: 3.3%
Inflation: 5.4%

Inward direct investment
$m

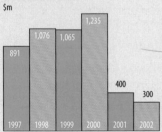

The government's determination to retain tight political control could provoke a backlash, though not strong enough to threaten the regime. Curbing the influence of political Islam, after recent parliamentary successes by the Muslim Brotherhood, will be the focus.

Investors will want further economic reforms, after the achievements of 2001. Their wish list for 2002? Better management of the currency, and more clarity, speed and transparency in government decision-making.

If the Israeli prime minister, Ariel Sharon, remains in power following an election in 2002, anti-Israeli sentiment within Egypt will grow, damaging relations between the two countries.

IRAN

GDP: $87bn
GDP per head: $1,330
Population: 65.7m
GDP growth: 4.0%
Inflation: 16.0%

American concerns over Iran's alleged links with international terrorism will flare up in 2002 as the United States prosecutes its anti-terrorism campaign. America's European allies will take a more charitable view of Iran's activities.

Despite his overwhelming victory in the recent presidential election, the reformist president, Mohammed Khatami, will face staunch opposition in 2002 from hard-line conservative clerics, slowing the pace of political and economic liberalisation. Younger Iranians will become restive.

IRAQ

GDP: $32bn
GDP per head: $1,320
Population: 24.5m
GDP growth: 11.0%
Inflation: 50.0%

American and British efforts to pressure the Iraqi government will intensify in 2002: Iraq's alleged sponsorship of terrorism will once again bring Saddam Hussein into their cross-hairs. While another Gulf war-style invasion is unlikely, some kind of American military response seems inevitable.

With the sanctions regime still in place, Iraq's only economic policy will be to find new smuggling routes for its oil. Economic growth will track the changes in oil production. GDP shrank by some 10% in 2001; it could rebound in 2002, but Iraq's decrepit oil production facilities are badly in need of spare parts and the American mood is far from charitable.

ISRAEL

GDP: $114bn
GDP per head: $17,400
Population: 6.5m
GDP growth: 2.2%
Inflation: 2.5%

A fresh election is likely in early 2002. As more Israelis realise that massive retaliation against the Palestinian uprising will not ensure security, the public may turn against Ariel Sharon, the Likud prime minister. However, the deeply divided Labour Party will have to campaign hard to win votes.

The security situation will remain a threat

Inward portfolio investment
$m

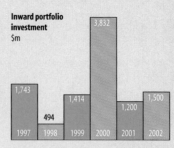

to the stability of Israel's financial markets. The economy is likely to perform better in 2002, but only if the violence begins to abate, and if a recovery in the United States—so critical to Israel's burgeoning IT sector—takes hold.

The risk that the Israeli-Palestinian conflict will spread into a broader Israeli-Arab confrontation is not great. No Arab state can afford to wage war with Israel.

To watch
Pressure from the United States. America will turn up the heat on Mr Sharon to negotiate with the Palestinians, and make concessions—such as a freeze on illegal settlement-building in the West Bank.

JORDAN

GDP: $9bn
GDP per head: $1,310
Population: 7.1m
GDP growth: 3.6%
Inflation: 2.5%

King Abdullah is popular with the majority of Jordanians—both Palestinians and East Bankers—and will face no serious threats in 2002. But social pressures are building. The "anti-normalisation" campaign seeks to curb improved relations with Israel. Careful management will be required if support for radical Islam is not to emerge.

Investment should improve in 2002. Encouraged by gradually declining lending rates, new domestic investment is expected in the Aqaba free zone, in telecommunications and tourism, while investment in the industrial zones should also continue. In addition, a parliamentary election should encourage domestic demand.

Gross fixed investment
% growth

LEBANON

GDP: $18bn
GDP per head: $4,890
Population: 3.6m
GDP growth: 2.0%
Inflation: 3.0%

The rivalry between the prime minister, Rafiq al-Hariri, and the president, Emile Lahoud, will continue. It is rooted in the tension between Mr Hariri's elected government and the Syrian-backed Mr Lahoud, whose authority stems from control of the military forces.

Mr Hariri will push ahead with economic reform, but the economy will grow very slowly in 2002. Without budget cuts, international confidence will not return, and the stability of the entire economy could be put at risk.

To watch:
"Paris II". This meeting of aid donors, scheduled for late 2001, has been delayed. It will determine the extent of financial support Lebanon receives in light of its large budget deficit.

SAUDI ARABIA

GDP: $176bn
GDP per head: $8,110
Population: 21.7m
GDP growth: 2.6%
Inflation: 1.0%

Petroleum production
b/d, m

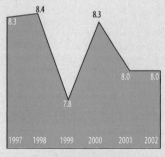

America will put pressure on Saudi Arabia to support more fully its anti-terrorist campaign. This could exacerbate anti-American sentiment in the kingdom. But the strategic and economic importance of the relationship will hold sway.

The need to continue economic reform will grow as unemployment rises, but political factors will limit progress. However, Crown Prince Abdullah bin Abdel-Aziz al-Saud will persevere.

To watch
The volatile price of oil. Barring a major conflict in the Middle East, oil prices will fall as global economic growth remains weak. But American military strikes against terrorist targets outside Afghanistan would push up prices dramatically.

The world in figures: Industries

General trends

Spreading the wealth
Capital flows to developing countries, $bn

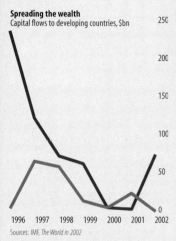

Sources: IMF, *The World in 2002*

Interesting times. The world economy will teeter on the brink between recession and growth. Attention will be focused on America. The IMF predicts 2.2% growth, but there is a significant risk of much worse if consumers stop spending, if productivity falls or if business investment does not pick up.

Economists hope for a V-shaped recession: a fast slowdown followed by a fast recovery. But if the bounce fails to materialise there would be turbulence in financial markets and a run on the dollar. Europe and Japan's fragile economies would be hit badly; developing countries would suffer even more.

Looking to the long term, the economic wonders of the information technology (IT) revolution should roll out into Europe and elsewhere. The long-term trend rate of growth, which depends on productivity, was 2.5% a year in the United States. But IT-related productivity increases have probably pushed this up to 3-3.5%. The challenge for European and Japanese firms is to repeat the feat. Economic hard times may just help, as competitive pressures are ramped up and costs are forced down.

Shareholders become less docile in downturns. Annual general meetings will be noisier as managements face more demands to justify their actions. Calls to allow shareholders to vote on the remuneration of senior management will grow louder.

Production

AEROSPACE

A new generation of passenger planes is on the drawing board. EADS' Airbus and Boeing, the world's duopoly makers of 100+ seat planes, have different visions of the future. Airbus's 555-passenger superjumbo, the A380, is due to enter service in 2006. Costing over $10bn to develop, the A380 will take passengers along major routes. Far sexier is Boeing's "sonic cruiser", a smaller plane that will fly close to the speed of sound. It will carry fewer passengers but will provide more frequent, point-to-point services.

The market for executive aeroplanes almost died. But then came time-share and the industry, worth $10bn a year, boomed. There will be 11,500 planes flying in 2002, four-fifths of them in the United States.

Russia hopes to make money out of its Soviet-era space technology. The market for satellite launches is worth $2bn a year. Russia's cosmodrome in Kazakhstan is too expensive. It hopes to launch satellites from Christmas Island in the Indian Ocean by 2003. MirCorp may build a private minispace station for tourists.

To watch
Star wars, the prequel. America already has 150 defence-related machines, mostly satellites, in orbit. In 2002, it will research land-to-space weapons that destroy ballistic missiles. By 2010, the Pentagon fears that its satellites could be vulnerable to enemy attack. The first space-to-space laser weapons could be tested in 2012.

The world fleet doubles
%

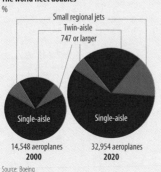

14,548 aeroplanes
2000

32,954 aeroplanes
2020

Source: Boeing

AGRICULTURE

Advanced economies find it hard to leave agriculture—and farmers—behind. Agricultural tariffs across most of the world remain at 40-50%; those for manufactured goods are below 10%. Within the OECD, annual government handouts to farmers exceed Africa's GDP. This harms developing countries. Welcome then an agriculturally heavy round of trade talks.

A wilting sector
World export volume
1990 = 100

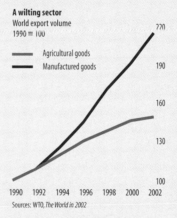

Sources: WTO, *The World in 2002*

Market access will dominate the agenda, as developing countries seek the fulfilment of promises made in the Uruguay Round. The EU will defend its export subsidies to farmers, worth about 4bn, and will reduce them only if America, India and other big exporters also cut their export-credit guarantees.

Reform of the EU's common agricultural policy (CAP) is scheduled for 2005. The system of subsidies will not be extended east upon enlargement of the Union, says the European Commission: that would be far too expensive. In 2002, CAP will cost European taxpayers 46bn.

A long-awaited recovery will come to some food commodities in 2002. Prices for grains, oilseeds and sugar will lead the pack, with price rises of 15-20%.

To watch
The world go by. Coffee culture in America and Europe is ripening. America will drink $18bn of it. Starbucks plans to open 1,200 new stores, including its first in France, Spain and Italy. McDonald's will open 200 McCafes. But the market is floundering as overall coffee consumption is not rising. Prices will plummet to 30-year lows.

CARS

Detroit will tremble under the onslaught of Japanese sport-utility vehicles (SUVs) and vans. General Motors, Ford and Chrysler have about 65% of the new-vehicle market but only sell to half of all first-time buyers, down from 60% in 1997. Nissan aims to manufacture 80% of the cars it sells in the United States there, up from 65% at present, to avoid currency risks and tariffs. Back home, the Japanese car industry will bear the brunt of economic hard times. Up to 140,000 jobs could be lost by 2005.

America's National Academy of Sciences wants to raise the Corporate Average Fuel Economy (CAFE) standard 47% over the next 10-15 years. CAFE currently requires passenger cars to do 27.5 miles per American gallon (11.7 kilometres to a litre). Car manufacturers are worried, arguing that the increase will result in smaller, less safe cars. Scientists say that there is the technology to make large cars guzzle less gas.

All the major firms will research fuel cells. These react hydrogen and oxygen together to produce electricity. An alternative, one that BMW is exploring, is to burn hydrogen in a conventional internal-combustion engine (ICE). Conversion to allow a car to run on both petrol and hydrogen is simple. However, it is inefficient: for the same amount of hydrogen, a fuel-cell powered car can travel 60% farther than a hydrogen-powered ICE.

To watch
The road, at night. Raytheon, the defence contractor, will sell night-vision equipment for cars. It estimates that sales will hit 300,000 a year by 2005.

The one in front
The top-selling passenger vehicles in the United States

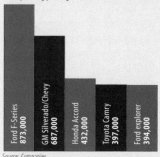

Source: Companies

ENERGY

Oil production
m b/d

2002		2010	
		United States	9
United States	9	Developing countries	13
Developing countries	11	Eurasia*	15
Eurasia*	11	Other OECD	16
Other OECD	15		
OPEC	32	OPEC	42

Source: Energy Information Administration
* Former USSR, China and Eastern Europe

With slower economic growth, expect OPEC to cut production in an attempt to keep oil at above $25 a barrel. Such price manipulation is all but impossible to do with any precision. So expect spikes in prices and criticisms from western governments. Military conflict outside Afghanistan would cause a rise in price.

If relations between India and Pakistan improve, long-standing plans for a 2,400km pipeline, costing $5bn, from gas-rich Iran to gas-poor India, via poor Pakistan, will be dusted off. BP will drill its first well in Azerbaijan's Alov region of the Caspian Sea, a project that will be plagued by Iran's claims of sovereignty over the area. The Caspian area should have three big oilfields by 2015, yielding 4m b/d. Getting the stuff out will present the challenge. American oil companies want to build a pipeline to take oil from Kazakhstan through Iran to world markets. But they cannot act on with American sanctions on Iran in place.

Demand for electricity should rise 45% by 2020 in the United States, creating the need for another 1,300-1,900 new power stations. But even with George Bush in the White House, nuclear power will not be the answer. Natural gas, at $3-4 per million British thermal units (BTU), is much cheaper. A gas plant can be built in two years for $500 per kw produced. A nuclear plant costs $1,600 per kw and can take six years to build. The advantage of nuclear power is its lack of greenhouse-gas emissions. Nuclear enthusiasts will not be beaten easily. Researchers in the United States hope to create a new generation of reactors and fuel cycle technologies, to be deployed by 2030.

Britain is currently self-sufficient in energy and exports North Sea gas. However, by the end of 2005 it will need to start importing gas. There will also be pressure to revive nuclear power. Environmentalists would prefer hydro-electricity. The government plans for 10% of energy to come from renewable sources by 2010.

Distributed power is the future. That is, households, or small communities, making their own power, in an environmentally friendly manner, when they need it. Fuel cells may arrive in the home before they get to cars. General Motors hopes to have a TV-sized cell capable of producing seven kilowatts of electricity in production in 2003-05.

To watch
Super-conducting power cables, to be installed in Detroit in 2002. Carrying between two and ten times more power than traditional copper wires, these will become an important part of every modern city's energy infrastructure.

INFORMATION TECHNOLOGY

Moore's Law looks set to hold. Proposed in 1965, it states that the number of transistors that can be packed on to a microchip, and thus the chip's capacity, doubles every year. Most lines on chips are now 0.25 microns wide, one four-hundredth the width of a human hair. Experiments in printing circuits less than 0.1 micron wide using ultraviolet light will get under way in 2002. Motorola's new gallium arsenide chips are more efficient than silicon chips and will replace them in mobile phones.

Falling investment in IT will hit Asia hard. Half of Singapore's exports are in electronics. Taiwan produces about half of the world's laptops. Only China has enough domestic demand to defy a global downturn. In five years it will be the world's second-largest IT market after America; in ten it will be a rival in size, if not in technological prowess.

Do not expect a break-up for Microsoft; just continuing legal wrangles. The company will face antitrust challenges to its new web initiatives. There are also concerns that Windows XP, its new operating system, contains illegal "bundling", the co-mingling of codes that prevents PC makers from replacing Microsoft's software with those of competitors.

As with past downturns, this one will trigger price wars. Prices and margins have further to fall in the PC computer market. One of the big names, Gateway

Handy
Sales of personal digital assistants, m

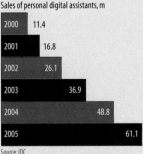

2000	11.4
2001	16.8
2002	26.1
2003	36.9
2004	48.8
2005	61.1

Source: IDC

perhaps, may have to quit the business. The chip glut will also get larger, keeping prices low. China plans to build more than a dozen new fabrication plants.

To watch
Your web rage. Traffic on the Internet is doubling every six months, partly driven by corporations moving off private networks to cut costs. It will become harder to find the information you are looking for, and easier to get frustrated. Search engines will become ever more important. Google is the biggest, hosting a quarter of all searches. With text advertising and licensing its search technology to companies such as Yahoo! and Cisco, it will have revenues of $50m in 2002.

Priceless?
Health-care spending as % of GDP

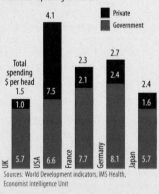

| | Private |
| | Government |

	UK	USA	France	Germany	Japan
Private	1.0	4.1	2.1	2.4	1.6
Government		7.5			
Total spending $ per head	1.5		2.3	2.7	2.4
	5.7	6.6	7.7	8.1	5.7

Sources: World Development indicators, IMS Health, Economist Intelligence Unit

PHARMACEUTICALS

Drug companies are in for a tough year, even if they will be largely immune to a recession. Their pain will come from three other complaints. Drugs with annual sales of $28bn are due to lose their patent protections by the end of 2005. Companies will try to prolong these rights, and the attendant revenues, through exploiting legal loopholes, much to the disgust of America's Federal Trade Commission. It will launch a probe into anti-competitive practices.

Slick branding of drugs will also be questioned. Around two-thirds of patients who ask their doctor for a drug, get it. In other words, drug advertising, now totalling $2bn a year, works. Generic medicines usually do as good a job, but account for only a tenth of all drug spending in America.

To add to the pain, America's Food and Drug Administration will be slow to register new drugs for public use. A number of high-profile failures have made it cautious. Approvals were down 40% in 2001 and will be slower in 2002. Delays in approval mean delays in drugs rolling out and less money rolling in.

American and European companies have failed to make a dent in Japan. This will change. Western drugs do not now need to undergo special trials to ensure they work on the Japanese. Foreign firms will line up to register their drugs and buy local competitors. They will be cheap: few have a market capitalisation of more than $10bn.

To watch
Your sex life. Lilly ICOS has submitted IC351 (brandname: Cialis) to the European and American regulators. Like Viagra, Cialis is a PDE5 inhibitor. Unlike Viagra, it remains effective for 24 hours. It could start selling in 2002.

RAW MATERIALS

The American steel industry will be in trouble. Prices will be at their lowest for 20 years. Not averse to the odd touch of protectionism, the Bush administration will respond with quotas and tariffs. This will hurt European firms, who export 5m tonnes of steel a year to America.

Metals are in for a tough 12 months. Energy prices will be high and industrial demand subdued. Diamond prices are set to fall too. China will provide the only sparkle. Demand for iron ore is growing at 20% a year there and the country is guzzling aluminium, copper, zinc and tin.

Consolidation in the paper industry will result in falling capacity and higher prices, notably for newsprint paper. The benchmark pulp (northern softwood bleached kraft) is not expected to fall below $650 a tonne. By 2030, some 80% of industrial round wood will be grown in fast-growing plantations in the southern hemisphere.

To watch
Vector, an American tobacco company. It has developed a genetically modified tobacco that contains virtually no addictive substances. Their "Omni Free" cigarettes will be aimed at America's 47m adult smokers in 2002 as a stop-smoking aid. Research is also targeted at removing the major carcinogens.

TEXTILES

On January 1st, stage three of the WTO's Agreement on Textiles and Clothing kicks in. 49% of the members' total textile imports should come under GATT rules. At the beginning of 2005 all restrictions should be eliminated. America and Europe used this agreement to slow down the opening of their markets to developing countries. With full implementation, clothes will get cheaper in the West, and developing world producers will become richer.

Services

ADVERTISING

Advertisers take economic downturns on the chin. Newspapers and television suffered a miserable 2001 when advertising revenues fell dramatically after a volatile 2000. In 2002, newspaper spend will rise 2% and spending on television will fall again, by 4%. Magazines will fare even worse.

Online advertising is having a difficult childhood. It represents only 3% of total advertising spend, half that of radio. Average click-through rates have fallen to less than 1 in 200, half that in the boom years of 1999-2000. But the market has not collapsed and as the medium matures, blue chips will increase their online presence. Not in 2002 though. Expect the downturn to eat into the $8bn spent on online advertising in 2001.

Fewer commissions
Total advertising spend, USA, France, Germany, UK, Italy, Spain, Japan
$bn

1999	
2000	
2001	
2002	
2003	245

Source: Zenith Media

To watch
Less television. Since 1985, the average number of hours watched by Americans under 18 fell 20%. Even hit shows fail to reach 10% of Americans, well down from 50% in the 1980s. With new channels dividing audiences, television is becoming a perilous place to advertise.

AIRLINES

Hit hard in 2001, 2002 will offer little respite for the airline industry. Passenger numbers are still scheduled to grow at 5% a year to 2020. But squeezed corporate travel budgets and high fuel bills will cause turbulence. The security headache will not go away quickly. The result should be long-overdue consolidation, especially in Europe, which has 28 scheduled airlines, excluding the small regional players. America has seven big carriers serving a much larger market. More medium-sized carriers such as Swissair will not survive without the help of public money. Governments will refuse to bail out unprofitable firms.

The NASA-financed "Highway in the sky" project will transform flying. By simplifying the manifold controls and dials inside a cockpit into a video-game-like screen, planes will become as easy to drive as cars.

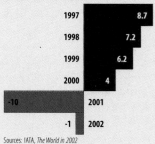

Better, but still not good
Profits of IATA members, $bn

1997	8.7
1998	7.2
1999	6.2
2000	4
-10	2001
-1	2002

Sources: IATA, *The World in 2002*

New runways will be needed to meet the increase in passenger traffic. Heathrow will get the go-ahead to build a fifth terminal. Costing £2.25bn, it will allow the world's busiest international airport to handle 80m passengers, compared with the 64m at present. Expect noise from environmental groups about noise and much else. Aeroplanes are big greenhouse-gas emitters, accounting for around 10% of world emissions.

To watch
Your budget. Low-cost air travel is forecast to grow 25% a year, with Ryanair, Go and easyJet out in front. The model that works so well in Britain will be introduced to continental Europe, causing prices there to plummet.

E-COMMERCE

B2B exchanges, places where businesses transact goods and services online, are not a fad. By 2004, one in three business transactions will be conducted online in America, one in five in Europe. But B2B development will be slower and less lucrative than predicted. Of the 1,000 or so B2B exchanges established in the past 18 months, less than 100 will host transactions in 2002. The most successful will be those set up by major corporations. Covisint, a car-industry B2B, will handle $750bn in annual purchasing. The long-term trend, however, is for companies to establish private exchanges, where they can reveal sensitive information to suppliers on a need-to-know basis.

Credit cards are getting clever. Although not yet clever enough to tell you when to stop spending. Magnetic-strip technology is on the way out. Migration to chips is moving fastest in Europe where Visa is spending 168m to put 180m cards into people's pockets by the end of 2004. The hope is chips will be more secure, reducing fraud.

The e-book revolution is moving at a worm's pace. Estimates of digital books accounting for 10% of all book sales by 2005 are optimistic. Another online leisure activity will be far more popular. There are now over 1,400 gambling sites on the Internet, at which 1m users regularly dabble. Industry revenues will rise to $3bn a year by 2002.

The topography of the Internet is changing. Popular sites are now "cached", duplicated and stored, by content delivery networks on their servers. This allows frequently accessed content to be "nearer" to viewers and quicker and cheaper to deliver. By 2005, 50% of all traffic will flow through these "edge aggregation points".

To watch
Your bills. By 2005, more than 40m American households will pay some of their bills on the Internet. Telephone companies, public utilities and financial-services firms will spend $1bn in 2002 on improving bill-paying technology.

Adult sites
Minutes spent per visitor a month

Italy	37
Britain	46
Sweden	54
United States	57
Germany	59
Taiwan	72

Source: NetValue

ENTERTAINMENT

The music industry will have more rhythm and fewer blues in 2002. CD sales, worth $37bn worldwide, levelled off years ago and the Internet shook the industry to the core. But 2002 will prove that its nemesis has been tamed. Bertelsmann, a German media giant, controls Napster, an online music site, while Vivendi Universal owns MP3.com. Two new music subscription services will be launched. Sony and Vivendi are setting up pressplay, a retail download service for Internet users. AOL Time Warner, Bertelsmann and EMI will launch MusicNet, a wholesale operation for online music retailers. Expect to pay $10 a month for the ability to download all the music you want, legally.

The battle for the $20bn games console market—between Sony's PlayStation 2, Microsoft's Xbox and Nintendo's Gamecube—will be gladiatorial. Sony has a huge lead in games but Microsoft has the technological edge. Do not be deceived, however. They are not just fighting over games, but over the future of home entertainment. Sony has teamed up with AOL Time Warner to deliver e-mail and movies to its consoles. Microsoft will spend $500m in marketing and subsidising the Xbox. Small change: the company has $30bn of cash and short-term investments with which to play. The Xbox will not win out this time, but there will be a version 2.0.

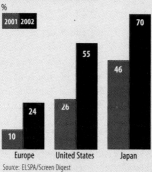

Gaming nations
Households with 128-bit consoles
%

	2001	2002
Europe	10	24
United States	26	55
Japan	46	70

Source: ELSPA/Screen Digest

66% of American and 72% of British homes will have digital TV by 2005, compared with 25-30% now. The switch from analogue will be driven by your demand for clearer pictures and more channels, and the industry's belief that you want interactivity. Broadcasters want to sell you things "in the broadcasting stream", providing opportunities to buy while watching TV. Expect to be offered two thousand and two ways to bet on the sport you are watching.

It will be another five, perhaps ten, years before video on demand (VOD)—films streaming over the Internet into your home—becomes a reality. The current backbone cannot support the massive data demands, and the costs are enormous. To send one movie—about 1,000 megabytes of data—down a pipe to one viewer costs about $10. In 2002, geeks will expand bandwidth. Lawyers will deal with copyright issues. And some bright spark will be dreaming up a credible pricing model.

To watch
DVDs. 2002 will see a messy rerun of the VHS-Betamax battle for a new standard in home video. Some digital video disk (DVD) recorders allow a disk to be recorded only once. Many do not play disks recorded on other machines. Philips and Pioneer will have new DVD machines in the shops. Sony claims its all-compatible machine will be available in the summer. Until there is a clear standard, consumers will be reluctant to buy.

FINANCIAL SERVICES

The new currency takes hold
Bonds issued in euros, $bn

Year	Value
1999	487
2000	471
2001	512
2002	550

Source: Thompson Financial Securities Data, *The World in 2002*

Investment banks suddenly look vulnerable. Their underwriting and M&A business will take time to recover from the slump. And they will also have to deal with new competitors. With access to savings deposits, universal banks can afford to offer cheap-rate loans to corporate clients. With such enticements, they will steal traditional investment business. In 2002, investment banks will fight back. Expect them to follow Morgan Stanley and funnel money into lending and acquiring small commercial banks. It will cut profits—lending is a small-margins business—but it will aid survival in the lean times.

With funding sources dry, the IPO market moribund and no one interested in trade sales, venture capitalists will have a bad 2002. America's 3,000-odd venture-capital firms will consolidate with abandon, leaving only a dozen or so large companies. They also will have to be more realistic about how profitable they really are. Returns in the 1990s averaged 13.4%, only marginally more than the 12.1% provided by an investment in publicly traded shares.

NASDAQ wanted to link up its European and Asian boards with its American operation in 2003. But NASDAQ Japan and NASDAQ Europe have faltered with the meltdown in tech stocks. New chairman, Hardwick "Wick" Simmons, will establish a common clearing and settlement system in 2002 but the "global exchange" project will take longer than expected. The year will also see renewed activity in consolidating European exchanges. It is unclear whether the London Stock Exchange will acquire or be acquired.

Corporate bond markets in Europe will not do too badly. European companies will move towards an American-style liability structure; less bank loans, more debt. An easing of interest rates will give the sector a further boost.

How much capital should banks put aside to cover their risks? Basel 2, a framework to answer this tricky question, should have been agreed by the end of 2001. Odds are, however, that disagreements and horse-trading will continue into

2002, postponing the implementation that was planned for 2004. Banks are critical of the Basel Committee's proposals. Insurers hope that one day banks will buy insurance policies to cover all their risks.

To watch
Rich people. The world has 425 dollar billionaires, 269 in America. 7.2m millionaires control about a third of the world's wealth. These high net-worth individuals own $27trn, and that pool will grow 8% a year. Private banking will grow with it. The nouveau riche like to shop around so there is competition for business. Fees will drop but private banking will remain exclusive. You will need investible assets of $5m before you get special treatment. Having between $250,000 and $5m just makes you one of the "mass affluent".

HEALTH CARE

Only 15% of Americans say they have a great deal of confidence in their health-management organisations. Electricity companies (which deliver blackouts) enjoy double that level of support. Such loathing will help the Democrats drive through radical changes to America's health-care system. With a patients' bill of rights already on the statute books, they will push for subsidised drugs for the elderly, free health-care coverage for uninsured children and a reduction in the age of eligibility for Medicare.

Just lie down
Hospital beds per 1,000 people

Japan	16.5
Norway	14.2
Netherlands	11.3
Hungary	8.1
United Kingdom	4.0
United States	3.4

Source: OECD, *The World in 2002*

INSURANCE

American property and casualty insurers will enjoy stronger premiums in 2002. But costs will rise too. Car insurers will report rising medical and legal costs. European insurers wanting to enter the United States will target life business.

Everything was going so well for Lloyd's, London's venerable insurance market. They were hoping to be profitable in 2002, for the first time in years. But after September 11th 2001, the market was left facing $30bn of losses.

In Britain, stakeholder pensions—which cap fees to 1% of funds under management—started selling in 2001. Good news for those with modest earnings, but not for insurers; they will not make any money from them until 2010. With take-up disappointing, and with private-pension provision still insufficient, the government is likely to get tougher. Employer contributions to private-pension schemes may become compulsory, with the cost offset through tax-cuts. Where Britain goes, there follows the rest of Europe.

India and China will be the big growth stories for the 2000s. India, where foreign insurers can hold 26% stakes in joint ventures, will have a market worth $33bn-39bn in premiums by 2010. With one of the world's lowest insurance penetrations, some 0.3% of GDP compared with 7% in developed markets, there is plenty of room for growth.

TELECOMMUNICATIONS

The revolution takes another step forward, but with fewer breathlessly optimistic devotees. The likelihood is that, like 19th-century railroads, telecoms will be valuable for the economy but not for its investors.

Broadband, technology that allows fast Internet access, is already here; it's just unevenly distributed. South Korea leads. It has 9.2 broadband connections per 100 inhabitants. America has only 2.25, Luddite Britain 0.08. There are two types of broadband links; digital subscriber lines (DSL), an upgrade on the telephone wire, and cable. Roll-out of both has been blocked by poor regulation and incumbents. The good news is that competition will start to bite in 2002. The number of DSL lines will grow 50-100% in many European countries.

New technology will bring more data and acronyms to your mobile. Japan's DoCoMo will iron out problems with FOMA, its new third-generation (3G) mobile phone service introduced in late 2001. 3G UMTS (Universal Mobile Telephone System) will start in Europe. It will take over from GSM (Global System for Mobile Telephony), and GPRS, so-called 2.5G, which added fancier software to the GSM backbone. By sending data in packets, UMTS will allow web pages to be downloaded at 50kbps. But UMTS will not generate revenues until at least 2005, a delay which will cause pain for indebted telecoms firms. American firms dodged the debt bullet that came with Europe's 3G bandwidth auctions in 2000-01. They will use a different 3G technology known as CDMA 2000 (Complex Division Multiple Access), incompatible with Europe's UMTS and learn from the mistakes of the Japanese and Europeans. Sprint will

launch 2.5G services in the United States in 2002. If CDMA is successful, the United States will not continue to lag behind Europe in mobile technology.

The nightmare for telecoms firms is that 3G will be caught in a squeeze. 2.5G technologies already allow data to be transmitted at speed. New technologies such as 802.11b, which links laptops to office networks at high speeds, will also diminish demand. Whisper it softly, but 3G's big selling point—video on the move—may not be a killer application.

Nearing saturation
% of population with mobile phones

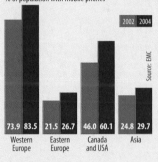

2002 2004

Source: EMC

Region	2002	2004
Western Europe	73.9	83.5
Eastern Europe	21.5	26.7
Canada and USA	46.0	60.1
Asia	24.8	29.7

To watch
Messages. By 2004, the world will be sending 82bn text messages a year. America will catch the trend too. Only 36% of young Americans currently own mobiles, compared with 77% in Britain. By 2005, that will rise to 75%.

TRAVEL

The European online travel market will soar from $2.9m in sales in 2000 to $11bn in 2002, thanks to more web access and improved online-payment systems. Airlines take half of all online ticket sales, but this will decline as tailor-made holidays offered by independent agencies become more popular. Opodo, an online travel service backed by nine European airlines, and its American equivalent, Orbitz, will fight back.

The United States is the world's most visited country. China will be in 2020. In the same year, Japanese tourists to America will outnumber those from Canada and Mexico.

The tourist economy
% of GDP

Nigeria	2.0
China	9.7
United States	11.6
France	12.0
United Kingdom	12.2
Anguilla	87.6

Source: World Travel & Tourism Council

A global briefing needn't cost the earth.

Subscribe to The Economist and save 50% on the normal subscription price.

Includes FREE access to www.economist.com with online Library

✂

Subscription Invitation
Introductory offer to new subscribers

☑ **YES.** I would like to subscribe to *The Economist* and **save 50%** on the normal subscription price.

☐ Mr ☐ Mrs ☐ Miss ☐ Ms ☐ Other title

Initials _____ Surname _____

Job title _____

Company _____

Address _____

_____

Country _____

Telephone _____

Fax _____

E-mail _____

Prices One year – **Save 50%** of the Subscription Price

		Local currency	€			Local currency	€
Austria	Asch	1,128	82.00	Netherlands	FL	181	82.00
Belgium/Luxembourg	BF	3,308	82.00	Norway	NKR	619	–
Denmark	DKR	677	–	Portugal	Esc	14,234	71.00
Finland	FiM	461	77.50	Spain	Pts	11,813	71.00
France	FF	538	82.00	Sweden	SKR	655	–
Germany	DM	160	82.00	Switzerland	SF	154	–
Irish Republic	I£	57	72.50	Other Europe	£ St	46	–
Italy	Lire	140,380	72.50				

Payment options

☐ **Cheque** enclosed, payable to The Economist Newspaper Ltd.
Local currency cheques accepted

☐ **Credit/Debit Card**   ☐ American Express   ☐ Diners Club
                              ☐ Eurocard/Mastercard   ☐ Visa

Card number ☐☐☐☐ ☐☐☐☐ ☐☐☐☐ ☐☐☐☐ ☐☐☐☐

Signature _____   Valid until _____

☐ Invoice me   ☐ Invoice my company

VAT No (if in EC) _____

(Only subscribers registered for VAT may deduct VAT at the local rate from their payments.)

The Economist Newspaper Ltd may wish to use your personal information to contact you with details of offers and products which we think may be of interest to you and/or for the purpose of market research. Please tick the box if you would prefer not to be contacted for these purposes by: ☐ The Economist Group and/or ☐ Other organisations selected by us.
Please allow up to 28 days for your order to be processed. **Offer closes: 31st March 2002**

To subscribe today

 Fax this form on:
+ 44 (0)1444 475647

 Credit card Hotline:
+ 44 (0)1622 778111
Quoting reference: **M172A**

 Email us at: **economist.subs@qss-uk.com**

 Or, post this form to:
**The Economist Newspaper Ltd,
PO Box 471, Haywards Heath,
RH16 3GY, UK.**

YOU COULD PREPARE YOUR COMPANY FOR TOMORROW

BY HIRING A 'CALIFORNIAN FUTUROLOGIST'

Or you could face the future confidently with a scaleable network from BT.
Networks that can grow instantly and are the choice of 18 of the U.K.'s 20 major banks.
To find out more **Freefone 0800 800 997** or connect to **BT.com/business**

BT Business. Connections that get results. **BT**

Business and management

Hail to the chief executive

Edward Carr

Nobody said 2002 was going to be simple: but did it have to be this hard? Chief executives who cut their teeth in the exuberant bull market will be grappling with redundancies, stagnant profits, low share prices, tight capital markets and international tension, as well as the relentless technological and managerial demands that kept them awake at night in the 1990s. But they should not despair. For, in one important respect, their jobs have just got much easier.

The paradox of the bull market was that as stockmarkets rose, chief executives became less secure. According to Challenger, Gray & Christmas, a recruitment consultancy, senior managers last an average of only 4.7 years in the job. That compares with eight years in 1991, when the economy was last in recession. Much of this management churn is concentrated on the chief executive. Rakesh Khurana, of the Sloan School of Management, has found that chief executives appointed after 1985 are more than three times as likely to be fired as those who took the job before it.

The downturn will throw this trend into reverse. Fifty-seven American chief executives left their companies in August 2000, only half as many as departed in August 1999. This was the third time in four months that the number of departures was lower than it had been a year earlier. Companies have suddenly begun to question whether the chief executive really is at fault when things go wrong.

Will this prove only a reprieve, or will the chief executive's chair become permanently more secure? For an answer, look first at why chief executives depart before the date shown at the bottom of their contracts. A share of the departures is inextricably linked to the business cycle. When two firms merge there is room for only one chief executive. As the bull market charged ahead, so did the volume of deals; when it died, the deals by and large died too. You can be sure that, as night follows day, the deal-makers will return and executives will once again merge themselves out of a job.

However, a second—secular—trend is harder to predict. Perhaps running a company has simply become too hard for one person to do alone. Accenture, a consultancy, has drawn up a list of 14 qualities, such as "personal mastery" and "living the values", that the consultancy believes leaders of the future will need—and that only a superhuman could possess. A chief proponent

The chief executive meets the shareholders

of this "too big for one person" theory is Jeffrey Garten, dean of Yale School of Management. In his book "The Mind of the CEO" he explains: "I believe historians will conclude that the pressures of the era have proved much greater than anything most of these leaders could surmount. As a group, global CEOs will be seen as captains of small ships in turbulent seas—rarely able to chart a steady course and to maintain control of their own fate."

Today's chief executives are often appointed in their late 30s or early 40s, and have probably risen through a single function, such as finance, or sales. Anonymous interviews with chief executives confirm their unease. Thirty told a study by part of Ogilvy & Mather, an advertising agency, that they were troubled not by doubts

2002
Weak global economic demand and pressure from the American administration will mean the price of oil will struggle to reach OPEC's target of $25 a barrel.

Edward Carr:
editor, Inside Track,
Financial Times

about their company, but about their own performance. They felt constrained by the bureaucracy of head office. Some confessed they had been persuaded to take decisions that went against their instincts.

The chief executives themselves are partly to blame for their predicament. Ever since Lee Iaccoca became a celebrity manager (for writing an autobiography and saving Chrysler, in that order), the world's great corporate bureaucracies have succumbed to the cult of the individual. General Electric has 313,000 employees in more than 100 countries. But the world puts most of its success down to only one of them. Executives behave as if they have become brands in themselves, managing "Me, Inc" as assiduously as they manage the fourth-quarter sales.

Because chief executives have been so keen to claim the credit, they have inevitably caught the blame. And there is plenty of blame to go round. Once composed of the chief executive's golfing partners and his dentist, the board is now more sensitive to investors' unhappiness and the growing threat of shareholders' lawsuits.

When boards feel they have to be seen to act, the chief executive is often the first to be shown the door. However, in a downturn, "action" means cutting thousands of jobs on the shop floor, instead of one on the top floor. Indeed, sacking the boss suddenly smacks of panic. Whether this endures in the upturn depends on which is the most po-

tent, economic efficiency or the appetite for drama.

Sacking the boss is often a poor remedy for a company's woes. Total shareholder returns in most of the companies examined by three consultants from McKinsey fell when a new person arrived. Jack Welch, who spent 20 years at the top of GE, has argued that it takes a decade for a chief executive to make his mark. In other words, the company that succeeds is the company that appoints the right chief executive, not the company that sacks the wrong one. And this suggests the need for boards that know how to find a chief executive as well as how to watch the share price. Warren Bennis and James O'Toole, at the University of Southern California, offer a guide: the board should be of one mind, look beyond the obvious candidates, take its time and resist the temptation to hand the search over to professional headhunters.

However, there is something unconvincing in the idea that the world's largest companies will be run by self-effacing team players, eager to remain in the same job for a decade or so. Most chief executives thrive on risk; they have big egos and ambitions to match. If the prize is glory, they will try to seize it, despite the danger of failure. Meanwhile, boards need chief executives as scapegoats; and the media and the analysts who conspire in their ascent also relish their fall. Chief executives should enjoy their brief moment of security in 2002 while it lasts. □

2002

The world's largest pumping station starts up in Egypt. It will take water from Lake Nasser to irrigate 560,000 acres of desert.

Something to change your life

Tom Standage

Tom Standage:
technology
correspondent,
The Economist

A new technology will arrive in your office, and perhaps your home, in 2002 that will change the way you communicate. The technology has a terrible name: 802.11b. It is also known as "wireless Ethernet" or "Wi-Fi". But don't make the mistake of thinking that this is merely something for geeks. It isn't. It will become as much a part of your life as has the fax, the Internet and the mobile phone. 802.11b took

off in America in 2001, and is spreading fast, with hardware sales growing by around 40% a year. To set up an 802.11b network in your home or office, you simply buy a base station, plug it into a phone socket or a high-speed Internet connection, and hang it on a wall. Using unlicensed radio spectrum, the base station then communicates with computers within 45 metres (150 feet) or so, provided they are equipped with suitable plug-in cards.

In effect, 802.11b lets you flood a building with wireless connectivity. This has a number of advantages: it is often cheaper and easier to link several PCs together wirelessly than it is to run cables all over the place. And if the PCs in question are laptops, they can be picked up and carried around, still connected to the Internet.

Offices and university campuses have been quick to adopt the technology, since it allows users to remain connected, exchange files, and have information at their fingertips during meetings and seminars. 802.11b "hotspots" providing free access have sprung up in airport lounges, hotels and coffee shops. Scandinavian Airlines is testing the technology as a convenient way to provide Internet access on aeroplanes, without the need to run cables to every seat. In major cities including San Francisco, London and Seattle, enthusiasts are building "guerrilla networks", also

High-flying Wi-Fi
Worldwide sales of 802.11b
m

○ Network interface cards

○ Access points
(including gateways)

5
4
3
2
1
0

2000   2001   2002

Sources: Dell'Oro Group, Glasswave

known as "parasitic grids", in an attempt to provide blanket Internet coverage. Firms such as MobileStar in America and Jippii in Europe are doing the same, but on a commercial basis. MobileStar, Starbucks and Microsoft plan to make 802.11b available to paying customers in most of Starbucks' coffee shops by the end of 2002.

802.11b is not perfect. For a start, it has serious security shortcomings: its built-in encryption standard has been proven to be flawed, and tall tales abound of malicious hackers prowling Silicon Valley car parks, looking for wireless networks to attack with their laptops. Another drawback with 802.11b is that it does not allow you to roam from one hotspot to another. But work is under way to fix these problems, and a new version of the standard, called 802.11a, offers improved range and transmission speed, and will become widely available.

As the momentum behind the technology builds, some 802.11 enthusiasts, in America in particular, have suggested that 802.11 eliminates the need for the "third generation" (3G) mobile-phone networks now under construction around the world, which will make possible all kinds of whizzy data services on mobile phones. 802.11 is cheap and works today, whereas 3G is expensive and has yet to materialise. "3G is so far off in the United States that people are looking at 802.11 and saying it's here now, let's deploy it," says Joe Manget at the Boston Consulting Group. Already, 802.11 displays all the hallmarks of a "disruptive" technology—an innovation that unexpectedly spreads like wildfire, and threatens to overturn established ways of doing things. Could it kill 3G?

The answer is no. For a start, 802.11 is designed for use with fully-fledged computers, and transmits data at high speed over short distances. 3G is slower, but was specifically designed to handle a far larger number of users, and to work with small, handheld devices over longer distances. 802.11 is intended to provide coverage in hotspots; 3G is intended to provide blanket coverage. In short, while computer users will happily use 802.11 to access the Internet from their laptops when it is available, they will still need a cellular connection, such as a 3G connection, if they want to roam beyond 802.11 hotspots or make voice calls.

As a result, the technologies are widely seen as complementary, rather than competitive. Many equipment vendors, such as Nokia, Nortel and Ericsson, make both cellular and 802.11 equipment. Tero Ojanpera of Nokia even suggests that the success of 802.11 will drive demand for 3G networks. "Once you get used to wireless data in the office, you start to want it everywhere," he says. Nokia has launched an "operator" version of 802.11b, aimed at existing network operators, which supports subscriptions and billing using technology borrowed from existing cellular networks. And a report from Analysys, a consultancy, backs the idea that mobile-network operators should consider building 802.11 networks alongside their 3G networks. In America, several wireless operators, including AT&T Wireless and Cingular Wireless, are already looking into doing just that. The idea is that your laptop could use 802.11 to access the Internet when you are at the office, switch to 3G while you travel to a conference in a taxi, and then switch back to 802.11 when you enter the conference centre.

This sounds great for laptop-toting business users.

What's your rank?

The world just loves league tables. In 2002 there will be thousands of organisations producing statistics, charts and tables, most of them delightfully bogus. The human development index, produced by the United Nations, has the grandest sweep: it measures nothing less than overall quality of life. In 2002, European countries will dominate, along with Japan, the United States and Australia. It is Canada that will be out in front though, with its people enjoying a fantastic quality of life. African states will fill all of the bottom 20 places. Again.

Money doesn't buy everything though. Sweden is ranked sixth in terms of human development, but only 21st in the league that measures GDP per head. Singapore is eighth in this GDP league but only 24th in the human development one. Then there is the "Who lives longest?" league. Six of the top ten countries are Mediterranean, including relatively poor Greece and Spain. For longer life, sunshine and olive oil would seem to be more important than GDP. Tellingly, the countries that will do best in overall quality of life will be less corrupt and more open than many that have higher levels of wealth. The 20 least corrupt countries, as measured by Transparency International, will also occupy at least 16 of the top 20 places in the UN's index of human development. Down near the bottom of both leagues will be much of the Arab world. To add to their troubles, many will have oppressive governments too. According to Freedom House, only five Arab states will be "partly free" in 2002. All the rest will not be worth ranking at all; they will simply be "not free". □

Mummy says that we're 21st richest, sixth best developed and sixth least corrupt

But what about consumers? Assuming that consumers want to use data services while on the move—and the popularity of text messaging suggests that they do—the mobile-data device of choice is the mobile phone. In 2001, sales of Internet-capable mobile phones are thought to have overtaken sales of PCs for the first time, and outnumbered sales of handheld computers by a factor of ten. The problem is that 802.11 is unsuitable for use in phones, in its current form at least, since it consumes too much power, and does not support voice calls. 3G, on the other hand, has been explicitly designed to support consumer data services.

It is true that 3G is currently unwell, but reports of its death at the hands of 802.11 are premature. While 802.11 is where the action will be in 2002, it will eventually end up working alongside 3G, rather than killing it. □

Our home country.

We don't just travel to the countries where we do business. We live in them – working together with local people to develop, produce and sell our products. In fact, right now there are over 200 countries we call home. Find out more at www.daimlerchrysler.com.

Sir Christopher Bland, chairman of BT, says the telecoms companies have their biggest changes still to come

Flexible phones

"Broadband is the second wave of the communications revolution. It arrives in earnest in 2002"

The communications industry is undergoing a period of rapid evolution. And it is therefore worth remembering what Charles Darwin, the theorist of evolution, meant by "the survival of the fittest": not that the biggest would always win, but the most adaptable. When climates change, organisms adapt or die: and the climate in communications is certain to change dramatically in the year ahead.

It has been changing since the mid-1990s, which saw the end of a long and stable era—before the Internet and wireless technology had hit the mass market, before the full liberalisation of telecoms markets in Europe, Asia and North America and before the development of broadband networks and services.

Since then, the forces of technological innovation and competition have been unleashed, creating turbulence in the industry and dramatic mood swings among investors. At first it seemed that the technology would generate an endless spiral of growth. But now it is clear that while the potential remains enormous, both the economics and the timing are more complex. Broadband infrastructure will need a massive investment. Technological advances such as wave division multiplexing, in which light of different frequencies is sent down the same fibre, have brought down the cost of bandwidth, leaving much of the world's optical fibre unlit and challenging the carriers' economic models.

A new world is being born, but it is not the easy birth that some anticipated. However, in time, the new communications technologies will drive up growth, enhance the quality of individuals' lives, and bring unprecedented efficiency to the private and the public sectors.

Already, the main ex "telcos" are adapting: AT&T, Deutsche Telekom, France Telecom, NTT and BT. The nature of the adaptations vary—spin-offs, de-mergers, acquisitions, financial restructuring—but for all, there has been a similar pattern. Decades of relative stability in the old telecoms world, followed by a frenzy of acquisitions and joint ventures, and now a whirl of restructuring and transformation.

So how will the climate develop in 2002? Watch out for these things:
● the move to a broadband world;
● the convergence of telecoms, IT and broadcasting;
● the role of management in changing the direction and culture of organisations.

Broadband represents the second wave of the communications revolution. It arrives in earnest in 2002. The first was the narrowband wave, which brought mass market uptake of Internet access and mobile telephony, attended by heady growth rates. But inevitably, as market penetration has increased, the growth of subscriptions has begun to plateau.

This makes life more challenging. Network usage is now the goal, rather than subscriptions. Instead of a quest to be the fastest and biggest, there is a race to be different, to provide the most sought-after, personalised applications. And as adoption rates tail off in narrowband, broadband is only just starting to take off.

Demand not supply

For major communications businesses, broadband means giant investments: equipping exchanges with the DSL technology which transforms copper wires into high-speed broadband lines, and building third-generation mobile networks for which the licence fees, never mind the actual infrastructure, have cost over £80 billion ($117 billion) across Europe.

It is a massive undertaking, but one worth pursuing. Broadband brings the ability to access video and audio online with ease, to download large files at speed, and to maintain an "always-on" link with customers or colleagues. There are new entertainment possibilities for consumers and more efficiencies for businesses.

But it is not simply a question of providing the infrastructure. Operators have striven to create the capacity, yet most of it remains untapped. The focus has to shift in 2002 from supply to demand. Increasing broadband uptake will depend upon building compelling content. It will depend on increasing awareness of the benefits, especially among small and medium-sized enterprises. And it will depend on the public and private sectors working in partnership to deliver social goals where commercial logic alone cannot justify the levels of investment required.

The broadband environment is also encouraging the convergence of previously separate sectors. In Britain, for example, BT is competing head to head with cable-television companies, both for telephony and broadband services. BT's lines are being used to channel on-demand news and video to customers. Cables are being used to provide high-speed access to the Internet via a PC. Ex-telcos are competing or collaborating with satellite companies to deliver broadband. The distinctions which matter are no longer the vertical lines between telecoms, broadcasting and publishing, but the horizontal lines between content, network, service provision and equipment.

This has ramifications for policymakers and regulators as well as the commercial players. To evolve, to survive and thrive, companies need to reshape themselves. Positioning in today's communications world is a proactive management choice, not an act of fate. There is no iron law saying that a telecoms company must run fixed and mobile networks, run voice and data services over both, serve every conceivable type of customer, operate nationally and internationally, and create or aggregate content at the same time. The challenge to managements in 2002 is to decide what to do—and what not to do. □

Why wire your world?

...when you can connect it by satellite

We have made global wireless solutions our business for 37 years. In an instant, our satellites across the sky can connect to anyone, anytime, anywhere on earth.

Whether your business needs Internet, corporate networks, worldwide television coverage or voice and data communications, we can provide the solution.

Where the earth meets the sky, Intelsat inspires connections.

- Internet
- Corporate networks
- Broadcast services
- Voice and data transmission

To connect, visit our website at **www.intelsat.com**

When films become franchises

Peter Bart   *Beverly Hills, CA*

Hollywood in 2002 will further explore the question: Why innovate when you can replicate? Sequels like "Rush Hour II" and "American Pie 2" propelled the motion picture industry to record box-office takings in 2001—spurred by rising ticket prices—and the studios stand ready to raise the ante in 2002. Enshrining what may once have been one-shot hits into "franchises" suits the new corporate Hollywood, dominated by behemoths such as Vivendi, Sony, Viacom and News Corp.

The movie business suddenly seems more controllable and marketing-friendly. Of course, sequels can further inflate studio budgets through high talent and production costs—Sony's 2002 release of "Men in Black II" may end up costing more than $140m to produce, with another $60m required for opening ads—but the rationale is that "franchise" movies will at the very least generate a banner during the first weekend. Whether business will hold up beyond this is open to question.

The studios learned in 2001 that limited shelf life was now a fact of life, a trend that will become more dire in 2002. Movies like "Jurassic Park III" produced first week totals ranging up to $70m in the United States only to plummet by over 50% by the second weekend. Studios have to burn millions of dollars on their film launches, circulating as many as 5,000 prints to the nation's multiplexes, because by week two another wannabe blockbuster will push them aside.

As a result, the once-cosy relationship between distributor and exhibitor will be put into further disarray in 2002. Cinema owners, their balance sheets already troubled because of over-building, depend for their profit on longer-running films. Their piece of the pie may be as little as 10% to 20% of the box-office takings during the first weekend, but that share grows to as much as 60% if the movie "holds". Such holds will be increasingly rare.

In the era when a film like "ET" would remain atop the charts worldwide for ten or more weeks, Hollywood focused on creating broad-based "audience pictures" that appealed to a wide demographic spectrum. Given the evanescence of film making circa 2002, however, distributors will target movies for specific sections of American society. The 2002 screening of "American Pie 3" will be aimed at teens and the young date crowd, while "Rush Hour III" will look towards urbanites who like action and special effects.

Global entertainment companies will set the pace of change in 2002. Viacom has been especially aggressive in force-feeding cross-promotions between its films, television and MTV divisions. The overlap between film and the burgeoning universe of video games will become a stronger lure to these companies. But not without risks. Viacom's film "Lara Croft: Tomb Raider" brought in over $250m worldwide, but Sony's "Final Fantasy" served as a reminder that the PlayStation and the multiplex do not necessarily overlap.

While the United States has been slow to advance the cause of broadband or digital TV, 2002 will finally see an acceleration. The long-awaited roll-out of video on demand also will have an impact within the United States, as studios explore new ways to combat the market dominance of Blockbuster in the video retail business. Given their weak advertising sales, the networks will cut back on talent costs in 2002 and will be forced to engineer exceedingly complex deals in acquiring motion-picture rights. The model may resemble MGM's deal for its hit, "Legally Blonde", when late in 2001 the studio managed to sell successive runs on the Fox Network, TNT and Comedy Central—three separate deals where a single, far richer one formerly prevailed.

Since advertising drives the media economy, the big guessing game in 2002 will focus on how quickly a recovery may take place. Advertisers may not loosen their purse strings in 2002 until they are completely persuaded that a significant economic recovery is taking place. Once budgets are cut, corporate committees are slow to restore them. So expect more low-budget reality shows, less hour-long drama and fewer movies. Though entertainment in the past has been oblivious to economic downturns—during the Great Depression the highest paid executive in America was MGM's Louis B. Mayer—that will prove not to be the case in 2002.

One media investment banking firm, Veronis Suhler, estimates that the entertainment industry's compound annual growth for the next five years will be a good 30% lower than for the previous five-year period. Here and there technology may provide a sudden blip. The DVD may create an instant impetus for the video industry, provided issues of pricing can be hammered out. Certainly new technology such as Napster has utterly confused the music industry and will continue to do so through 2002. Arguably the only corner of the entertainment economy that will be predictable is that of interactive entertainment, where all indicators point straight down. In a world of double-digit expectations, the dotcomers may help their brethren in the entertainment industry relate to a new era of single-digit reality. □

Peter Bart: editor in chief, *Variety* magazine

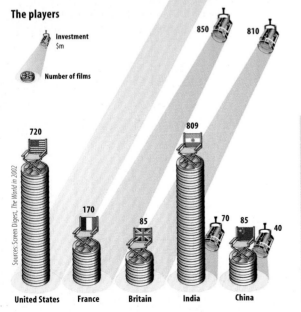

The players

Investment $m

Number of films

9,500

850   810

720   170   809   85   70   85   40

United States   France   Britain   India   China

Sources: Screen Digest, *The World in 2002*

2002

"Scooby-Doo" and "Spider-Man" hit the big screen. A sequel, "Men In Black II", a sequel to a sequel, "Terminator III", and a sequel to a prequel, "Star Wars II", will share the box office takings.

Get your gadgets here

Nicholas Valéry

Once Palm Computing owned the market for personal digital assistants (PDAS). Its neat palm-sized PDA—with its nifty handwriting software, electronic diary, address book, to-do list, calculator and memo pad—was the gizmo of choice for techno-trendsetters everywhere.

No longer. The iPaq H3670 from Compaq has relegated the Palm, along with clones from Sony and Handspring, to the bottom draw. Three design features have contributed to the iPaq's runaway success. The first is its brilliant back-lit screen, which displays images with a full 65,000 colours. The second is its speedy StrongARM microprocessor from Intel. Breezing along at 206 megahertz (MHZ) compared with the Palm's pedestrian 33MHZ, the iPaq never skips a beat. The third is the sheer amount of memory—a walloping 64 megabytes compared with Palm's eight.

But the thing that makes the iPaq a hands-down winner is its use of Microsoft's Pocket PC operating system. With all the look and feel of its Windows big brother, this runs stripped-down versions of all the popular applications (Word, Excel, Power Point, Access and Outlook) that have made Microsoft Office the standard throughout the world. The iPaq can even double as a tape recorder, an e-book reader, and an MP3 "Walkman". Retail price: $649.

Forget Razor scooters and their lookalikes—they're kids' stuff. Real men ride Citybugs. With its 24-volt battery and built-in computer to monitor the battery charge and automatically cut out when the brakes are applied, the Citybug will zip along silently at 14mph and travel for up to 15 miles before needing a recharge. Plugged back into the mains, it is ready to go again within four hours. At $599, the Citybug is not the cheapest electric scooter on the market, but it is one of the cleverest and most comfortable.

When digital video disc (DVD) players hit the market six years ago, the recordable versions were supposed to be only a year or so away—spelling an end to the era for the video cassette recorder (VCR) and its bulky old tape cassettes. Not only were DVDs slimmer, easier to store and offered a vastly better picture than VCR cassettes, users could jump from track to track in a trice instead of having to rewind or fast-forward a tape that would soon jam or snap. Even without any recording facilities, DVD players have still been a great success. Some 20m were sold around the world in 2000, taking a serious bite out of the VCR market (now down to 60m units a year). In 2002, more DVD players are expected to be sold than VCRs.

So, what ever happened to the recordable DVD machines? The answer is that they were sneaked on to the Japanese market two years ago—to shake the bugs out of them. But Japanese manufacturers did not learn any lessons from the bloody VHS versus Betamax battle they fought over video-recording standards in the late 1970s. This time there are no less than three competing standards.

The Matsushita camp, whose VHS won the previous video battle, has backed DVD-RAM. Together with Toshiba and Hitachi, Matsushita all but got its standard adopted by the whole industry until Sony proposed an alternative called DVD+RW and Pioneer went its own way with DVD-RW. The manufacturers point out that, no matter which video-recording standard they use, all DVD recorders have no trouble playing back pre-recorded DVDs bought or rented from a store. What they do not say is that their recorders do not play back DVDs recorded on a different type of machine.

Which to plump for? In terms of picture quality, there is nothing to choose. The Sony camp's DVD+RW has collected powerful backers in the shape of Philips and Hewlett-Packard. Gadget freaks and other early adopters rarely bother about such things. These customers buy the best and the brightest now, cheerfully replacing it when a better one comes along. In Europe, the machine of choice is currently the Philips DVDR 1000 which sells for around $1,500, excluding tax.

Meanwhile, Matsushita is in the process of launching models designed specifically for America and Europe. And Sony plans to launch a dual-format recorder in the United States and Europe sometime later in 2002. None of these will cost less than $1,000 initially, but prices will quickly tumble. Expect also to pay around $20 to $25 apiece for recordable discs.

And, finally, for the man who has everything—the Gulfstream jet, the Hobart racing yacht, the McLaren sports car—watch out for the ultimate in digital photography: the Hasselblad Dfinity. Where the best of the rest of the digital cameras boast three or four mega-pixels (that is, 3m or 4m picture elements per frame), the Dfinity delivers a staggering 16.8m pixels. Pin-sharp does not begin to describe this camera's awesome resolving power.

The key is a light-sensing chip unlike any other. In designing the chip, engineers at a young Silicon Valley firm called Foveon rejected the conventional CCD (charge-coupled device) technology employed in other digital cameras for the CMOS (complementary metal-oxide semiconductor) approach used to make computer memories and microprocessors. That way they could take advantage of the enormous improvements made over the years in packing millions of memory cells into CMOS chips. Much clunkier CCD devices, by comparison, hail from the dark ages of chip making some four generations ago.

More intriguing still, the Dfinity's light-sensing chip is not even digital. It is actually an analog chip. Instead of building a blocky image using the ones and zeroes of binary digits, Foveon's analog chip imitates the way the human eye works, taking advantage of the biological short-cuts that nature has learned over millions of years of evolution. Needless to say, the new Dfinity has all the bells and whistles beloved by professional photographers. It takes Canon's standard L-series lenses, has an electronic shutter with speeds from two seconds up to an 8,000th of a second, and packs a socket for a fast cable connection (IEEE 1394) to offload the huge 16.8 mega-pixel pictures from the camera to a laptop. How much? Well, as they say, if you have to ask... □

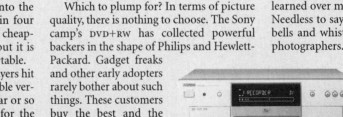

Nicholas Valéry: editor, *The Economist* Technology Quarterly

[hp photosmart 715 digital camera]

Film. Man, the 1900s were fun.

Presenting digital photography's leap from infancy to adulthood. Pictures are artfully
captured with the help of hp's remarkable technology, by mimicking
the most sophisticated lens of all: the human eye. For more information on our entire
collection of digital imaging products, visit www.hp.com

[hp pavilion home PC]

[hp photosmart p100 printer]

[hp psc 950 printer/scanner/copier/fax]

® invent

hp PCs use genuine Microsoft® Windows® www.microsoft.com/piracy/howtotell
Some of the products/models featured in this advertisement are only available in certain countries.
For further product details, please visit www.hp.com

2002

Another link is forged in Asia's energy grid as Malaysia starts importing gas from Indonesia's West Natuna field. Indonesia has 158 trillion cubic feet of gas reserves, and wants to sell to India and China.

Fly me, I'm desperate

Iain Carson

Air travel will begin to bottom out during 2002 in the depression caused by the economic downturn and the aftermath of the terrorist attacks in New York and Washington. The year will also see the rise and rise of low-cost airlines in America and Europe. They will even spread to Australasia.

Before the terrorist attacks, airlines in America were headed for a loss of about $3 billion in 2001; they will have finished the year with losses of up to $10 billion. The federal bail-out of $15 billion will allow most to stagger on, but in the first half of 2002 at least one, and possibly three, American carriers will go bust. Although traffic will recover to near normal levels by the middle of the year, the cash drain in the interim could prove too much for the likes of America West or US Airways. Northwest and Continental are also badly exposed. A full recovery in traffic will take until early 2003 to occur.

In a normal world, as soon as economic clouds gather, companies cut back on business travel; so volume declines, and more business travellers move back into the economy seats from business class. This will be seen throughout 2002.

IN SICKNESS AND IN HEALTH

The airlines that will hold up best in terms of traffic are low-cost, low-fare carriers. Nowadays economy-minded travellers even have the option of opting for the much cheaper flights available on low-cost carriers, such as Southwest and JetBlue in America, easyJet, Go and Ryanair around Europe. Southwest will soon carry more passengers inside America than any of the big airlines. In Europe, the relentless growth of the low-fare carriers is leading them to set up bases in continental Europe. One new airline, Blue Fox, will start low-fare business-class flights across the Atlantic in March.

The volume of air traffic worldwide will fall by around 5% in 2002 before bouncing back dramatically in 2003, with growth of nearly 20%. The revenues that airlines receive for every seat occupied will fall faster. Over

Iain Carson: industry editor, The Economist

the longer term, this is declining at a rate of 1% a year but discounting, to lure back lost passengers, will depress it even further.

The combination of a structural change—the big push of the low-fare airlines—and the conjunctural economic downturn will put huge pressures on the big airlines to change. Consolidation along conventional business lines is not possible because of the regulated nature of air travel. A petty, out-of-date nationalism will do economic harm. It is nearly impossible for one nation's "flag carrier" to take over another. And no airline can operate freely in a country that is not its own. Theoretically this does leave some scope for consolidation within the two biggest aviation markets, America and Europe.

In America the scene was set for considerable consolidation when United Airlines launched an agreed bid for US Airways in May 2000, followed seven months later by another deal whereby American Airlines would rescue the ailing TWA, while taking over the bits of US Airways that United thought it wise to divest in order to placate the antitrust authorities in Washington. In the event, the regulators blocked the United deal tout court, and American waltzed off merrily with TWA to become the largest airline in the world.

In Europe, consolidation was supposed to follow Swissair's bold expansion in which it took a stake in Belgium's Sabena and bought shares in several smaller French carriers. That turned to dust because all the airlines Swissair bought proved to be severe cash drains. In the event both Swissair and Sabena went bust. They will re-emerge from bankruptcy much diminished, if at all. Similarly, plans by British Airways (BA) to hook up with KLM Royal Dutch Airlines came to naught.

So does this mean consolidation is out of the question in 2002? Far from it. Expect BA and KLM to try again, and in America, something will have to be done about US Airways. Delta and Continental will merge, while United might acquire Northwest. Regulators will smile on such deals. Meanwhile the old saga of BA and American Airlines trying to pool their transatlantic businesses is back in fashion. They have two hurdles to clear: one is assuaging fears in Europe that a combination, which would give them 60% of traffic on some key routes, would not be anti-competitive. The other is the creation of an open-skies agreement between Britain and America, without which Washington will never allow the two airlines the antitrust immunity they need to pool services, fares and revenues. If the airlines do not pull off their deal quickly they will find that Britain will soon lose the ability to negotiate such deals, as the European Commission wins the right early in 2002 to handle air agreements for the EU as a whole.

The other big change is in the use of the Internet. The low-fare carriers are leading the way in using the Internet to cut distribution costs. The established airlines are moving fast too, with their joint online booking services such as Orbitz and its European equivalent, to prevent too much of the distribution side of air travel slipping away to non-airline online agencies such as Expedia. The aviation business (with its perishable product, seats on a flight) and the Internet (with its instantaneous information flow) were made for each other. This will be the year when the two learn how to live together. □

THE INDUSTRY STANDARD HAS JUST GONE UP.
THE INTEL® PENTIUM® 4 PROCESSOR.

Back in 1965, Intel founder Gordon Moore predicted the number of transistors on a chip would double every 18 months. Guess who's just broken "Moore's Law"? Gordon Moore's company. Intel continues to lead the industry, breaking down barriers in chip performance and developing and defining new technologies. But at 2 GHz (and with 42 million transistors) the Intel® Pentium® 4 processor is so far ahead, even we're not sure we can beat it. Find out more at www.intel.co.uk/4

Single currency, many prices

Daniel Franklin

Remember Europe's single-market project? The EU's internal frontier-free market was officially "completed" in 1992. Trade barriers did indeed come down. But a decade on, the EU market is still far from seamless. Now, some hope, the euro will finish the job: a single currency for a truly single market. Will it?

The fragmentation of the EU marketplace is reflected in its prices. Survey after survey shows that prices can vary hugely across the EU. One study of 53 products in the euro area revealed an average price differential of 24%. A poll of European marketing directors showed an average variation of 80% between companies' highest and lowest price points. In Portugal, normally one of Europe's cheapest countries, researchers found the price of salt to be 12 times higher than in Italy.

The euro is meant to change this. When euro-cash arrives in 2002, price comparisons will become thoroughly

ent countries, making comparisons between their prices all but impossible.

For many products, the sheer variety of models complicates comparisons. Take the humble fishing reel. A single manufacturer, Abu-Garcia, makes 53 models of just one type of reel. Since local preferences and conditions abound in Europe, strict product standardisation is often ruled out. Southern Europeans tend to have narrower feet than northerners, so shoes have to be tailored accordingly. Spaniards are used to washing machines with lower spin speeds than elsewhere in Europe. Germans like built-in fridge-freezers, whereas Britons prefer free-standing models with the freezer at the bottom (and the French like free-standers with the freezer at the top). And so on, from kettles to cookers.

Suppose you manage to find some really comparable products: a certain CD, say, or a particular golf ball. Two

One market, many prices
Price, €

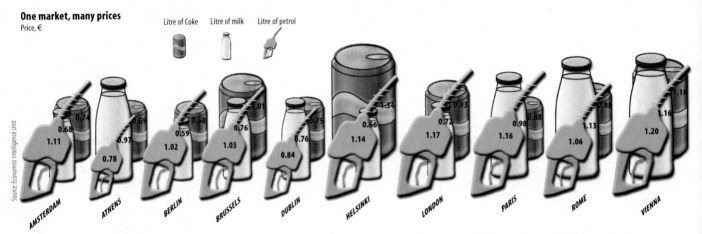

Litre of Coke   Litre of milk   Litre of petrol

AMSTERDAM ATHENS BERLIN BRUSSELS DUBLIN HELSINKI LONDON PARIS ROME VIENNA

Source: Economist Intelligence Unit

transparent, at least in the 12 euro-zone countries. From Athens to Dublin, fussy consumers will be able to shop around for the best bargains far more easily. Market pressures—helped where necessary by government regulators—will make prices converge. Or so the theory goes.

The reality will be more complicated. Yes, the euro removes one difficulty in cross-country comparisons. But plenty of others remain. When the Economist Intelligence Unit was asked recently to select some identical branded consumer goods available in several countries, so that prices could be compared, this proved surprisingly tricky. For many products, purely local brands dominate: a pan-European T-shirt, for example, barely exists. Even where trans-national brands can be identified, comparing like with like across countries is extraordinarily complicated.

Local colour

One problem is that manufacturers change product specifications from country to country. Bicycles with the same model number use different components. The "same" Adidas trainer may turn out to be a slightly different version, with subtle alterations of tread, shape or composition. Panasonic says each of its microwave models is manufactured to a different specification for differ-

things can still frustrate straightforward price comparisons. First, the packaging may differ. How many golf balls are sold per pack? Does the CD include a "bonus track" (the sort that can add 50% to the price in Britain)? Second, the distribution channels can change the picture. In France, for example, the main channel for sales of audio products, televisions and videos is hypermarkets, whereas in Germany sales are mainly through specialist stores; although they are costlier, Germans often prefer these shops because of their quality of service. If all this was not complicated enough, there are still many other fiddly factors that influence prices: different seasons between north and south, different tax rates, the timing of sales and stock-clearance, the distance from manufacturer to retailer.

The euro will help, but just a bit. The prices of some products—simple things like petrol and milk, or fairly standardised trans-national goods like IKEA furniture, Zara clothes, Big Macs and, of course, *The Economist*—will be easy to compare across the euro zone, and should converge toward a European standard. But these will be the exceptions. Producers will still have a whole arsenal of ways of making distinctions, and keeping price differences, between countries. Europeanisation, let alone globalisation, has a long way to go yet. □

2002

Another nail in the coffin of geography. New broadband technology allows real time, DVD picture quality video-conferencing. The market will quadruple in value to $8 billion by 2006.

Daniel Franklin: editorial director, Economist Intelligence Unit

EXPERIENCE AND INNOVATION POWER

Understanding and consistently enhancing leading-edge technologies. Experience and perfect teamwork. And the unreserved desire to achieve the extraordinary, time and again. In both racing and private banking, these are the vital factors for long-term success. For now and in the future. Contact us and you will soon be on the winning side. **www.cspb.com**

CREDIT SUISSE | PRIVATE BANKING   IT'S TIME FOR AN EXPERT.

Finance and economics

Just a whisper of recovery

When nerves recover

Hamish McRae

> **2002**
>
> Expect a record level of corporate debt defaults in America. Probably some $150 billion, and more in 2003. Don't expect to recover a jot: in a downturn, there are few buyers at asset auctions.

Hamish McRae:
associate editor of
The Independent

The valley of 2001 was deeper and darker than anyone could have imagined. The financial markets marched through it, trying to explain to themselves the inexplicable, and were towards the end of 2001 beginning to recover some of their sense of order. But the composure is fragile. It will remain so through 2002.

The light that the markets hope to see in front of them will be a secure, sustainable and profitable recovery in the world's major economies. Since this looks like being a synchronised downturn they will look for a synchronised recovery too. Once they are confident that recovery is secure, they will stop fretting about the deeper-than-expected valley and be prepared to scale the uplands. But they may experience some false starts. A recovery that seems secure in, say, the summer may stutter out in the autumn. And it may not be synchronised after all, as some countries are held back by structural problems and weak consumer confidence, and will struggle to crank up growth.

Once the "when?" question is answered, the markets will move on to the "what sort?" one. They have to figure out whether we are at the early stages of another long boom, akin to the 1990s version, or whether there will be several years of somewhat disappointing growth, though associated with virtually no inflation. They will have to judge whether the burst of public spending in response to September 11th supports long-term growth, or whether, however necessary it may be, undermines it. They will have to reach some sort of conclusion about the different responses to the crisis by Alan Greenspan, Wim Duisenburg and other central bank chairmen—a judgment complicated by the arrival of the physical euro, not just the theoretical one. Above all, they will try to understand what makes consumers tick: will Americans go back to their hard-spending ways and what might make Japanese and Germans loosen up?

That is a lot of imponderables but ponder the markets must. Expect that by the end of 2002 they will be confident about the durability of the recovery but less sure of the longer-term growth of the world economy. Once companies start to show some growth in earnings, the markets can start making sensible calculations as to the appropriate price/earnings ratios to trade their stocks. But they will find it hard to sell their views to increasingly sceptical investors. The investment community has been deeply wounded by the poor quality of advice it received during the past two years.

Expect the year to divide into two halves. The first half will be spent watching, waiting and learning. Investors will want secure signs of recovery, not just promises. Equities may perform quite well but these will be dangerous days. Any sign that the recovery is delayed, or insecure, will cause a disproportionate reaction. The exchanges will make their first real judgments on the euro. More important, European consumers will make their judgment on it. Expect the first few months to be twitchy and tough.

The second half of the year will be different. This will be long-haul time. The markets should be catching a feel for the answers to the imponderables noted above. If concerns about personal and national security are assuaged, then consumers should be starting to recover their cool. Do not expect them to be buoyant, though, until they are a little surer of their jobs. If governments are cautious in their spending and do not use this emergency to over-commit themselves, expect the benign low inflation, low interest rate environment to be sustained. As demand picks up, the slimmed-down corporations will start to post a recovery in earnings. If there are no serious policy mistakes by governments or central banks, the world will look much brighter. Even those dismal Japanese markets could lighten up.

For equities those are a lot of "ifs". A sensible hope (it can be no more) is that equity markets in general will by the end of 2002 have recovered any ground lost during 2000 and 2001 and will have a secure base to go forward. But this will not have meant two wasted years. They were two years when lessons needed to be learnt. Expect the American and British equity markets to improve in line with earnings; expect continental European equities to reflect the success (or otherwise) of the euro. And expect, at last, a better year for Japan's investors.

For bonds the key is whether governments will now feel they have a licence to spend. The markets will wear some rise in fiscal deficits—this is a time when the world needs secure, well-funded national governments—but if they feel their respect is being abused, then watch long rates rise. But as investors realise that the world will continue for a while yet, expect spreads to narrow. There will be a recovery in confidence in both junk bonds and emerging-market debt. Bonds will increasingly be analysed as though they were equities, instead of investors forced to rely on formal, rear-view-mirror credit ratings. So some of the great investment opportunities in 2002 will be in bonds.

And currencies? The first big decision will be to think through what a euro is really worth. That decision is a European one, initially taken by European citizens: is this a currency you save or spend? That will affect the European recovery. But in the longer term it is a decision for the world's citizens: has Europe created a real rival for the dollar—or a currency that will weaken the European economies rather than strengthen them? If those decisions go well in the first months of 2002, expect a broad parity for the dollar and the euro. If not, all bets are off. Other currencies? The dollar will remain adequately secure—no crash but no triumph either. The yen will slide in the first half of 2002 but recover in the second. And sterling will play its usual game: two-thirds of the time it will pretend it is the European dollar and move with the American one, and one-third a north Atlantic euro and move with the euro.

In short, 2002 should be a calmer year for world financial markets, a year of putting it all back together again, a year of being sensible. And not before time. □

Pam Woodall: economics editor, *The Economist*

Farewell eurosclerosis

Pam Woodall

The European tortoise will gain further ground on the American hare in 2002. In 2001, the economies of the euro area grew more rapidly than the United States for the first time in ten years. However, according to conventional wisdom, once America's recession ends, it will again resume much faster growth than Europe. Europe's sclerotic economies, strangled by high taxes, red tape and rigid labour markets, are, it is argued, no match for the flexible American economy. Conventional wisdom is likely to be wrong: over the next decade GDP per head, the best measure of economic prosperity, will grow more rapidly in the euro area than in America.

The notion that Europe will be more sluggish than America for years to come is based upon two fallacies. First, that America greatly outperformed Europe during the 1990s. Second, that the euro-area economies are incapable of change. The truth is that America's superior economic performance during the past decade has been exaggerated. And, thanks to recent reforms, there is good reason to expect growth in the euro area to perk up.

America's GDP growth averaged 4% during 1995-2000, well ahead of the euro area's 2.6%. Conventional statistics also show faster labour productivity growth. But this was a mere five-year period during which the United States enjoyed an unsustainable boom. If we instead look at the whole of the past decade in order to strip out the distorting effect of the economic cycle, America's edge over Europe looks more modest. GDP growth was still stronger, but mainly because of faster population growth. If we take GDP per head, America's grew by 2.2%, only a whisker ahead of the euro area's 2%. Labour productivity growth was exactly the same over the ten years in the two economies.

What is true is that America's productivity growth accelerated between the first and second halves of the 1990s, while that in Europe slowed. It is argued by many, therefore, that the past five years offer a better guide to their future relative prospects. However, part of America's spurt in productivity growth was due to an unsustainable increase in investment. Different statistical methods also flatter America's growth performance. If we recalculate growth in America and the euro area using the same method, and exclude capital depreciation, the difference between productivity growth in

Piling up the work
GDP per person, %
(average annual growth)

2.7   2.2
2001-2010

2.0   2.2
1991-2000

2.1   2.2
1981-1990

2.8   2.1
1971-1980

4.4   2.9
1961-1970

Sources: European Commission,
US Dept. of Commerce, *The World in 2002*

America and Europe virtually disappears in the second half of the 1990s. America's productivity did indeed accelerate over the decade, but the result was simply that its productivity growth caught up with that in Europe.

Not only has Europe's past economic performance not been as dire as popularly presented, but there is also reason to expect its productivity growth to spurt over the next decade. It is often argued that Europe's more sluggish investment in IT has left it at a big disadvantage, and America's superior IT systems will help its economy to thrive once growth returns. However, there are two advantages in going second in the IT revolution. Unlike America, the euro economies are relatively free of the economic imbalances, such as excessive private-sector debt and over-investment, that have dragged America into recession. Second, European firms can avoid America's mistakes, and copy what works. There is no reason why Europe cannot in future reap similar gains.

At this point the sceptics argue that to reap the gains of IT spending, labour and product markets need to be flexible to allow the necessary shift in resources. Strict job protection laws make it hard to lay off workers and so may prevent Europe from enjoying the full productivity benefits of IT. But there has been much more reform in the euro zone than governments are typically given credit for. In most euro-area economies labour markets have been made more flexible. Personal income-tax and corporate-tax rates have been reduced. Product markets are also being opened up through deregulation and privatisation. As a result, the unemployment rate in the euro zone has fallen by more than in previous upturns, from almost 12% in 1997 to a low of 8.3% in 2001. Indeed, in the four years to 2001, total employment increased faster in the euro area than in America.

Germany is the euro zone's slowcoach on reform. But even Germany has made significant tax reforms and relaxed its outdated retailing laws. The introduction of the euro has also unleashed a financial revolution, creating a deeper, more liquid capital market across Europe. The increase in corporate bond and equity issuance has started to make firms more responsive to shareholders and put pressure on managers to lift rates of return.

Europe's markets are still more rigid than America's. But Europe does not need to be as flexible as America to enjoy a spurt in productivity growth, as long as it is moving in the right direction. Moreover, the United States is far from perfect. Inferior education and a run-down public infrastructure are a drag on growth. Germany's better-educated workforce compensates for its more rigid labour market.

Looking ahead, Europe can boost its growth in GDP per head either by increasing productivity growth or by tapping its large pool of unused labour. In the euro area only 62% of the working-age population have jobs, compared with 74% in America. Europe therefore has huge scope to boost its labour force. If, thanks to on-going reform, it increased its employment rate to United States' levels over the next 20 years this could boost the region's potential growth rate by almost 1% a year. If productivity growth also rises, then the gain would be greater still. The prospect of such rewards is surely sufficient motive for European governments to press eagerly on with reform in 2002. □

David Shirreff:
capital markets editor,
The Economist

The sky ain't the limit

David Shirreff

2002

The deadline for Japan's banks to mark their ¥38 trillion worth of shareholdings to market prices is March. The government wants them to sell off at least ¥10 trillion worth by September 2004. This should make banks less risky, and the stockmarket more so.

This is the year when the internationally active banks will downsize: the start that was made in 2001 was just a toe in the water. They will look more closely at the risks they run which are not related to credit or market fluctuations. Citigroup and JPMorgan Chase, the products of merger upon merger, are truly global financial institutions. Citibank has assets of $902 billion and 1,400 branches or subsidiaries in 46 countries. JPMorgan Chase has assets of $713 billion and offices in more than 50. There was a scare in early September 2001, when Citibank experienced sudden breakdowns with its ATM cash machines. Had Citi simply got too big to manage?

Financial regulators were relieved to see, in the week following the destruction of New York's World Trade Centre, that the biggest banks relocated their damaged operations reasonably easily. It was the smaller firms that proved more vulnerable. However, that was an unusual financial crisis, not involving credit quality, or a disaster at any big bank. It should not give us much comfort about what can go wrong at a single big institution and the wider impact that might have on the entire sector.

It seems surprising that neither bankers nor their regulators had suggested before that such banks might have grown beyond their optimum size. Through the 1980s and 1990s, the urge to merge was irresistible. Apart from those that went bust or were closed down, very few banks ever downsized voluntarily or spun off divisions.

Now things may change. A new set of proposals on bank capital adequacy, due to be published in a revised form in January 2002 by the Basel Committee of rich-country bank supervisors, will set high capital charges for the operational risks run by banks, to be applied by early 2005. Bankers are worried that this will add to the overall cost of businesses where they have huge turnover—foreign exchange, securitisation, credit derivatives, even asset management—and make them uneconomic. That, secretly, seems to be the regulators' intent: they want to curb the unbridled growth of these markets which, they fear, harbour risks that have not been adequately provided for. The destruction of the World Trade Centre has

Money makes reform go round

Stephen Green

Before Liberation in 1949 Shanghai was Asia's financial centre. 2002 will see the city make great leaps towards regaining that illustrious title. With China in the World Trade Organisation (WTO), the financial industry will start opening up to foreign ownership and greater competition.

About time too. Despite this being China's 25th year of reform, its financial system is still chronically inefficient. All but a tiny handful of financial institutions are state-owned. Against all commercial sense, bank credit is still directed towards value-destroying state-owned enterprises (SOEs). The big four state banks lend 70% of their money to them. Expect the non-performing proportion of these to reach 65% in 2002, although no one at the central bank will admit it. Private firms will still have enormous difficulties getting loans. Even the stockmarket does not offer a reprieve; it too is dominated by SOEs. Over 200 of the 1,200-odd listed companies will make losses. But they too will be coy about coming clean.

Foreign retail banks are poised to make the greatest gains from China's WTO entry. They will start lending to Chinese firms in 2003 and to retail customers in 2006. An average Chinese earns only $800 a year and will initially be an unappealing target for financial services. But that figure disguises concentrations of wealth. China already has 1.3m households with annual incomes of over $50,000. Foreign banks will target them with home, car and education loans and, of course, credit cards. Expect the central bank to keep foreign banks in check by limiting the number of branches they can open.

Foreign insurers will also gain. Total premium income will grow 12% a year to total $34 billion by 2005. Life insurance will be lively as the state pulls away from being the only provider of health care and pensions. By 2010, 110m Chinese will have life policies, up from 40m now. In 2002, watch out for big moves in fund management too. The Investment Fund Law should be passed in the summer. The first foreign fund management firms will also start. They

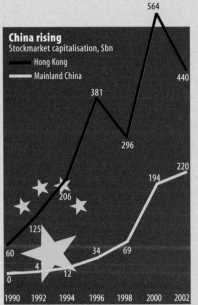

China rising
Stockmarket capitalisation, $bn

— Hong Kong
— Mainland China

564

381

440

296

206

194

220

125

60

34

69

4

0

12

1990 1992 1994 1996 1998 2000 2002

Sources: Thomson Financial Datastream, *The World in 2002*

will sell open-ended mutual funds. The government may even roll out stock-index futures.

The real problem is China's growing debt. This will probably exceed 100% of GDP in 2002. And with pensions increasingly being funded out of the budget, some form of fiscal crisis looks inevitable. China's leadership will have few ways out of this trap. One would be to print money, making the debt cheaper to pay off. That would trigger inflation. The other would be to cut back on spending, pensions and other welfare payments. That would be grossly unpopular with the people. Expect accelerated asset sales and efforts to increase tax revenue to fund the debt. Money makes reform go round. When it runs out, it won't be just the financial sector that opens up to competition but the political arena too. Not a popular idea in Beijing. □

strengthened their hand. Banks have until June 2002 to respond to the proposals, after which they will horse-trade with their regulators until the end of the year. A new Basel capital accord will be decided by early 2003.

This is the background against which banks of all types and sizes are trying to compete and find a profitable niche or two. From 2005, Basel 2 will affect them all. Few banks now, apart from the global giants, are trying to provide a full array of banking services. Most have decided that the entry cost is too high, or the competition is too fierce, to offer everything. ABN Amro, for example, cut back its investment banking from January 2001, Dresdner Bank shrank its global ambitions from July. Almost all the banks which had diversified into private equity in the late 1990s were chastened by huge losses in 2001. Arguably, commercial banks should not have got into this business in the first place.

Defining a bank, and what it does, has become increasingly difficult. Insurance companies, such as AIG and Allianz, and industrial companies, such as GE or Enron, are carrying loans on their balance sheet and dealing in securities and derivatives more heavily than many regulated banks. This worries regulators because they do not have oversight. Investment banks make corporate loans like commercial banks, as an entry to other business; and commercial banks, like investment banks, are bundling their loans into securities. Yet most commercial banks continue to enjoy the protection of deposit insurance,

and the biggest ones are regarded as safe counterparties because they are "too big to fail".

Regulators are in a fix: they need to ensure the safety of bank deposits, and the stability of the financial system. Banks continue to be the transmission mechanism for most national and international payments. Yet they are also involved in all kinds of risky business on their own account. Regulators are trying to keep track of this activity but they will always be several steps behind.

They do not relish recessions, however. Investment banks are the leading indicator at such times, since their people costs are high. When recession, or even a hint of it, looms, they cut jobs. They began in mid-2001: CSFB, JPMorgan Chase, Dresdner Bank cut deepest, with only Goldman Sachs and Lehman Brothers resisting the trend.

The cuts come at a time when investment bankers are under attack for paying themselves enormous bonuses, and for being cavalier about internal conflicts of interest when advising share issuers and investors in those shares. Expect 2002 to see a deep change in the way these banks operate and reward their employees. They are rebuilding Chinese walls within their firms, under threat of regulation and litigation. Bonuses in 2002 will be tiny, at least by the industry's standards. Might this indicate reality returning to a sector which, until recently, rewarded employees at the expense of shareholders? Perhaps. It is unlikely that this issue will be redressed all in one year but at least a start will be made. □

2002

Federal subsidies for Amtrak, an American train operator, are due to run out in September. If it cannot survive on its own, it could be sold off, closed or, more likely, receive more public money.

BUYING A DOZEN ROSES FOR HER BIRTHDAY?

Baby is suddenly 60

Paul Wallace

Pension reform generally moves at tortoise-like speed. By this standard, steps to enhance the role of private funding will be positively hare-like in 2002. The reason for the rush? All of a sudden, retirement is looming for the big baby-boom generation.

As early as 2008, the first post-war baby-boomers will be eligible to take early retirement in America. In France, where the state retirement age is 60, they start to swell the pensioner ranks even sooner, in 2006. Throughout the developed world, the trajectories of old-age dependency ratios—the number of people who are 65 or over as a proportion of the working-age population—are poised for take-off.

In America, population ageing will be less intense than in Europe or Japan. Even so, by 2030 there will be barely two workers to support one pensioner, compared with the current ratio of about three-and-a-half to one. The bipartisan commission established by President George Bush to map a way ahead for American pensions has spelt out why this trend matters. With fewer work-

A green old age
Pension assets per person, 2005
$

United States 36,881
Britain 33,383
Japan 14,087
14,900 Australia
1,829 Germany
1,207 Italy
1,083 France

Source: InterSec Research Corp.

ers to support each pensioner, either benefits must fall or contributions rise.

Is there a way out of this bleak pension arithmetic? Not while you are locked into a pay-as-you-go scheme like Social Security in America where each generation of workers pays for today's pensioners in the increasingly forlorn hope that tomorrow's workers will pay for its own pensions. That is why reform looks to financial markets and the creation of privately funded pension rights.

Private funding offers a way out of the demographic trap because returns on financial assets should be higher than the implicit return on a pay-as-you-go scheme when populations are ageing rapidly. As important, it reduces the political risk that a future generation of workers will renege on an unenforceable pledge to pay retirement benefits to a future generation of pensioners. But it does not offer a free lunch. Investment returns are volatile, as the bursting of the stockmarket bubble demonstrated in 2001. And there is a transition cost as

one generation of workers has both to pay for today's pensioners and to fund its new pension accounts.

That is why pension reform in the developed world is evolutionary rather than revolutionary. The idea is to graft a new funded branch on to the pay-as-you-go trunk. In America, for example, Mr Bush envisages a scheme that will allow younger workers to start building up their own private retirement funds through Social Security. These accounts would be voluntary but the incentive to save through them would come from the prospect of benefit cuts in the 2020s and 2030s when the finances of Social Security become seriously unbalanced.

Actual legislation is unlikely in 2002, this being a mid-term election year, but the report of the president's commission will give fresh impetus to reform. In Germany, by contrast, the debate is now over and a new private-funding scheme will start in 2002. Private-sector workers will initially be able to put 1% of their earnings into retirement funds, rising to 4% by 2008. The government expects that four-fifths of eligible employees will eventually participate in the scheme, making a total of 25m employees. This reform is too timid, say advocates of private funding, but Holger Bonin of Bonn University calls it the most radical change to pension financing in Germany in over 40 years.

The German reform points the way to the rest of the EU, where private funding still plays a negligible role in most member states' pension provision. The European Commission's proposal to establish a common framework for supplementary pensions throughout the EU should finally get the green light once the political logjam caused by the French presidential contest clears in the spring. The election will also open the way to much-needed pension reform in France, although this is unlikely to involve private funding. By contrast, Italy is poised to exploit a distinctive feature of its job market, whereby employers withhold 7% of the pay packet of their employees until they leave the company. This severance pay could instead be diverted into private retirement accounts, which would be especially useful for younger workers.

In Japan, too, private funding will get a fillip in 2002 from new tax-advantaged schemes which allow employees to build up their own portable pension accounts for the first time. Emerging-market economies like India are also restructuring their public-pension systems to enhance the role of private funding. According to the World Bank, there will be 29 countries with a privately funded pillar supporting pension provision by the end of 2002, up from 22 in 2000.

The pace of reform may be erratic but the direction is clear. More and more countries are turning to private funding to rescue over-stretched public-pension systems. It is the only way to relieve the tax pressure on workers in pay-as-you-go schemes and to offer pensioners a future that is less vulnerable to political risk. □

Paul Wallace: economy writer, *The Economist* and author of "Agequake" (Nicholas Brealey)

NO, ORDERING 50,000 FLOWERS FOR A CHAIN OF STORES.

WIRELESS SOLUTIONS FROM COMPAQ MAKE IT HAPPEN. NOW.
To implement Wireless successfully you need a company with proven expertise.
And no one has the experience, devices, infrastructure, services and partners that
Compaq has. If your company deals in perishables, a Compaq wireless solution lets
you check inventory and buy and sell in an instant, thereby cutting wastage and
increasing revenue. And isn't that what IT is all about? If you think so, visit
compaq.co.uk/wireless

[INNOVATIVE PRODUCTS,
INTEGRATED INTO SOLUTIONS
& DELIVERED GLOBALLY

COMPAQ
Inspiration Technology

Andrew Crockett, general manager of the Bank for International Settlements in Basel, runs through the risks of 2002

Eyes wide open

"How robust will the financial system be in a downturn?"

Will 2002 be a year of financial crisis? This is a reasonable question because, even before the attacks on the United States, global growth was slowing to its lowest rate in more than a decade and corporate profits as well as share prices were falling sharply.

The combination of slower growth and unforeseen shocks has often brought vulnerabilities latent in the financial system to the surface. The pace of developments in financial markets during the past five years means that many new financial structures have yet to be tested in a downturn. For example, a whole new range of financial risk insurance and transfer products has developed to spread risk more widely. How robust will these prove if default rates rise? Will insurance companies hurt by the events of September 11th continue to buy credit risks from banks? Another example is the financing of "new economy" firms. The tech-sector collapse has shaken several large financial institutions. Further impacts on the financial system cannnot be excluded.

Such vulnerabilities in the financial system attract attention as the world economy is more susceptible to financial risk than ever before. Increased financial leverage serves to intensify both booms and slumps. Deeper international linkages mean that crises in even medium-sized countries can disturb the whole global system. And because financial markets now play a bigger part in allocating resources than in the past, the microeconomic consequences of any dislocation could be profound.

At first sight, the experience of the previous decade is not encouraging. The 1990s saw a series of financial crises, each seemingly worse than the last. The costs of banking crises in many countries have been enormous and many are still far from resolved. Markets have remained volatile. Many investors have suffered huge losses. There have been several episodes when liquidity evaporated in even the largest of markets. Several financial firms have been caught with massive, ill-judged market positions. Yet it should not be forgotten that the 1990s was also a decade of robust growth. This was helped by the development of new financial mechanisms in a liberalised environment. In this sense, freer and more innovative global markets have "worked".

Good grounds for optimism

Why have they worked? I would suggest three reasons, each of which gives some ground for optimism about the future and each of which points to unfinished business.

The first reason is that crises—even those exacerbated by over-reactions in international markets—have not led governments, particularly those in developing countries, to retreat into financial autarky or repression. On the contrary, economic reforms are being accelerated in many developing countries. Good governance, transparency and disclosure are words that may sound a little dry but they nevertheless characterise a radical change of mind-set for much of the world. The major policy challenge will be to maintain the momentum of reform once the immediate crisis has passed.

The second reason is that the ability of the financial system to prevent crises has improved. Most major banks are well enough capitalised to absorb shocks. This was not true for much of the 1980s. The original Basel Accord agreed in 1988 was instrumental in raising capital-adequacy levels at banks worldwide.

Once more to Basel

There is now a greater awareness of the need for co-ordination between those responsible for different bits of the financial system. The Financial Stability Forum provides one such mechanism, bringing together as it does the main bodies responsible for financial stability in all of the major countries. In the past, it has often taken a crisis to force action to strengthen the financial system. In the future, we should be pre-emptive.

A final reason for optimism is the pragmatism demonstrated in the handling of crises. Belief in the general superiority of financial markets in the allocation of capital has not degenerated into "market fundamentalism". The response has not been to envisage only market solutions in a crisis, but has often also involved collective action, by both the private and public sectors. Large institutions, normally fierce competitors, recognise their collective self-interest in jointly agreed action. In addition, prompt and large official support for countries or industries (the airline business after the attack on the World Trade Centre, for example) has defused crises before they got out of hand. Such rescue packages must of course be exceptional. If investors were to rely on them as the norm, market discipline would soon be undermined.

Satisfaction about the past must be tempered by a sober recognition of the risks that now face the financial system. One is the increased concentration of risks, as firms become larger. Another is that of herding, which results in sudden huge destabilising movements in prices. What is needed is the growth of a culture of informed and independent investment decisions. The proposed new Basel Accord, incorporating modern credit risk management techniques in the regulatory framework and emphasising the responsibility of individual banks for assessing credit risks, is a major step forward.

For all these reasons, then, a message of cautious optimism for 2002 is not out of place. The resilience of financial markets and institutions in the face of severe shocks and the record of pragmatic policymaking in recent years give good grounds for optimism—provided we keep our eyes wide open to the risks. □

IN METAL, BIG IS BEAUTIFUL

SO WHO'S THE BIGGEST AND MOST BEAUTIFUL

Norilsk Nickel supplies a wide range of base and precious metals, and is the world's No. 1 in nickel and palladium. As a vertically-integrated company, Norilsk Nickel explores, mines, processes and delivers their metals themselves.

The beauty of all this is the opportunity Norilsk Nickel represents to the West. The company's products are of the very highest quality, and they have the enviable reputation for reliability. Their prices are globally competitive and their business practices Western in their transparency.

Whatever the prevailing market conditions, Norilsk Nickel remains committed to both the production of traditional metals and the fulfillment of the various programmes that the company has approved and is carrying out in the manufacturing, investment, import/export and socio/environmental sectors. Already occupying a strong position in both domestic and international markets, Norilsk Nickel, in accordance with its adopted development strategy, intends to increase its capitalisation and become an even bigger player in those markets.

All this bears witness to the unique competitive edge Norilsk Nickel enjoys in the global markets, and the beautiful opportunities open to those who do business with Norilsk Nickel.

NORILSK NICKEL

www.nornik.ru

Source Inglehart & Klingemann

The greatest gift that we possess

Alun Anderson

2002

The first complete sequence of the human genome will be published in 2003. Fifty years since Watson and Crick discovered its double-helix structure.

Alun Anderson: editor-in-chief, *New Scientist*

Humans have a terrible tendency to think that the world is going down hill. The "good old days" always seem better. We might be particularly tempted by pessimism in 2002 as worries about terrorism and recession mount. What better time to turn to a largely unnoticed field of scientific endeavour—the study of happiness. Unlike doctors and psychiatrists, scientists studying happiness do not just focus on depression and the darker side of mental life. Instead they look at the full spectrum of mental states from mild happiness to outright joy. And they have some good news for a potentially gloomy 2002. First, the world has been growing happier and it is likely to continue doing so. And second, if you live in one of the advanced nations and are struggling to earn a lot more money in tough times, you may be focusing on the wrong ingredient for happiness.

Geneticists, evolutionary biologists, psychologists, physiologists and political scientists are all involved in studies of happiness. Not all of them like the word. Instead they prefer the more technical "subjective well-being" (swb), even though it is the same thing. How do they assess happiness (or swb)? One method is simply to ask people if they are satisfied with their lives. That is only a start as humans are quick to rewrite history. A long, bad

day that ends in a happy outcome will be remembered as happy, even though it was not. So scientists add "experience sampling". People are equipped with pagers and beeped at random times to record their momentary feelings. Further evidence may come from friends and family, or even from measuring how often you smile.

Some go a step further and explore physiological correlates of happiness. The amount of the adrenal hormone cortisol in the saliva can indicate stress levels. Electrical recordings from face muscles can help tell a fake smile from the real thing and catch fleeting give-away expressions of emotion. Asymmetries in mid-frontal brain activity can indicate agreeableness. Put together, all this research helps dissect different components of happiness and provides fodder for thousands of academic papers. But fortunately for those who want to look at the big picture, the different measurements correlate well enough to provide reliable scores of happiness, both across cultures and through an individual's life.

The World Values Survey, co-ordinated by Ronald Inglehart of the University of Michigan, must be the biggest study of them all. Since 1981 it has sampled the changing beliefs and happiness levels of people in more than 60 societies representing 75% of the world's population. One surprising principle emerges: an increase in wealth per head of population makes a big difference to the happiness level of the poorer nations but has little impact on those that are reasonably well off. This means that as the poorer nations grow in wealth, they can look forward to rapidly ascending the happiness scale. That is good news for the former communist countries, which are deeply depressed even for their levels of wealth. Moldova holds the world record for misery with only 32% of the population saying they are happy, and Russia and Belarus are not far ahead. India and Poland, however, are zooming up the charts.

The lesson for the wealthier nations is that even more money does not necessarily buy more happiness. Iceland, Holland and Denmark are the happiest nations of all, with over 92% of their populations happy, even though they are not nearly as rich as the gloomier United States and Germany. The Japanese do not do very well either, despite their wealth. Like other Confucian states, they seem to spend too much time worrying about what other people think rather than enjoying life.

What is true for the wealthier nations as a whole also holds for the individuals within them. Income is not significantly correlated with happiness in western countries and even millionaires are only slightly happier than the average. The key to happiness must lie elsewhere and long-term studies provide a clue. They show that people are remarkably adaptable to both good and bad circumstances. Lottery winners are happier than the average but only for a year or two after their win. Marriage makes people happy but only for a similar period. Children do not bring permanent happiness. Pay rises and promotions have even more transitory effects before people sink back to their former happiness levels. On the reverse side of the coin, misfortunes do not necessarily spell an end to happiness. Even people with disabling injuries regain their sense of well being. Only long-term unemployment seems really to sap happiness levels.

Overall these studies suggest that most people oscillate around a happiness "set point". Is happiness really a matter of temperament then? Genetic studies show it is important. David Lykken, professor of psychology at the University of Minnesota, measured the level of happiness of hundreds of pairs of middle-aged twins. His data shows that identical twins report similar levels of happiness, even when they have been brought up apart and have had different life experiences. Your genetic makeup is clearly significant but it cannot explain everything.

What is important? We know that individual happiness is not strongly linked to wealth, age, sex, race or education. Nor do key theories about happiness provide simple answers. Ideas that our happiness derives from comparing ourselves favourably with others, our recent past, or how well we are achieving our own goals all fail to explain much of the variation in happiness.

The conclusions of Ed Diener of the University of Illinois at Urbana-Champaign are decidedly folksy. He lists good friends and involvement in activities that we enjoy as important keys to happiness. Folksy it might be, but there may be something to it. As studies show that ever-increasing wealth does not create ever-increasing happiness, more people will turn to the "post-materialist" values of community, belonging and self-expression. □

Molecular anthropology

Steve Connor

Some intriguing discoveries will be made in 2002 in the relatively new field of molecular anthropology. The findings will lead to a greater understanding of human evolution as a result of studying the DNA of indigenous peoples and ethnic groups. By analysing the differences in the DNA of people living now, scientists hope to open a window into the past, thereby helping to nail down the ultimate origin of humankind. Already, minuscule genetic differences between indigenous groups are pointing to a mass exodus of anatomically modern humans out of Africa about 100,000 years ago.

It is in these tiny differences between genes that the clue to our history lies. Unfortunately, the history locked up in our genes is being lost as once-isolated tribes and ethnic groups become homogenised in a global economy marked by mass migration and urbanisation. Based on the number of discrete languages, there are between 5,000 and 8,000 indigenous groups who have experienced centuries, and in some cases millennia, of genetic isolation and inbreeding. It may of course not have been total isolation—it rarely is—but it has been enough to make them sufficiently different from other groups.

Geneticists have long realised that human diversity is being narrowed as a result of migration, intermarriage and genocide. Although they may not be able to stop this, they believe that they can preserve what diversity there is by collecting tissue samples from as many indigenous peoples as possible. The aim is to establish a standardised databank, which would effectively be a molecular museum of mankind representing the genetic variation of our species at the turn of the 21st century. This vision,

| 2002 |

The first football cup for humanoid robots is organised in Japan and South Korea. Boffins aim to build a team able to beat professional human players by 2050.

Steve Connor: science editor, *The Independent*

My DNA is a collector's item too

▷simple, & friendly ~~not~~ *not formal*

High-flying mandarins

The World Space Congress that will meet in Houston, Texas, in October 2002 will be agog: a new nation will be arriving at the frontier.

In 1961, the Soviet Union rocked the world by putting Yuri Gagarin in *Vostok I*, the first manned space flight. It has taken them 40 years to catch up with their erstwhile communist comrades, but in late 2002 *Shenzhou-6* will carry China's first *yuhangyuan*, or astronaut, into orbit. Expect an outpouring of national pride at the achievement. The Chinese leadership will announce plans to build its very own space station. No expense will be spared. Competition like this might wake up NASA again.

During the cold war, space was a frontier worthy of huge budgets. It hosted fierce competition between hostile nations. How times have changed. 2002 will see NASA struggling with a budget of only $14.5 billion. Both the president and Congress believe that public money is better spent closer to home. Politicians will be frustrated by the $25 billion International Space Station. Cost overruns, potentially amounting to $4 billion by 2006, if the White House's calcula-

One small leap

tions are to be believed, have already forced fancier parts of the project to be jettisoned. For example, budget cuts have made NASA scrap its Pluto mission.

Mars, in contrast, will prove to be hot stuff. NASA's *Mars Odyssey* will begin mapping the planet in 2002. On earth, as part of the preparations for landing missions planned for 2003, scientists will experiment with a robotic mole in the Alaskan permafrost. The suspicion is that water might exist deep below the surface of Mars. Powered by solar panels, the mole will drill down to find out. If liquid water exists, life may not be far behind.

Under pressure to cut costs, what could be better for NASA than exploring space from the comfort of the earth's own atmosphere? The world's largest portable telescope will fly into action in 2005 when a modified Boeing 747-SP takes off with a 99-inch diameter telescope on board. The great advantage of the Stratospheric Observatory for Infrared Astronomy will be its ability to rise above the earth's atmospheric water vapour. Clear pictures of space ten billion light years away will be the result. □

---

called the Human Genome Diversity Project, was meant to be run in parallel with, but independent of, the better-known Human Genome Project.

Unfortunately, the diversity project has run into problems as a result of the sensitivity attached to studying any racial differences. The scientists themselves have already been accused of pandering to racism. Kenneth Kidd, a human geneticist at Yale University, says that trying to justify the genetic diversity project in terms of preserving DNA differences is counterproductive. Many indigenous people say "our culture is dying and you're willing to preserve our DNA, but what about us?"

Despite such problems, a databank of some 200 tissue samples is being compiled. At some point in 2002 the first "withdrawals" from the databank will take place. Using human DNA to study human origins is already well advanced. Svante Paabo, a Swedish DNA sleuth, is leading the way with a team based at the Max Planck Institute for Evolutionary Anthropology in Leipzig, Germany. In 2002 the group will move into a $30m laboratory where DNA analysis will be carried out. In addition to teasing out the genetic differences between human groups, the Leipzig team will investigate the differences between the DNA of humans and chimpanzees, man's closest living relative. Although the difference is known to be less than 2%, next to nothing is known about what constitutes the distinction. Unravelling it might resolve the issue of how and why the first humans emerged from our primate ancestors, about 2m years ago.

Molecular anthropology, and its more conventional cousin, suggest that the first human migrations came out of Africa about a million years ago. But their tiny num-

ber meant that they were totally usurped by a relatively recent migration of anatomically modern humans around 100,000 years ago. It is this group of people that are the direct ancestors of all humans today.

Genetic studies have shown that native groups in Asia, Europe and the Americas are far less diverse than groups living today within Africa. This suggests that a relatively small number of people—perhaps no more than a few thousand—emerged from Africa to populate the world, thereby creating a "genetic bottleneck" that persists in the DNA of all non-Africans today. Other studies of DNA differences between native groups are revealing equally intriguing results. Mark Stoneking, another member of the Max Planck team, is investigating tribal groups in Thailand to see whether he can detect differences in the prehistoric movements of men and women. His results, show that—unexpectedly—it is the women who tend to migrate farther than the men. By analysing Thai tribes with two distinct social cultures—one patrilocal, where men stay in the village of their birth, and one matrilocal, where women tend to stay put—Dr Stoneking has the first evidence to support this view. The men in patrilocal tribes have significantly greater Y chromosome variation than men in matrilocal villages. These differences in diversity accumulate over time because in villages where men do not move, the Y chromosomes becomes genetically isolated from other groups. In the rarer instance where tribes are matrilocal, it is the maternally inherited mitochondrial DNA that shows the wider variation. Unfortunately during 2002 the rate at which this sort of work will proceed will be more than matched by the rate at which human diversity is being lost for good. □

> ### 2002
> The UN has designated 2002 the International Year of Mountains. A conference, High Summit, takes place at the foot of the world's highest peaks in each of the seven continents.

Fertility rights

Shereen El Feki

O n October 15th 2001, the "Pill" celebrated its golden anniversary. The world's first oral contraceptive had an unlikely birth 50 years ago—its key ingredient created in a Mexican laboratory from native yams by a group of European émigrés. But as the Pill well and truly enters middle age, just how fertile is the field of contraceptive development?

It depends on whom you ask. Carl Djerassi, one of its original developers, reckons that pharmaceutical companies have lost their appetite for birth control. The worldwide market for female contraceptives—from pills to sheaths to coils—is worth $16 billion, or less than 5% of the total prescription drug market. Presented with the opportunity to produce yet another drug for controlling,

One born every minute
% of married women using modern contraception

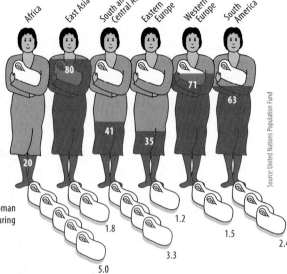

Source: United Nations Population Fund

Fertility rate
(number of children a woman is expected to produce during her reproductive years) 2000-05

say, cholesterol, or a new way of regulating reproduction, pharmaceutical firms are more likely to go where the money is.

In the rich world, at any rate, this means treating the conditions of creeping old age, such as arthritis or heart disease or, indeed, problems of infertility. It is a rather different story in many developing countries, where women are still bogged down by unwanted pregnancies and childbearing. Worldwide, there are roughly 100m unintended pregnancies each year, a fifth of which end in an unsafe abortion. Women around the world need not only better access to existing contraceptives but also new methods better suited to their financial, cultural and physiological constraints.

But contraception is a tough field for drug and device makers. Unlike medicines used to treat dread diseases, contraceptives are given to healthy people, rather like vaccines. As a result, they must pass through expensive and time-consuming tests to prove their long-term safety before entering the market. Once there, they run a high risk of litigation as the makers of intra-uterine devices and Norplant, an implantable contraceptive, have dis-

covered to their cost. No wonder most drug companies have deserted the field, leaving only four main firms and a few plucky biotechnology ventures to continue research and development.

That said, Elof Johansson at the Population Council in New York, can point to a few bright spots in female contraception. Among them are more convenient delivery systems for improved cocktails of sex hormones which regulate the normal female reproductive cycle. Better implants, which are easier to get into and, critically, get out of the body are now entering the market. Also on their way are vaginal rings, following on the recent introduction of souped-up intra-uterine devices, to release synthetic sex hormones exactly where they are needed. Such methods not only make it easier for consumers, but also produce other health benefits, such as easier menstruation.

Also in the works are better spermicidal and microbiocidal compounds, which are more effective at stopping unwanted intruders, be they sperm or viruses. And many researchers are excited about the prospect of mifepristone, or RU-486, as a contraceptive to block both ovulation and implantation. But there is a hitch: mifepristone was first introduced on to the market as an abortifacient and has run into trouble with the right-to-life lobby in America. Such political sensitivities, along with the commercial difficulties of contraceptive development, mean that translating new scientific advances into products is much slower in contraception than in other areas of drug design.

Male contraception, on the other hand, is moving more quickly. In 2002 two drug companies, Organon and Schering A6, will move forward with sizeable clinical trials of hormones to regulate male fertility. Researchers at the MRC Human Reproductive Sciences Unit in Edinburgh, Scotland have already managed to turn off sperm production in small groups of volunteers and, critically, to turn it back on again. Their trick is to give daily hormonal pills to shut off activity in the testis, where sperm are made, in combination with a long-acting testosterone implant to put back some of the hormone men need to maintain their machismo. At the Institute of Reproductive Medicine at the University of Münster, scientists are taking a similar tack, using hormonal injections alone. Ideally, researchers would like to use compounds known as GnRH antagonists along with improved versions of testosterone to gain finer control over sperm production with fewer side-effects, and several such molecules are in the early stages of development.

Other approaches are in the works too—among them vaccines to prime a woman's body into producing antibodies to stop sperm in their tracks, molecules which might inhibit sperm function rather than just production and substances to block the formation of new blood vessels in the uterus, so there is no cosy womb for an embryo to take root. But these are still far from the clinic. In the meantime, the big question is whether men will be ready to take a male oral contraceptive. Certainly opinion surveys conducted by the Edinburgh group suggest that, in the post-AIDS era, men are more willing to shoulder the responsibility for contraception, and women more willing to trust them. Will the male Pill prove as popular as Viagra? Fertile ground for debate indeed. □

Shereen El Feki: health-care correspondent, *The Economist*

JUST BECAUSE IT DOESN'T HAVE A CORD DOESN'T MEAN IT SHOULDN'T BE PLUGGED IN.

CA Wireless Partnership

NOKIA • EDS • KYOCERA WIRELESS • SYMBOL • AETHER™ • MOTOROLA • PALM

Capitalizing on opportunities in mobile eBusiness depends on successful integration of wireless technology with existing infrastructures. That's why CA is proud to be partnering with wireless market leaders and global professional service providers to create enterprises without boundaries. CA's security, infrastructure, and information management solutions are not only industry leaders, they're also hardware and software neutral. So future wireless initiatives will be limited by nothing but the imagination.

Computer Associates™

Bill Gates, Microsoft's chairman and chief software architect, predicts that companies will look even more closely at the benefits of digital technology during a recession

Tech in a time of trouble

"The first ten years of the 21st century will be the digital decade"

In the wake of the dotcom meltdown and terrorist attacks, and among 2002's economic miseries, all the excitement about the personal computer and Internet revolution of the 1990s can seem like a distant memory. While the enthusiasm over the digital revolution has been overshadowed by recent events, its significance has not. The phenomenon that made digital technology an essential part of the workplace, home and classroom is not subject to fashion. The digital future is more important than ever.

Like every technology revolution, this one will come in waves. The first, which spanned the 1990s, transformed how we communicate and get information. Almost overnight, the PC and the Internet enabled businesses and people to exchange e-mail, ideas and data instantaneously. The next wave will have a far broader impact. As the PC is joined by a growing range of intelligent devices, all connected by faster, cheaper and more reliable network connections, we'll see a vast transformation of products and services into digital form, from books to movies to business billing systems. The first ten years of the 21st century will be the digital decade.

We've already seen how atoms have been transformed into bits in many different media: that is to say huge chunks of the world's output have dematerialised from the physical to the virtual. But this decade is when we'll start to think of this digital metamorphosis—and the productivity gains that will accompany it—in a whole new way. Take music. It has been in digital form since analog long-playing records gave way to compact discs in the early 1980s, but until recently you still needed some kind of disc to carry the musical data. Now, though, music is freeing itself completely from its physical form. As bits, it can be accessed wherever you want it, from any intelligent device that can decode the bitstream.

We will see this phenomenon replicated in products as diverse as software, photographs, video and books. Software has been sold online since the earliest days of the public Internet, but only recently has bandwidth been capable of carrying the enormous number of bits required for sophisticated business, personal, educational or entertainment programs. In the years ahead, as more people have access to cost-effective high-speed lines, the Internet will become the primary way in which software is distributed, updated, maintained and even managed. Software that once came in shrink-wrapped boxes and was updated infrequently—if at all—will be transformed into dynamic, living code that can update and repair itself over the network.

Take another, domestic, example. Millions of people are now using digital cameras to capture their families' lives, and using digital photo frames to share memories with family and friends around the block or around the world. The ability to store and share high-quality digital video as easily is just around the corner. And while e-books have yet to take off, I'm confident that they will within the decade. New text-display software and new kinds of devices, such as tablet-sized PCs, will make onscreen reading, annotating and searching easier and more enjoyable than ever.

The long-term consequences of this digital revolution will be far-reaching and overwhelmingly positive for many industries, fundamentally transforming the economics of the marketplace. In part, this will occur simply through a decline in costs. Digital goods are cheaper than their material counterparts. And you only have to make them once. Inventory costs will also fall, a result of improved efficiency, and of being able to create a "virtual" distribution network. E-publishing, for example, offers an incredibly efficient business model, with almost no manufacturing, packaging or distribution costs.

Along with virtual distribution will come an increasing trend towards online billing and payments. According to Jupiter Research, a consultancy, American companies alone spend a combined $18 billion a year preparing and delivering paper bills. Jupiter estimates that online bill payment could eliminate 80% of this expense.

Digital bespoke

The digital revolution will create an entirely new concept of self-service and an unprecedented degree of customer control. Do you want to buy a product, or rent it and receive automatic updates? Do you want the bits now, at a premium, or streamed to your PC overnight, at a discount? The variations are endless, as are the opportunities.

These advances will be equally welcome to both large and small businesses alike. The Internet has already greatly enhanced the ability of small businesses to sell their products globally. The next wave of the digital revolution, powered by technologies such as XML (eXtensible Markup Language), will enable those small firms to tap resources from around the world, combining their expertise with those of others to customise their products and services for customers. In a digital world, product or service development increasingly becomes collaborative. And the factors of production themselves become fluid, because it is the processing technology, rather than the goods themselves, that is being reproduced.

There are some potential pitfalls as the digital revolution advances. As it becomes easier to make perfect counterfeit copies of an increasing number of products, the issue of how intellectual property rights are protected will be of growing concern—especially in those countries where enforcement remains inadequate.

Clearly, some industries have struggled to make the jump to a digital world, but far more are reaping the benefits of this transition. Investing in tomorrow's technology today is more critical than ever to future competitiveness. □